Praise for This Book

"I am very enthusiastic about the book's clear and forthright vision of systemic crisis, involving the social institutions of media and government. Prof. Exoo takes a very strong structural approach in his explanation; this is the most detailed analysis of media representations of the current war that I have seen. The chronological development of the journalistic narrative of the war is engaging and persuasive . . . This work is a good example of how responsible academics can contribute to the public dialogue."

—Harry W. Haines, *Department of Communication, Trinity University*

"The writing is fantastic: Very easy to read, to understand, and to synthesize. The arguments are well crafted and well documented. This is the most up-to-date analysis of the media coverage of the Iraq War I have read, and it would put news coverage of the run-up to the War into context. . . . It's a fun read, it's accessible for students, and it's timely. What more could a professor ask for?"

—Alison D. Dagnes, *Department of Political Science, Shippensburg University*

"The news media pay a lot of lip service to the importance of objective reporting and to their role in maintaining a healthy democracy. This book successfully challenges both assertions. . . . Exoo's book provides an exhaustive illustration of what's wrong with the news media, using a very relevant and timely example."

—Robert Heiner, *Department of Social Science, Plymouth State University*

"This text will challenge students to reexamine their beliefs about the news media, helping them to become more critical citizens. In doing this, the text would engage students' attention in crucial developments in the media, in politics, and in the intersection of the two."

—Paul R. Brewer, *Department of Journalism and Mass Communication, University of Wisconsin-Milwaukee*

The Pen and the Sword

For Diane.

The Pen *and the* Sword

PRESS, WAR, *and* TERROR
in the 21st CENTURY

CALVIN F. EXOO
St. Lawrence University

Los Angeles | London | New Delhi
Singapore | Washington DC

For information:

SAGE Publications, Inc.
2455 Teller Road
Thousand Oaks,
 California 91320
E-mail: order@sagepub.com

SAGE Publications India Pvt. Ltd.
B 1/I 1 Mohan Cooperative
 Industrial Area
Mathura Road, New Delhi 110 044
India

SAGE Publications Ltd.
1 Oliver's Yard
55 City Road
London EC1Y 1SP
United Kingdom

SAGE Publications Asia-Pacific
 Pte. Ltd.
33 Pekin Street #02-01
Far East Square
Singapore 048763

Printed in the United States of America

Library of Congress Cataloging-in-Publication Data

Exoo, Calvin F.
The pen and the sword: press, war, and terror in the 21st century / Calvin F. Exoo.
 p. cm.
Includes bibliographical references and index.
ISBN 978-1-4129-5360-3 (pbk.)
 1. Terrorism—Press coverage—United States—History—21st century. 2. War—Press coverage—United States—History—21st century. 3. Journalism—Objectivity—United States—History—21st century. 4. Press and politics—United States—History—21st century. 5. Afghan War, 2001—Press coverage. 6. Iraq War, 2003—Press coverage. I. Title.

PN4784.T45.E96 2010
070.4'49363325—dc22   2009029090

This book is printed on acid-free paper.

09   10   11   12   13   10   9   8   7   6   5   4   3   2   1

Acquisitions Editor:	Todd R. Armstrong
Editorial Assistant:	Aja Baker
Production Editor:	Astrid Virding
Typesetter:	C&M Digitals (P) Ltd.
Proofreader:	Andrea Martin
Indexer:	Kathy Paparchontis
Cover Designer:	Gail Buschman
Marketing Manager:	Jennifer Reed Banando

Contents

Preface

This book is about the politics of the mass media in a post-9/11 world. Since that fateful day, terrorism and international conflict—the wars in Afghanistan and Iraq—have been the number one subject of American news. The book's goal is a comprehensive review of how the media have told these momentous stories, and why they've told them in that way.

The stakes in this matter could not have been higher. War and peace, life and death—indeed hundreds of thousands of lives and deaths—swayed in the balance. The thesis of this book is that, at this most crucial moment in American history, the mass media have failed, miserably, in their capacity as watchdog of the people. What's more, the book argues, this failure is not an aberration, but an especially vivid illustration of the chronic failure of contemporary media in performing their indispensable democratic function.

Unlike other books that have told parts of this story, this one is in position to see it whole, to tell it from start to finish—from 9/11 to the Obama moment—to explain why it happened, and to use this chronicle of tragedy as a doorway to a critical perspective on mass media.

We hope that this compelling subject will be of interest to students in courses on the mass media, popular culture, journalism, and American foreign policy. The years following 9/11 have been crucial in the history of these subjects and will probably be remembered, like the McCarthy era or the Vietnam War, as a dark night of American politics. The students who will become our future mass media, journalism, and foreign policy professionals will want to know what happened and why.

A major pedagogical hurdle, in such courses, is getting students to see the news as something other than "the way it is," as Walter Cronkite used to call it, something other than a naturally occurring set of objective facts that are good for us to know. This book's case study is a tonic for that problem. Indeed, students may be shocked by the record of tendentious, mendacious news coverage they find here, and led to ask, Why? This is how teachable moments begin.

We also hope that some unique features of this book will help students understand this momentous subject.

- In addition to examining what the press has said about war and terror, each chapter will also offer a "reverse content analysis" of what the press did not say—the important stories that were somehow deemed "not news." We'll see that these excised stories tend to be part of a larger untold story of America in the world—the story of American empire.

- Explanation is the work of theory, and this is the only politics and media text firmly grounded in social theory. We begin with the theory of democracy and the press advanced by Madison and Jefferson, and proceed from there to Antonio Gramsci's theory of cultural hegemony. With these tools, we can see both the promise and the peril of our mass media: the power to open minds, and the power to close them.

- Because not just news media but all media affect our thinking about war, this book also examines the war stories told by the press's corporate first cousins, the non-news media: movies, advertising, and entertainment TV.

- An Introduction and Conclusion to each chapter will show students the chapter's argument and main points in miniature before they begin, and help them think about what to take away from the chapter at the end. Because this book diagnoses the media's condition as chronic, our final conclusion will offer thoughts on how, in this time of enormous flux, we might reform our media to better serve democracy.

❖ A MAP OF THE BOOK

To help us understand how the news covers war and why, we'll begin with the building blocks of serious thinking about social issues—political theory. In Chapter 1, we'll be introduced to theories about the media and

—democracy, and the press's unique capacity to enable it, and

—hegemony, and the media's capacity to disable democracy.

We'll also meet the media's hegemonic message about American foreign policy—the dominant, press-preferred story of America's role in the world. This is the story of a beneficent America, carrying the torch of freedom, like Prometheus, to the world. And finally, we'll turn to the alternative, untold story of the United States' role in the world—the chronicle of American empire. This account will be our first use of "reverse content analysis," a method employed throughout the book, which asks, What important stories are *not* in the news, and why? In these two stories of American foreign policy—the press-preferred and the untold tale—we'll begin to see that the press's post-9/11 errors of omission and commission are not an acute attack of one-sidedness, but a chronic condition.

With Chapter 1 as our introduction, we'll be ready to begin our study of how the press has covered war and terror in the 21st century. Our story begins, unavoidably, on September 11, 2001. In Chapter 2, we'll meet the horror of that day head-on; we'll examine coverage of the ensuing debate and of the war in Afghanistan. Here we'll see a pattern emerging: At a moment when America most needed the media to be a marketplace of ideas, offering many sides of the story, the press instead became a censor of ideas, offering only one side, one story.

This was the uplifting and entertaining story of American right and might overcoming a powerful and incomprehensibly evil enemy. Meanwhile, as our ongoing reverse content analysis will show, the argument that war in Afghanistan might have been ill-advised, costly in terms of money and mayhem, and dysfunctional in its outcome appears only as a forlorn parade of unreported facts and uncovered stories. In the end, our argument is not that the war in Afghanistan was wrong or right. The argument is simply that there were two sides to this story, and only one was told.

In Chapter 3, we'll examine coverage of the public relations campaign for war in Iraq. It is a tumultuous tale with a colorful cast and would be a ripping good yarn altogether, if only it weren't so tragic. It is a story of foreign policy Vulcans ascendant; of agendas hidden and false; of the *New York Times,* duped like a rube by hidden persuaders; of a nuclear tale that went down the tubes; of an infamous "sixteen words"; of a cabinet member's "web of lies"; and of an entertainment media enlisting.

It is also a story of protestors crying in the wilderness; of profiles in courage: reporters who bucked the tide and got the story right; of Cassandras treated as traitors; and of scoundrels treated to promotions. Through it all, the story is one of an obeisant press in the face of a deceitful White House, leading to a simple truth both had forgotten: War is hell.

But that truth was not yet in view as the war broke out and "concluded" in the spring of 2003. Instead, as we'll see in Chapter 4, coverage of the war was a patriotic hymn to the thrilling power of America, and an entertaining fascination with the techniques and technologies of battle: war as football, war as PlayStation.

We'll see that, more than ever, the experts chosen to explain the war came from a very selective, pro-war Rolodex. For "balance," one writer said, there were retired generals as well as active ones.

In this chapter, we'll also review the history of press and Pentagon relations since Vietnam, which led to the "sheer genius" of embedded reporting. We'll examine the dynamics and results of embedding, as well as the news from the "Platform for Truth," and the military's treatment of unembedded, and thus unwelcome, reporters.

We'll also continue our reverse content analysis by asking, What happens, in a "good war," to "bad facts," like civilian casualties? Finally, we'll focus on the war's iconic moments: a "daring rescue" that wasn't; the "pure emotional expression—not staged, not choreographed"—of a toppling statue that was, in fact, both staged and choreographed; and the moment of "Mission Accomplished." We'll see that, indeed, truth is often war's first casualty.

In Chapter 5, we'll follow the news coverage from the "Mission Accomplished" moment to the present. We'll see that something about our mass media has changed—and not for the better. In Daniel Hallin's definitive account of the Vietnam War, the press begins in its default position, which is pro-war. But as public opinion and elements of elite opinion begin to turn against the war, the press also discovers an anti-war story (1986). In Iraq, that doesn't happen. Instead, as Iraq descends into the chaos of Abu Ghraib, Fallujah, ethnic cleansing, and civil war, the press clings to an increasingly untenable, pro-war story.

In Chapter 6, we'll ask perhaps the most important question of all: Why? The unsettling answer will be that the media's failures of post-9/11 coverage were not a temporary lapse of judgment. That, indeed, these failures grow from deeply rooted structures and practices of the news business: from U.S. news' commercial imperative, from its continuing overreliance on officials as sources, its susceptibility to the machinations of the public relations industry, its vulnerability to advertisers and owners, from the emergence of a tendentious and powerful right wing within the mainstream media, and so on. These factors, together with the crucible of fear created after 9/11, have placed us, in Matthew Arnold's ominous words, "On a darkling plain . . . where ignorant armies clash by night."

This diagnosis means that the prognosis is not good. As the media status quo persists, coverage and knowledge of our world and our options are likely to be woefully incomplete. For that reason, Chapter 6 concludes with some thoughts about media reform, suggesting that our current system of "rich media, poor democracy" can be improved.

❖ OUR OMNIPRESENT MEDIA

"Imagine," Plato asks, "the condition of men living in a sort of cavernous chamber underground. Here they have been from childhood, chained by the leg and also by the neck, so they cannot move and can see only what is in front of them. At some distance higher up is the light of a fire burning behind them; and between the prisoners and the fire is a track with a parapet built along it, like the screen at a puppet-show, which hides the performers while they show their puppets over the top. . . . Behind this parapet imagine persons carrying along various artificial objects, including figures of men and animals in wood or stone or other materials, which project above the parapet. Prisoners so confined would have seen nothing of themselves or of one another, except the shadows thrown by the fire-light on the wall of the Cave facing them. . . . Such prisoners would recognize as reality nothing but the shadows of those artificial objects."

Little did Plato know how prescient his parable was. It is almost as if, unwittingly, he had peered into the future and seen that our lives would one day be dominated by a shadow show of flickering images. A show controlled by fewer and fewer, more and more powerful puppeteers.

Does it stretch the truth to say so? Does Plato's allegory overstate the media's hold on our consciousness? You could, as Casey Stengel used to say, look it up. Here's what you'd find:

- In the average American household, the television set is on more than seven hours a day. The family of that household will spend about 70% of their nonworking, waking evening hours watching it. When asked where they learn about "what's going on in the world," a sizable majority of Americans now answer, "Television."

- This is particularly true when we are at war: 80% of Americans said they "watched TV more closely" during the Iraq conflict.

- Almost all of those close viewers were tuned to one of just five networks, each owned by one of the handful of companies that now control most of the magazines, book publishers, movie studios, and radio and TV networks and stations in the United States.

- On an average day, a majority of American adults will flip through a newspaper. A majority of them will be reading a paper owned by 1 of just 10 major corporations.

Although our main focus, in this book, will be on the news media, we will also pause occasionally to look at what the non-news media, such as movies, ads, and prime-time TV, are saying about war and terrorism. We'll do this because, as we'll see, these media, like the news, are important sources of our thinking about politics. As we do this, we'll find that often the same few companies, guided by the same corporate goals, own both the news and entertainment media. Once again, we'll learn that we spend a lot of our time and resources in their cave. Consider the following:

- On an average day, the individual American sees about 3,000 ads. By the time of high school graduation, she or he will have spent about one-and-a-half years watching TV commercials. More than three quarters of this advertising, now costing over $260 billion a year, is "brought to you by" just five giant advertising agencies.

- On a recent weekend, Americans paid $155 million to share a single cultural experience: the opening of *The Dark Knight*. In any given year, Americans make the pilgrimage to their local movie theaters about one and a half billion times. Most of those visits will be to only a handful of "blockbuster" movies produced, once again, by the six largest media corporations, which altogether claim over 90% of the film industry's revenues. At the time *The Matrix Reloaded* was released, 95% of Americans knew something about the movie, but at the same time, two thirds of our population could not name any of the Democratic candidates running for president.

- Four firms now own 90% of the music released in the United States. One company, Clear Channel Communications, Inc., owns 70% of all U.S. concert venues, plus 1,240 radio stations.

- The number of companies now commanding half of all U.S. Internet user minutes is four.

- Altogether, Americans now spend about $1 trillion a year on media products.

Does Plato's parable exaggerate the media's power? Not by much.

❖ THE ARGUMENT IN BRIEF

It would seem important then to consider this shadow show. To understand it fully, we need to ask not just what the media is and does, but why. The latter question is the work of theories. This book will look at mass media through the eyes of cultural hegemony theory. It suggests that those who own or control a society's "idea factories"—like the media—can use them to urge their own ideology on others.

This process may sound simple and straightforward. It is not. It is complex and subtle. So subtle in fact that those who produce that hegemony are not, for the most part, consciously trying to. They are just doing their jobs. But written, as it were, into their job descriptions are needs, routines, and values that result in hegemony. Those demands and routines arise mainly from the "commercial imperative"—the media industries' voracious appetite for profit. So this book spends time trying to understand how that imperative shapes the process of making mass media.

Of course, a book about war, terror, and media is interested in more than the process by which those media are made. Ultimately, our interest is in the product that emerges from that process. In particular, we'll ask, What are the media's messages about international conflict? And what effects might those messages have on our political life?

Press messages about the Afghanistan and Iraq wars will be described in detail in Chapters 2 through 5, but here we can say this much: Those particular messages about war conformed to the general contours of the media's two foundational hegemonic messages:

1. The first message is a massage. With the tinsel and glitter of sex, violence, and celebrity gossip, the media divert our attention from the hard work of political and social problems. Of course, when problems go unaddressed, the status quo is maintained, which is just fine with

those who are prospering under it, and not so fine for others. As we shall see, even matters as weighty as war can be, and have been, spun into the cotton candy of infotainment.

2. When they do talk politics, the media tend to applaud the viewpoint of the powerful, a viewpoint that may not be best for everyone—especially not for working- and lower-class Americans, or for those people in the Third World who may find themselves standing like Indians on the plain of American global ambition. As we shall see in Chapter 3, the press played "Follow the Leader" in its 2002 and 2003 coverage, relentlessly framing Iraq the way the White House did, as America's enemy, even though other frames were readily available. The consequences for the Iraqi people have been devastating.

All of this is yet to come. But let us begin by acknowledging that a quiet coup has occurred in American life. We are its willing prisoners, watching its images by its firelight. Seeing it clearly and making out its meaning for our politics and society will not be easy. After all, it's dark down here. But it seems important to try.

❖ ACKNOWLEDGMENTS

Let me express my deep and heartfelt gratitude to the colleagues, students, friends, and family who are the *sine qua non* of this book.
Thank you:
To the reviewers of this book, for your keen insights and your gracious encouragement: Todd L. Belt, Department of Political Science, University of Hawaii at Hilo; Kenton Bird, School of Journalism and Mass Media, University of Idaho; Paul R. Brewer, Department of Journalism and Mass Communication, University of Wisconsin–Milwaukee; Alison D. Dagnes, Department of Political Science, Shippensburg University; James N. Druckman, Department of Political Science, Northwestern University; Michael M. Franz, Department of Government, Bowdoin College; Harry W. Haines, Department of Communication, Trinity University; Robert Heiner, Department of Social Science, Plymouth State University; Janet McMullen, Department of Communication and Theatre, University of Northern Alabama.
To Todd Armstrong, Senior Acquisitions Editor at Sage, for your wisdom and support; and to Aja Baker at Sage, for your efficiency and sanguinity.

To my dear colleagues in the Department of Government at St. Lawrence University. The testament of their work reeducates me every day about commitment to what we do, to scholarship and teaching.

To two colleagues, in particular, whose friendship has been with me in better and in worse, in sickness and in health. To Alan Draper, whose influence can be seen throughout this book, and who has shown me, by his wonderful example, how scholarship and leadership should be done. To Kerry Grant, my teaching partner, who has taught me so much about the media, about teaching, about life. Above all, thank you, Alan and Kerry, for the *filia* that Aristotle called a virtue, for the *amicitia* Cicero wrote a book about.

To Patty Ashlaw, secretary for the Department of Government, for your infinite patience and your unfailing good cheer.

To my students at St. Lawrence University, for making mine the most wonderful job in the world. When I say, "This is my truth, now tell me yours," you let me hear your voices, which are by turns so brilliant, so thoughtful, so funny, so decent, so humane. Thank you for reassuring an aging man that the future is in such good hands.

To my beloved mother and brothers and sisters, whose love taught me about the *caritas* that "beareth all things, believeth all things, hopeth all things, endureth all things."

To my sons, Joshua and Christian, and to the daughters I wished for, Brigette and Kate. When the time is right for "pessimism of the mind," your infinite spirits are my "optimism of the heart."

Above all, thanks to my coconspirator, yokemate, best friend, love of a lifetime: the pilgrim soul to whom this book is dedicated.

The news media's story of U.S. foreign policy is one of a beneficent America, bringing human rights and democracy to the world. But through the grainy pixels of this 1983 television image, we begin to see that there is another story of America's role in the world. Here we see Donald Rumsfeld arriving in Baghdad to cement the U.S. relationship with Iraq—after Hussein has used poison gas to kill his own people, as well as Iranians. Subsequently, the United States provided Hussein with "a veritable witch's brew" of chemical and biological agents, as well as technology for biochemical weapons and the Bell helicopters used to spray deadly toxins on Iraqi Kurds, killing an estimated 5,000 in the village of Halabja in 1988.

1

Media, Democracy, Hegemony

This chapter argues that the press is full of promise and fraught with peril: It can be an instrument of democracy, or of hegemony. We'll apply this maxim to the subject of American foreign policy by examining the dominant, press-preferred story of American foreign policy and offering an untold story about America's role in the world.

We begin by asking, How important is a free press to democracy? It's so important, we'll discover, that democracy is simply not possible without a free press, which is why the Founding Fathers and the Supreme Court have given the press a privileged place in our Constitution.

Next we'll ask, What do a people who mean to be their own governors need from the press? Again, the Founders, their Constitution, and its interpreter, the Supreme Court, will help us with the answer: For democracy to work, the press must be a "watchdog of the people" and a "marketplace of ideas."

But what happens when the media's power, "the power to tell a society's stories," falls into the hands of "a shrinking group of global conglomerates with nothing to tell but a great deal to sell" (George Gerbner, in Jhally 1997). This question will lead us to the theory of "cultural hegemony." The word *hegemony* can be briefly defined as "domination."

In this case, it is the domination of a people's culture—ways of thinking, believing, and behaving—by those who own the culture's "idea factories," such as the mass media. Our look at hegemony theory will focus on the thoughts of one of its pioneers, Antonio Gramsci.

We'll see that some of Gramsci's observations fit our media to a T. Once it is complete, he said, hegemony is institutionalized, built into the rules and routines of a society's institutions. In the case of the media, the rule that's rigged the game is the commercial imperative— the rule that says the main business of the media is business. This chapter begins the argument that the rule's long-established hold on the media has grown even stronger in recent years, as conglomerate corporations have taken ever-larger pieces of the ownership pie.

Next, we'll turn to the hegemonic message itself. What is the dominant story of American foreign policy told to us by our mass media? And is there evidence of this story's influence over our thinking? As we'll see, the hegemonic story is a tale of America's benevolence in the world and of an American "right to lead," by military force if necessary, that follows from this benevolence. We'll see that the "Bush Doctrine" of preemptive war was presented by the White House and accepted by the press as a logical and necessary extension of this hegemonic story of American foreign policy.

Finally, we'll do a "reverse content analysis," asking what stories are *not there* in press coverage of foreign policy. Here we'll discover the relatively untold story of American economic imperialism. We'll hear this story not because it is the one true account of American foreign policy. There are other accounts, and they too are tenable. Rather, we'll hear this story because, despite the press's professed devotion to telling "both sides" of the story, this is the side not told. In our "marketplace of ideas," this is the shelf that is empty.

In this story, we'll learn

- Why the corporate sector is sometimes called our "fourth branch of government";

- Why President Eisenhower warned us of a "disastrous rise of misplaced power" involving the "military-industrial complex";

- How the United States builds and maintains its empire, by means that Henry Kissinger said are "not missionary work"— and how this dark history, in particular of U.S. support for brutal repressions and regimes, has been met in the American press by an eerie silence;

- How American policy in the Persian Gulf has produced considerable suffering and massive "blowback" against the United States, prompting even more violent interventions—and how the press has spun this story into one of American beneficence and heroism;

- How our Manichaean media see the world in black and white, good and evil, creating a "mean world syndrome" that teaches us fear and hatred—and how useful that fear is to press and politicians alike;

- Why we should be less terrified of terrorism than we are—and how the fear of terrorism has been stoked beyond reason in pursuit of ratings and votes;

- Finally, how the "globalization" now facilitated by U.S. foreign policy has been a boon to wealthy Americans and a bane to many American workers.

With this chapter as prologue—the press and democracy, hegemony, a dominant story and an untold one about America's role in the world—we will be ready to begin our case study of how the press has covered America at war in the 21st century.

❖ DEMOCRACY AND THE PRESS

How important is a free press to democracy? To Thomas Jefferson and James Madison, the answer was simple: no free press, no free country—no democracy.[1] "A popular government without popular information or the means of acquiring it," said Madison, "is but a prologue to a farce or a tragedy or perhaps both. Knowledge will forever govern ignorance, and a people who mean to be their own governors must arm themselves with the power knowledge gives" (Madison 1822).

In case we were wondering where that "popular information" will come from, Jefferson chimes in. Liberty is not safe, he says, "without information." But "where the press is free, and every man able to read, all is safe" (1816).

What the Founders understood was that, in the modern world of printing press and nation-state, each of us lives in "two worlds" (Bagdikian 2004, p. xii). One is the world in which personal experience and face-to-face interactions help us form our beliefs and attitudes, just as they have done throughout human history.

And then there is another very important world that is beyond the horizon of our own eyes and ears. Journalist Walter Lippmann, writing

---

[1] Strictly speaking, the terms *democracy* and *freedom* are anachronistic here, because they were not in favor among the Founders. They preferred the terms *republic* and *liberty*. Madison explains why in *The Federalist Papers*, #10 (Hacker 1964, pp. 16–24).

in the wake of World War I, asks us to consider "Miss Sherwin of Gopher Prairie" as she grapples with this "other world." She is aware that a war is raging in France and tries to conceive it. "She has never been to France, and certainly she has never been along what is now the battlefield" (1922, p. 12).

Despite this formidable handicap, Ms. Sherwin is asked to make important decisions about the war in France. As one of Madison's "people who would be their own governors," Ms. Sherwin is asked to consider whether it is a just war, whether the United States should enter the war or not, and then to cast a vote, pass a petition, demonstrate, or write a letter to a congressman. But given her handicap—these events and debates are not happening in her ambit—how can she consider such life and death questions? How can she make such fateful decisions?

The answer to this crucial question is, of course, a free press that can serve as Ms. Sherwin's other-world eyes and ears, open to all the far-flung events and debates she cannot personally see or hear. And now we see why, for Madison and Jefferson, modern democracy is not possible without a free press. Because without it, Ms. Sherwin—and we are all Ms. Sherwin—is blind and deaf to the world she is asked to help govern.

What Does Ms. Sherwin Need From the Press?

The first crucial role the press is asked to play for democracy is that of watchdog of the people, guarding against the tendency of those in power to take more than their share of social wealth and influence.

Thomas Jefferson began his earlier-cited tribute to a free press with these words: "The functionaries of every government have propensities to command at will the liberty and property of their constituents" (1816). And it is in response to this concern that Jefferson offers up a free press, to act as a kind of people's watchdog, alerting us when there are powerful prowlers afoot.

This tendency of the powerful to overreach themselves is especially likely to emerge in one particular situation, adds Madison, and his observation implies the need for an especially alert watchdog in that situation—the moment of war.

> Of all the true enemies of liberty, war is, perhaps, the most to be dreaded, because it comprises and develops the germ of every other. War is the parent of armies; from these proceed debts and taxes, and debts and taxes are the known instruments for bringing the many under the domination of the few. In war, too, the discretionary power

of the executive is extended . . . and all the means of seducing the minds, are added to those of subduing the force, of the people. The same malignant aspect . . . may be traced in the inequality of fortunes, and the opportunities of fraud, growing out of a state of war, and in the degeneracy of manners and of morals, engendered in both. No nation can preserve its freedom in the midst of continual warfare. . . .

War is, in fact, the true nurse of executive aggrandizement. In war, a physical force is to be created, and it is the executive . . . patronage under which they are to be enjoyed. It is in war, finally, that laurels are to be gathered; and it is the executive brow they are to encircle. The strongest passions, and the most dangerous weaknesses of the human breast, ambition, avarice, vanity, the honorable or venial love of fame, are all in conspiracy against the desire and duty of peace. (1793)

The press's watchdog role is, in fact, so important to popular sovereignty that it was, in a real sense, written into the U.S. Constitution. Supreme Court Justice Potter Stewart explains that the First Amendment's free-press clause was intended to allow the "organized expert scrutiny of government" by the press, and "to create a fourth institution outside the government as an additional check on the three official branches" (1975, p. 634).

The Supreme Court has also endorsed this "watchdog" view of the First Amendment's free-press clause, in the landmark case of *New York Times v. Sullivan*. As it granted the press wide latitude to bark at public figures, the Court said that "public men are, as it were, public property," and that "discussion cannot be denied and the right, as well as the duty, of criticism must not be stifled." Laws that restrict this freedom, indeed, this "duty," of the press "reflect the obsolete doctrine that the governed must not criticize their governors."

In addition to people's watchdog, there is also a second vital role that democracy asks the press to perform: that of "marketplace of ideas"—a teeming bazaar of competing perspectives that Americans can weigh and balance, in order to come to their own conclusions. Once again, in granting the press wide latitude to do its job, the Supreme Court's *Sullivan* decision declared that the "marketplace of ideas" role was also important enough to warrant constitutional protection. The First Amendment, said the Court, "was fashioned to assure unfettered interchange of ideas for the bringing about of political and social changes desired by the people." Quoting Judge Learned Hand's ringing defense of democracy, the Court said, "The First Amendment proposes that right conclusions are more likely to be gathered out of a multitude of tongues than through any kind of authoritative selection. To many, this is, and always will be, folly; but we have staked upon it our all."

How important is a free press to democracy? It is simple: no free press—no watchdog of the people, no marketplace of ideas—no free country. Together, these two press roles stand as the necessary underpinnings of any successful democracy. They are the standard we shall set for the press as we assess its performance in the coverage of recent wars.

The Promise and the Peril of Mass Media

The pen, it is said, is mightier than the average sword. Indeed, the mass media's pen is no ordinary weapon, but a two-edged sword. It has the power to enable democracy. But wielded another way, it can also erode democracy, helping it to degenerate, as Aristotle feared it would, into oligarchy—rule by the few—or into plutocracy—rule by the wealthy.

Few have understood both the promise and the peril of modern media as well as media effects researcher George Gerbner. Gerbner begins his discussion of the media's power by observing that "the basic difference between human beings and other animals is that we live in a world created by the stories we tell" (in Jhally 1997). By "stories," Gerbner means more than a few fictional narratives. These stories are our ur-stories—the underlying beliefs and values that guide our thinking about what is and what ought to be, beliefs and values "woven together into an invisible web called culture." Indeed, Gerbner defines culture as "the stories and messages that govern our way of life and our behavior." The power to tell these stories is the power to control the culture, says Gerbner, quoting Scottish statesman Andrew Fletcher: "If one person were able to write the ballads of a country, he would not need to care who makes the laws."

And here is Gerbner's concern about that power. "For hundreds of thousands of years," he says, "a culture's stories were told face to face." Then, suddenly, with the invention of the printing press, there began "the industrialization of story telling, the ability to stamp out large quantities of stories." And an even more sudden shock was to come, in the early years of the 20th century, with the simultaneous advent of mass production and the advertising industry needed to sell all those mass-produced goods, together with the electronic revolution. A mere century later,

> For the first time in human history, a child today is born into an environment in which the television is on more than seven hours a

day, a home in which most of the stories, most of the time, to most of the children, are told no longer by the parent, by the school, or the church, but instead by a shrinking group of global conglomerates that really have nothing to tell, but a lot to sell. (Gerbner, in Jhally 1997)

Now Gerbner has brought us up to the moment, where we meet our next question: How will democracy fare when private corporations own most of a culture's storytelling apparatus? When in fact, "five corporations dominate one of the two worlds in which every modern person is destined to live" (Bagdikian 2004, p. 10).

❖ THE THEORY OF CULTURAL HEGEMONY

For an answer, we turn to a thinker whose life's work focused on that question, the Italian political theorist Antonio Gramsci.

As a Marxist, Gramsci's idea of popular sovereignty was that sooner or later working-class men and women would see the injustice of life under capitalism and band together to change that life. Indeed, Karl Marx had sometimes seemed to suggest that such a people's revolution was inevitable—a matter of history taking its course (Marx 1988).

But already in 1927, as Gramsci began his great work, *The Prison Notebooks,* the rooftree of history had fallen in upon the notion of "inevitability." Himself imprisoned by Mussolini, the fascist dictator who had just consolidated his power in Italy, Gramsci surveyed a Western world where socialism seemed everywhere in retreat. Already, in 1927, it was clear that there would be no "of course" about history. And so, amid the rubble of the Marxian prediction, Gramsci wondered why.

The basis for what sometimes seems like cavalier optimism in Marx was his assumption that our culture—ways of thinking, believing, and behaving—is determined by our material circumstances.[2] Thus for a while, a property-owning class would be able to command the compliance of working-class people, browbeating them with the coercive powers of government and the undeniable demands of making a living. Eventually, though, the tensions of working-class life—of losing control of the fruits of one's labor, of how one worked, for what—would draw the working class to consciousness of its plight, to

---

[2]In fairness, though determinism is certainly on display in some of Marx's writings, the whole body of his work is more balanced. This economism/inevitabilism becomes categorical only later, in some of Marx's disciples (Abercrombie, Turner, and Hill 1980, p. 9).

resistance and revolt. And, argued many Marxists in the 1920s, wasn't the proof in the historical pudding? Hadn't Marx's scenario just been acted out in Russia?

But as Gramsci looked around him, he saw a Western world very different from Lenin's Russia. In Russia, a state that had lived by the sword, died by it—force was undone by force. But here, in the West, nations were stronger than coercion alone could make them; here, they also rested on the consent of the governed. To achieve that consent, the capitalist ruling class had to do more than deploy the police. It had to build and hold the barricades of "civil society,"[3]—all those places where political ideas and instincts are made and remade. All those places, Gerbner would say, where our stories are made: the schools, the political parties, the churches, the interest groups. Oh yes, and one more—perhaps the strongest barricade of all in our time—the mass media.

The flag to be captured on this battleground of civil society is what Gramsci called the "common sense"—the usually uncritical, often unconscious way in which most people perceive the world (Gramsci 1971, p. 419). This "common sense" is what Gerbner referred to as our "stories about how things are, how they work, and what to do about them" (Jhally 1997). Gramsci adds that these basic stories are so ingrained in us that we take their truth for granted. He called the conquest of these heart habits *egemonia*—hegemony.

Hegemony. Domination. It is an old sin, older than the ancient Greeks who first used the term *hegemony*. But Gramsci's understanding of it was new. The Greeks had used the term to describe the military domination of one city-state by another. In Gramsci, hegemony was not just military, but cultural, a conquering of a people's hearts and minds.

The great genius of Gramsci's account of this struggle is that it is full of healthy respect for all the combatants, which is not true of some accounts of "false consciousness" that ascribe only self-interest to the dominant and stupidity to the dominated. In Gramsci, to be sure, the common sense does protect ruling class power and privilege. But the propertied class has only succeeded in capturing the common

---

[3]Of course, Marx himself planted the seedling of this idea, which would grow to challenge both economic determinism and inevitabilism. The most famous passage is from the *German Ideology:* "The class which has the means of material production at its disposal, has control at the same time over the means of mental production, so that the ideas of those who lack the means of mental production are subject to it" (Marx and Engels 1964, p. 61).

sense by wrapping its ideology around a core of "good sense"—a set of genuinely worthy ideals.[4]

For example, one might argue that the ideal of freedom, which figures so prominently in the American common sense, ought to, because that word represents a deep human need. But somehow, propertied-class ideology has conquered that word and wrapped it in a particular meaning (freedom to do as I please with my property, free enterprise, free markets). That meaning, of course, tends to exclude other meanings more favorable to working- and lower-class people (freedom from poverty, freedom of a people to choose its civic destiny—even if the choice is to abrogate property).

Herbert Marcuse put the point this way: In our society," speech moves in synonyms and tautologies" (1964, p. 88). Words that should begin debates, end them. Words whose meanings should be argued over are instead invariably defined by the status quo, where the "haves" have and the ruling class rules. The "free press" is our press, never mind that it is bound wrist and ankles by commercial imperatives (as Chapter 6 will argue), while news editors in other countries have no commercial overseers, leaving our press behind that of 30 other countries in the "Second World Press Freedom Ranking" (Reporters Without Borders 2003). "Success" is commercial success. "The American way" is the capitalists' way. "The good life" is their life. Good words, words whose only limits should be limitless imagination, are, for the moment, bound to the service of one idea, one class.

But other meanings remain in them, latent, like the strength of Samson, awaiting their moment for a "counterhegemony" when the "good sense" emerges to challenge the "common sense" that usually keeps it under wraps. When this happens, says Gramsci, a society's idea factories will try to "incorporate" the counterhegemony: to lasso it, tame it, and rewrap it in the embrace of the dominant ideology

---

[4]Is there "good sense" in the dominant ideology? As is often the case, Gramsci is ambiguous here. Clearly good sense involves a philosophical, critical mindset, as opposed to an unreflective one (Gramsci 1971, p. 419). But the conclusions such a mind will come to are not defined in the passages defining "good sense." Abercrombie et al. take the good sense to be only that part of the common sense that opposes the dominant ideology (1980, pp. 14–15). But Gramsci described his own argument as one that began by trying to find, in his bourgeois adversaries, that which "should be incorporated . . . in his own construction" (1971, p. 344). And in the passage that most compels a finding of good sense in the dominant ideology, he allows that his own Marxism "presupposes all this cultural past: Renaissance and Reformation, German philosophy and the French Revolution, Calvinism and English classical economics, secular liberalism. . . . The philosophy of praxis is the crowning point of this entire movement of intellectual and moral reformation" (p. 344).

(1971, pp. 395–398). For example, when the Women's Movement emerged to challenge, among other things, fundamental features of capitalism, capitalism moved to "incorporate" or "co-opt" feminism—creating countless advertisements that simultaneously celebrated women's empowerment and offered consumer products as the pathway to women's liberation: "You're tough, you're smart, you're driven. You've become the person you were meant to be. You've come into your own. . . . In colors for your eyes, lips, cheeks and nails, by Charles of the Ritz" (Barthel 1988, pp. 124–125).

Gramsci's heirs have also added a dose of respect and empathy to the understanding of another form of hegemony. In this form, the media's job is not to indoctrinate people into capitalism but to anesthetize them to its injuries. To carry them away from a world full of poverty, rapacity, and indignity, to a realm of undiluted pleasure—a world where laughter and sex and excitement are always available at the touch of a button; where the good guys, the ones like us, always win in the end and find true love; and where the endings are always happy. In our time, even the news media, as we shall see, have been asked to provide this kind of escape into "infotainment."

Again, in theories of "false consciousness," working people's willingness to "buy" this cornucopia offered by the media is viewed derisively—a selling of the birthright of resistance for a bowl of pottage. But this denies the obvious truth: the truth of how hard resistance to injustice is, of how good, really good, the confections of the media's ministering myths can be. "'False consciousness' always contains its truth," Todd Gitlin says, "the truth of wish, the truth of illusion that is embraced with a quiet passion made possible, even necessary, by actual frustration and subordination" (Gitlin 1987, p. 258).

For Gramsci, in other words, the capture of the common sense is not a matter of the strong hypodermically injecting their version of the truth into the weak. Human give-and-take does not work that way. Instead, the common sense is "negotiated by unequal forces in a complex process through which the subordination and resistance of the workers are created and recreated" (Simon 1982, p. 64).

Gramsci summarizes his position and hints at its implications in one of the most-quoted passages of *The Prison Notebooks:*

> In the East, the State was everything, civil society was primordial and gelatinous; in the West . . . when the State trembled a sturdy structure of civil society was at once revealed. The State was only an outer ditch, behind which there was a powerful system of fortresses and earthworks. (1971, p. 238)

In our time, this system of fortresses and earthworks is to be found in places like Hollywood, Madison Avenue, and the Manhattan headquarters of CBS, NBC, ABC, Fox News, *Time,* and *Newsweek.*

Hegemony and the Media

In case the hegemony thesis has begun to sound like a conspiracy theory, let me quickly add that it is not. Media magnates and managers do not huddle behind closed doors plotting to benight the masses. Today, hegemony is more complex than that. Today, as Gramsci predicted, hegemony is also more complete than that. Hegemony is now so complete that it is built into the very foundation of the mass media—into the imperatives, the norms, and the routines of the business—so that perpetrating hegemony is not deliberately benighting the masses. It is merely doing one's job. In our time, hegemony has become banal.

This was not always the case. In the beginning, these media were not a bundle of unquestioned assumptions, but of unanswered questions. Who would own these new possibilities? What was their function? Who would decide what they would say? By what criteria? The possibilities were endless. Titanic struggles over these issues ensued. And in one medium after another, capitalists emerged victorious (McChesney 1999). Certainly, their crucial victory was to make the capitalist purpose the media's purpose—that is, to define the media as a commercial enterprise.

With that commercial definition came these commercial imperatives:

1. **Maximize profit.** To do that,

2. **Maximize audience size.** To do that,

3a. **Do not bore the audience.** Entertain it. Avoid the arcana of social issues.

Instead, hit their pleasure buttons: sex, violence, laughter, and so on. Even the news can be enlisted in this project.

3b. **Do not offend your audience.** Do not challenge their common sense.

Reaffirm it. Indeed, decades of research have concluded that this is the most profound effect the mass media have on our culture: "reinforcing a particular way of seeing the world by telling the same stories over and over" (Gerbner, in Jhally 1994). In other words, to make the media commercial was not only to put ultimate power over them in the hands of capitalists; it was also to render their content either apolitical or reaffirmative of the common sense. This was a common sense the business community would be at pains not only to reflect, but to shape, especially in its formative years and in crisis times (Exoo 1994). Eventually, reaffirming the common sense meant reaffirming the "free enterprise" system and its corollaries.

Apolitical and pro-establishment. An opiate and an ideology in one syringe. What more could a hegemonic class ask for?

Media Hegemony in the 21st Century: A Turn of the Screw

Recently, the profit motive has tightened its grip on the media business even further. This happened as the media completed a transition foreseen by Thorstein Veblen at the turn of the last century. He called it the transition from "industry" to "business" (1904, chap. 3).

The founders of the media "industries" were intimately involved in the production of their newspapers, movies, or television programs. They wanted, of course, to make money. But as makers of products, they also indulged themselves in the pride of craftsmen.

Long-time White House correspondent Helen Thomas describes the pioneering CEOs of television this way: "Robert Sarnoff [of NBC] and William Paley [of CBS] had a great respect for news, and they helped democracy. They allowed their networks to be neutral and successful but didn't expect them to be big moneymakers. I think there's a different corporate view now in terms of the bottom line" (Borjesson 2005, p. 132). Under Paley, "CBS was the gold standard of American radio and television news," adds Ben Bagdikian. "It had the best documentary unit and the best news staff" (2004, p. 45).

But after this generation of founders has passed from the scene, after the industry proves its profitability, says Veblen, it is "acquired" by a purer form of capitalism—a form more interested in profit than in product, more interested in "selling the people" than in "telling the people" (Rubin 1981, chap. 3).

The transition Veblen describes has gone into overdrive in our time, the time of the takeover. Harvard's Rakesh Khurana has documented the change: In 1950, nearly 90% of corporate ownership was in the hands of the families and friends of the founders. By 2000, 60% of corporate equities belonged to "institutional investors" (Meyer 2004, p. 13). This era began in the 1970s, when American corporations were confronted with increased foreign competition. In response, they might have redoubled their efforts to make their own products better. But they chose an easier way: speculative investment instead of productive investment.

One form of this speculation is the takeover. Under this strategy, a company is acquired. Some divisions are sold to other speculators. Others are shut down, taking advantage of U.S. tax laws allowing companies to profit from the boarding up of productive enterprises and the creation of unemployment. Still other divisions are retained by the acquiring conglomerate and run, in the new corporate argot, "leaner and meaner."

By the 1980s, 12,200 companies, worth almost a half billion dollars, were bought and sold in a three-year period. "The merger-acquisition takeover business amounted to nearly a fifth of the 1986 market value of all traded stocks" (Harrison and Bluestone 1988, chap. 3). Ours had become a "casino" economy (Harrison and Bluestone, 1988, chap. 3). Since then, U.S. corporations have spent $20 trillion on mergers and acquisitions that are often "get rich quick" devices for senior executives and large stockholders, but they have spent only $2 trillion on the research and development that help companies compete and retain their employees (J. Brock 2005).

Among the favorite targets of the acquisition business have been the highly profitable mass media. But here, there was a slight wrinkle. Since the early days of radio, federal law has restricted the ownership of mass media, on the grounds that a diversity of owners would help produce the "multitude of tongues" required of our marketplace of ideas. But these restrictions stood in the way of some of the most powerful corporations in the world as they moved to acquire some of the world's most profitable media assets. Deferring, as we shall see in Chapter 6, to that corporate political power, the federal government obligingly removed most of these restrictions. For example, the Telecommunications Act of 1996 was a "Magna Charta" for multinational media corporations, unleashing a tidal wave of media mergers and acquisitions (McChesney 2004, p. 50).

The result is that since Paley's time CBS has been bought and sold by three different conglomerate corporations. Today, Sarnoff's NBC is the property of the General Electric Corporation—which also owns Universal movie and television studios, TV and radio stations in every major market, Universal Studios' theme parks, cable stations such as CNBC, MSNBC, USA Network, Bravo, and Telemundo, along with divisions that provide nuclear energy, military aircraft engines, plastics, financial services, oil and gas treatment plants, and, oh yes, lightbulbs.

Inevitably, these corporate acquisitions have concentrated the ownership of the mass media in fewer and fewer hands. "In 1983, there were fifty dominant media corporations. Today there are five. . . . [These] five global-dimension firms,[5] operating with many of the characteristics of a cartel, own most of the newspapers, magazines, book publishers, motion picture studios, and radio and television stations in the United States" (Bagdikian 2004, pp. 3, 16). To paraphrase Andrew Fletcher, "If one person were able to write the ballads of a country," these multinational corporations would be that person.

The CEOs of these sprawling empires have not usually apprenticed in the craft of media production. Their backgrounds are in law, finance, or other nonmedia businesses. They are not mainly interested in craftsmanship, quality, or product. They are mainly interested in profit, profit, profit. "I don't aspire to that Paleyesque role," a recent CBS CEO says flatly. "This is a business" (Baum 2003, p. 35).

These CEOs are not preoccupied with profit because they are narrow, greedy people. They are single-minded because they have to be, at this stage of advanced capitalism. For a variety of reasons, investors and stockholders have recently become an ever more fickle crowd.[6] They demand not just profits, but large profits—larger than last year's, larger than the other available opportunities. They do not suffer laggards gladly. Companies that don't produce are abandoned and raided. Today's climate is not one in which to worry about product at the expense of profit. Today, more than ever, profit is the king over television, the movies, and even the news. More than ever, the king's decrees are absolute law. More than ever, the resulting media fare is a toothless politics, a mindless entertainment.

❖ AMERICA'S PLACE IN THE WORLD: THE HEGEMONIC STORY

Because this book's focus is on media coverage of American foreign policy, let's ask, What are our culture's dominant beliefs about America's role in the world? Which "stories" about American foreign policy have currency in our media and in our minds?

"There are two fundamental presuppositions—actually articles of faith—that guide U.S. foreign policy," say media researchers John

---

[5]Bagdikian's list includes Time Warner, the News Corporation, Viacom, German-based Bertelsmann, and The Walt Disney Company. McChesney would add GE and Sony to this list of "top-tier" media firms (2004, p. 182). McChesney also lists a "second-tier" of 20 media conglomerates that "tend to be major players in a single area or two related areas" (p. 103). Examples are the Gannett newspaper chain and radio powerhouse Clear Channel.

[6]Among the reasons are U.S. tax laws and the computerization of the financial sector, which has made capital "hypermobile" (Harrison and Bluestone 1988, p. 58).

Nichols and Robert McChesney. "[These beliefs] are almost never questioned in major U.S. news media" (2005, p. 45).

The first article of faith is that "the United States is a benevolent force in the world" and that its role in global politics has been to make the world "a more just and democratic place" (Nichols and McChesney 2005, p. 45). In keeping with the press's belief in this precept, those moments when the United States is clearly *not* a benevolent force—the Iran Contra or Abu Ghraib scandal, for example—are framed by the press as deviations from the norm wrought by a few maverick miscreants—deviations that will soon be curbed, proving once again that our political system works. Reporting and editorials in the wake of these scandals were unabashed odes to the American way, to, as the *New York Times* put it, "the structure unshaken, the genius of American democracy renascent" (Exoo 1994, p. 61).

The other "article of faith" that goes largely unquestioned by the press is a corollary of the first: It is "that the United States, and the United States alone, has a 007 like right to invade any country it wishes" (Nichols and McChesney 2005, p. 47). The United States also reserves the right to "deputize an ally" to join an invasion, "but otherwise other nations are not permitted to join in the invasion business" (Nichols and McChesney 2005, p. 47).

This second basic tenet about America's proper role in the world became, in fact, the centerpiece of the Bush administration's foreign policy. In announcing the Bush Doctrine of "preemptive war," the president began with the first "article of faith," declaring that the "American flag stands not only for our power, but for freedom . . . We fight, as we always fight, for a just peace—a peace that favors human liberty" (Bush 2002a).

But he warned, in an age of

> terrorists and tyrants . . . if we wait for threats to fully materialize, it will be too late . . . the war on terror will not be won on the defensive. We must take the battle to the enemy. In the world we have entered, the only path to safety is the path of action. And this nation will act. Our military must be ready to strike at a moment's notice in any dark corner of the world. . . . All nations that decide for aggression and terror will pay a price. . . . While the United States will constantly enlist the support of the international community, we will not hesitate to act alone, if necessary, to exercise our right of self defense preemptively against such terrorists. (Bush 2002b)

America's role as champion of freedom, now threatened, implies an American right to invade, unilaterally and preemptively, the president asserted.

Recent work by Friel and Falk (2004) has demonstrated the media's acceptance of this belief in an American right to invade. Although the UN Charter prohibits the invasion of one country by another unless it is under armed attack, the U.S. press has been selective in its attention to such violations of international law—vigorously prosecuting the violations of unfriendly countries, but steadfastly ignoring blatant violations by the United States and its allies.

The press's acceptance of this story of American beneficence will also be on display in subsequent chapters. As we'll see, when there is debate about American foreign policy in the press, it tends to be about means, not ends. Because it is assumed that the United States is generally a force for good, serving well the people of America and the world, debate is limited to the question of *how*, not *whether*, to extend American power and influence around the world. As Iraq descended into a Hobbesian war of all against all, the news might have taken the opportunity to raise fundamental questions about *why* the United States invaded and *whether* it should have. But such questions would have disturbed the hegemonic assumption about America's benignity. Instead, letting the hegemonic assumption stand, press criticism focused on the question of *how*, not *why*, the war was fought, as we'll see in Chapter 5.

Not surprisingly, this message of the rightness of American might, regularly reinforced by American politicians and press alike, has left its tracings on the public mind. More than a year after the occupation of Iraq had begun, 77% of Americans still supported the Bush Doctrine of preemptive war—invading a country not actively hostile but considered threatening to U.S. interests.

The same survey respondents also asserted that "following moral principles" should be the most important value in American foreign policy (72%) and rejected the notion that "there is anything that the United States did wrong in its dealings with other countries that might have motivated the 9/11 terrorist attacks" (51%) ("Public Support for War Resilient" 2004).

This story, of American benevolence and an American right to lead around the world, with military force if necessary, is our story and we're sticking to it. It is a story that has been told over and over again and is now standard equipment in the American common sense.

❖ ANOTHER STORY: AMERICAN EMPIRE

Then there is another story of American foreign policy. This one is not so often told, perhaps because it is not as flattering to us as the first story. In this story, American foreign policy is not especially benevolent, nor is it interested above all in freedom and democracy. This is the story of American imperialism.

We'll hear this story, at some length, not because it is the only plausible story of American foreign policy; there are others, also plausible. Rather, we'll hear it as an exercise in what media research pioneer Warren Breed called "reverse content analysis" of the news—chronicling what's not there. Breed and Herbert Gans, in separate studies, found that stories like this one of American Empire, stories of social class and political power, and their uneasy truce with democracy, are a conspicuous lacuna in the news (Breed 1958; Gans 1979, p. 23). Making a similar point, Ben Bagdikian tells us that the press operates under a powerful imperative to "dig here, not there." This story of American imperialism is high on the list of "not there" (Bagdikian 2004, pp. 91–102).

Our "Fourth Branch" of Government

The story begins with a simple but crucial observation about the source of our material well-being, the American economy, made by Charles Lindblom in his classic book, *Politics and Markets* (1977). To an extent not matched in other developed democracies, Lindblom points out, ours is largely a privately owned and managed economy. This, in turn, means that most of the crucial decisions affecting the economy's performance will be made not by public officials, but by business executives.

And because ownership of American business is now, after many years of corporate acquisitions and mergers, quite concentrated, most of these crucial decisions will be made by relatively few, very large corporations. Today, eight companies control half the more than $100 billion oil refining business; just four command 90% of the $150 billion auto market; the four largest textile firms take 82% of a $20 billion market; and so on (Katznelson, Kesselman, and Draper 2002, p. 41). It is big business's decisions—whether to invest, what to invest in, what prices will be charged and wages paid—that will determine "jobs, prices, production, growth, the standard of living, and the economic security of everyone" (Lindblom 1977, p. 175). Thus, as Lindblom points out, "In the eyes of government officials, businessmen . . . appear as functionaries performing functions that government officials regard as indispensable" (p. 175).

In particular, it is U.S. presidents who find themselves, like it or not, in partnership with the business community. That is because research has shown that Americans take inflation, unemployment, and other "economic indicators" very seriously. And when these indicators tell of economic trouble, Americans do the most rational thing they can: They blame the president. Presidents who want to be reelected, or seen as successful by the history books, need to do something. But what? After all, presidents don't make most of the decisions that directly determine the health of the economy. So instead, presidents have done the next best thing: They *maintain business confidence*—that is, confidence that government will foster an environment in which business will flourish (Lindblom 1982, p. 327).

Former presidential adviser James Carville acknowledged this primordial power of big business, paying tribute to the stock and bond markets, where the business community registers its "thumbs-up" or "thumbs-down" on government policy: "The damned bond market. Who knew it was so powerful? If it gets nervous, everybody has to calm it down. If I'm ever reincarnated, I want to come back as the bond market. Then everybody will be afraid of me and have to do what I say" (*New York Times* 9/15/96).

The need to maintain business confidence was never more dramatically illustrated than in 2008, when a gigantic housing and financial bubble burst. Wall Street, together with unscrupulous mortgage lenders, blew the bubble, which, for a while, gave investment bankers a license to print money. But sooner or later, Wall Street and its regulators should have realized the "money" they were printing would be seen for what it was: counterfeit, worthless. At that point, the nation's investment banks, lousy with these toxic assets, would be insolvent.

Treasury Secretary Henry Paulson thought the big banks should pay for their own perfidy and announced that the government would not bail out Lehman Brothers, one of the most aggressive players in the game of get rich quick and let the future be damned. But even before Paulson finished speaking, all hell broke loose: Banks stopped lending, credit markets froze, the stock market crashed. Government had failed to maintain business confidence, and business registered its unhappiness. Within 48 hours, Federal Reserve Chairman Ben Bernanke would tell Paulson, "We need to bail out Wall Street." The two finance czars, both true believers in minimal government intrusion into free markets, then went to Congress with a blunt message: Unless you act now to supply Wall Street with nearly a trillion dollars, our economy will be "gone by Monday." Needless to say, Congress did act, preserving the privilege and positions of those who had caused the problem and handing the bill for Wall Street's greed to innocent taxpayers (Kirk 2009). Such is the power of big business in American politics.

In addition to its primordial power over the economy we all depend on, business has other political power tools. Big business, along with the wealthy Americans who profit from big business, control so much of the one asset every politician needs above all: money.

Mark Hanna, who is said to have run the first modern money and media campaign in 1896, put the point this way: "There are two things that are important in politics. The first is money, and I can't remember the second" (*New York Times* 4/1/01).

In recent years, money has climbed from *important* to *crucial* in the needs hierarchy of candidates, as campaigns rely ever more heavily on the expensive arts of political consultants and paid media. Between 1972 and 2000, spending on political ads increased by over 600% in constant, inflation-adjusted dollars. Over the past decade, the rate of increase in TV political ad spending has been 40% to 50% *every four years* (McChesney 2004, p. 127). In 1974, the average successful challenger for a seat in the House of Representatives spent an average of $100,000. By 2002, that figure was $1.5 million (both figures in constant, inflation-adjusted dollars; Pierson and Hacker 2005, p. 113).

And where is this mother's milk for candidates to come from? Just as Willie Sutton robbed banks because "that's where they keep the money," candidates go mainly to business and those made wealthy by it for contributions. In recent years, for example, business PACs have contributed about twice as much to congressional candidates as labor unions, the second largest contributors (Katznelson et al. 2002, p. 154). In the 2002 election cycle, a very wealthy one tenth of 1% of Americans provided 83% of all itemized campaign contributions (McChesney 2004, p. 131). In 2000, 95% of major individual contributors (giving $1,000 or more) to campaigns had incomes of $100,000 or more (Pierson and Hacker 2005, p. 114). These are the same Americans, roughly 10% of the population, who own most (78%) of U.S. corporate stocks (Wolff 2001, p. 15).

This story of America abroad continues, then, with this question: What might be the foreign policy interests of this business community, so politically powerful that it is sometimes dubbed our "fourth branch of government"?

American Empire: Act I

In the fresh wake of World War II, as European economies lay shattered, American business was in a unique position to expand into new markets in the Third World and to profit from its resources, its consumers, and its low-wage workers.

There was just one problem. According to historian David Callahan, this global expansion "was seen as requiring an international economic order that could only be guaranteed if the United States took over the position of a declining Britain" as the world's leading military power, to act as security guard for U.S. corporate interests worldwide (1994, p. 30). Fortunately for multinational corporations, President

Harry Truman was ready to maintain business's confidence that the United States would do all it could to facilitate this global expansion. Only one thing seemed to present itself as a threat to the vision of a U.S.-led capitalist world order: another emerging world power and avowed enemy of capitalism, the USSR. But as it turned out, the Soviet Union would not be much of an impediment. According to Soviet expert Adam Ulam, "The moment of [World War II] victory was to find the Soviet Union enfeebled and devastated on a scale unprecedented in the past by countries *defeated* in a major war" (1971, p. 11).

Exhausted and beleaguered by repeated invasions, the postwar Soviets had only a limited, if fiercely determined, foreign policy objective: to create a buffer zone under its control in Eastern Europe. There were no resources for fomenting a global rebellion against capitalism, and there was no attempt to (Gaddis 1972, p. 355).

And yet American politicians warned frantically of just such a Soviet scheme to spread communism across the world. Why? Perhaps Senator Arthur Vandenburg's advice to President Truman provides a clue: "The only way to get Americans to accept the United States' new role as world leader was to 'scare the hell out of the country'" (Katznelson et al. 2002, p. 305).

Truman's response to this situation was the "Truman Doctrine," which would define American foreign policy for the next half century: The United States would intervene in other countries' affairs, militarily if necessary, "to support free peoples who are resisting subjugation . . . by outside pressures" (Truman 1947). This sounds noble enough, but as historian Stephen Ambrose has pointed out, since the terms *free peoples* and *anti-Communist* were thought to be synonymous, the policy justified American intervention on behalf of any corporate-friendly dictator and against any popular movement, if the dictator merely claimed he was battling communism (Ambrose 1980, p. 305).

The Military-Industrial Complex

There followed a U.S. military buildup of a scale unprecedented in human history. Today, war production is the biggest industry in the United States. Over 4.5 million Americans are employed in the business of war. The U.S. Department of Defense (DoD) is the single largest consumer in the world. Total U.S. military spending now exceeds $800 billion per year—more than the next 12 highest-spending nations put together, and accounting for almost half the military spending world wide (Parenti 2008, p. 78).

Much of that spending goes to the huge corporations that are the DoD's top contractors. Among the country's 25 largest corporations, in fact, all but 5 are among the top 100 firms receiving DoD contracts. What's more, these firms are especially fond of their military contracts, which are often awarded without competitive bidding, involve no risk or competition, and pay for cost overruns that gallop into the billions (Johnson 2004, p. 309; Parenti 2008, pp. 79–81). These contractors, now doing business in all 50 states and employing millions of Americans, are another gale-force wind of lobbying power in the sails of more and more military spending.

Almost no other nation has even a single military base outside its borders. The United States maintains over 700, in over 70 countries all over the globe, along with a "military presence" in 153 of the UN's 189 member countries (Johnson 2004, pp. 167, 288; Nichols and McChesney 2005, p. 46). The U.S. Navy patrols every ocean, with a fleet larger than all the other navies of the world combined. American war planes "enjoy uncontested supremacy in the skies, and the United States has the best-trained, best equipped army in the world" (Katznelson et al., 2002, p. 317).

But perhaps the most important fact about the U.S. military is not its size, but its purpose. According to *New Republic* editor Gregg Easterbrook, the American armed forces are the only military in the world "whose primary mission is not defense. Practically the entire military is an expeditionary force, designed not to guard borders—a duty that ties down most units of other militaries, including China's—but to 'project power' elsewhere in the world" (2000, p. 24).

In his famous "Farewell Address" as president, former general Dwight Eisenhower warned the nation of the power of this "military-industrial complex":

> The conjunction of an immense Military Establishment and large arms industry is new in the American experience. . . . In the councils of government we must guard against the acquisition of unwarranted influence . . . by the military-industrial complex. The potential for the disastrous rise of misplaced power exists and will persist. (1961)

Empire Building: "Not Missionary Work"

Once again, this immense American firepower has been justified by U.S. officials, whose words are faithfully transcribed by the press as a defense of freedom and human rights against the specter of Soviet empire building. But a walk through the history of how the military has actually been used since World War II tells a very different story.

In a dispiriting parade of overt and covert U.S. excursions into other countries, it is clear that what is being defended are the raw materials, markets, and investments abroad of U.S.-based corporations. In case after case, it is painfully clear that human rights and democracy are not the point. Time and again, the United States has opposed peaceful and democratic social change in the Third World when it seemed to threaten U.S. corporate interests. Repeatedly, the United States has installed or propped up the most barbaric dictators, friendly to American corporations, but not above the use of torture, "disappearances," executions, and assassinations to crush their critics. When asked why his administration had first, as a favor to the Shah of Iran, encouraged rebellion among Iraq's Kurds and then, when that rebellion had outlived its usefulness, allowed them to be slaughtered while, via telegram, they literally begged him for help, Henry Kissinger replied, "Covert action should not be confused with missionary work" (Blum 1995, pp. 242–244).

In this way the United States imposed its will on Iran, Guatemala, Chile, the Congo, Brazil, East Timor, Greece, El Salvador, Bolivia, Nicaragua, Myanmar . . . this list could go on (Blum 2000). It is this dark history, in particular, of support for unconscionable repressions and regimes, about which the American press has maintained an eerie silence. "At the time of these events," says Ben Bagdikian, who edited the *Washington Post* at the height of the Cold War, "the accounts read by most Americans were the propagandistic reports issued by Washington, giving ordinary readers and viewers the impression that these moves . . . were either spontaneous or beneficent actions by the United States to oppose communism, further social justice or prevent threats to the security of the United States" (2004, p. 97).

Professor of journalism Lawrence Pintak, who has lived in Muslim countries during most of his long career, blames this press bias for the tragic disconnection he observed after 9/11: "The question that arose like a collective moan from the U.S. body politic after 9/11, 'Why do they hate us?' was mirrored by an equally bewildered, 'Why can't they see?'" from the Muslim world (2006, p. 15). After reviewing the particular injuries American foreign policy has inflicted on Muslim countries, Pintak answers the question about why Americans can't see: "In much of the mainstream U.S. media, there was only the most cursory effort to understand the motivations of those who had carried out the attacks or even the perspectives of the world's 1 billion plus Muslims." Instead, reporters were ordered to "tie facts to a pro-U.S. perspective." In other words, to frame the story in a way that cropped out the history of U.S. perfidy in the Middle East (Pintak 2006, pp. 40–41). "Dig here, not there" (Bagdikian 2004, pp. 91–102).

American Empire: Act II, "Globalization"

In the early 1990s, our question about the goals of American foreign policy was subjected to a fascinating natural experiment, when, quite suddenly, the Soviet Union imploded. Now that the reason given for our military escalation, the Russian Bear, was no more, would the United States melt swords into plowshares, redeploy some of the enormous resources devoted to the military, and use them for education or health care or tax cuts? Would there not be a massive "peace dividend"?

There would not. In a new National Security Strategy unveiled in 1990, the George H. W. Bush White House argued that the United States would continue to need a huge interventionist capability to deal with "threats to American interests" in the Third World. In particular, the Strategy foresaw a need to "reinforce our units forward deployed" in the Middle East, because of "the free world's reliance on energy supplies from this pivotal region" (Chomsky 1992, pp. 29–30).

So it was that, even in the post-Soviet 1990s, "Defense spending averaged . . . almost exactly the Cold War norm" (Johnson 2004, p. 56). Today's military budgets, adjusted for inflation, "exceed the average amount spent by the Pentagon during the Cold War," even when we exclude the special appropriations that pay for ongoing wars in Afghanistan and Iraq. In today's federal budgets, military spending continues to exceed all other discretionary spending combined (Hellman 2006).

And for very good reason. After all, the Cold War may have been ending in the early 1990s, but U.S. corporate "globalization" was just coming into full bloom. Global financial flows increased from several billion dollars a day in the 1970s to about $2 trillion a day at the end of the 1990s. U.S. exports increased from a value of $272 billion in 1980 to about $1 trillion by the late 1990s. Imports rose from $290 billion to $1.2 trillion during that period. In 1979, U.S.-owned assets abroad were worth $786 billion. By 1999, the foreign assets of U.S. corporations were worth $6 trillion (Scholl 2000; Wade 1996).

Once again, the vast majority of this business is being conducted by gargantuan companies—the multinational corporations (MNCs) that now control more than a third of the world's privately owned productive assets (Wade 1996). Once again, the global profit seeking of these MNCs relies heavily on their partnership with the U.S. government, as Bill Clinton's under secretary of commerce explains:

> We had a mission. [Ron] Brown [secretary of commerce] called it "commercial diplomacy"—the intersection of foreign policy, government power, and business deals. We used Washington's official muscle to help firms crack overseas markets. The culture was electric. We set up an economic "War Room" and built a "trading floor" that tracked the world's largest commercial projects. (Garten 1997, p. 16)

More than ever, the *sine qua non* of all this world commerce would be a global climate made safe for U.S. capitalism to do business. That kind of security could be ensured only by an undiminished U.S. military. As we shall see, no one made the case for continued military supremacy more ardently than the White House team that would lead the United States into a war-wracked 21st century.

American Empire: The Particular Case of the Persian Gulf

As the United States and its corporations surveyed their global opportunities after World War II, one region of particular interest was the Middle East, with its vast oil reserves. A classic study of the history of oil makes clear that this is no ordinary commodity for nation-states. This is the commodity on which their very survival depends:

> The First World War made all Western governments painfully aware of the importance of oil for survival . . . as the war extended—fought with planes, cars and tanks—and the oil tankers were critical for supplies. "We must have oil!" said [Allied Commander Marshal] Foch, "or we shall lose the war." "The allies," said Lord Curzon, "floated to victory on a wave of oil," as the Germans ran short. . . . After the war, there was a new rush of consumption . . . and the right to travel cheaply, to have cheap electricity and cheap heating became regarded as part of American democracy, and the whole landscape was transformed by the product. . . ." Oil," said Georges Clemenceau, "is as necessary as blood." (Sampson 1975, pp. 59–60)

More recent actions by U.S. presidents clearly demonstrate that oil and the Middle East are continuing priorities of American foreign policy. The "Carter Doctrine" puts the matter plainly: "Any attempt by any outside force to gain control of the Gulf Region will be regarded as an assault on the vital interests of the United States of America, and will be repelled by any means necessary, including military force" (Carter 1980).

In his turn, Ronald Reagan put muscle behind Carter's mouth, creating the U.S. Central Command (CENTCOM)—the first regional command created in 35 years—to police the broader Middle East, from Sudan to Kyrgyzstan.

Today, says U.S. foreign policy scholar Chalmers Johnson, "attempting to control as many sources of petroleum as possible" is one of the five post–Cold War missions that require maintaining a worldwide network of military bases (2004, pp. 151–152).

For their part, U.S. oil companies in the post–World War II period, like Tammany Hall philosopher George Washington Plunkitt, not only "'seen' their opportunities" in the Middle East, but with the essential help of the U.S. government, they also "took 'em" (Riordan 1905, pp. 3–6). In 1940, British companies controlled 72% of Middle East oil reserves; the United States, 10%; and several other countries divided the remainder. By 1967, Britain controlled 29%; the United States, 59%; and other countries, what little was left (Magdoff 1969, p. 43). How did the United States alter the balance of oil power so quickly and decisively?

Iran: Conquest and Blowback

In Iran, for example, where the only oil company was British after World War II, the CIA successfully conspired to overthrow the elected Prime Minister Mohammed Mossadegh, in 1953. Mossadegh was "neither pro-Soviet nor pro-communist; his nationalism was single minded" (Rubin 1980, p. 59). In fact, he had played a major role in driving the Soviets out of northern Iran after World War II (Prestowitz 2003, p. 184). But he had spearheaded a movement to nationalize Iran's oil fields, and this, the United States and Britain agreed, was unacceptable. Once he was out of the way, power was consolidated in the hands of Muhammed Reza Shah Pahlevi, who was "prepared to cooperate with the United States" (Sick 1985, p. 7).

Not long afterward, the Shah concluded an agreement, midwifed by the American government, with eight multinational oil companies, five of them based in the United States, to develop Iranian oil. There was also a clandestine "participant's agreement," kept secret from the American people, to restrict the flow of Iranian oil and thus maintain the fixing of the world price (Sampson 1975, pp. 128–132).

To help the Shah support the United States' interest in allowing U.S. corporations to do business in the Middle East, Washington also immediately agreed to sell him $80 billion (in today's dollars) of American weaponry (Prestowitz 2003, p. 185).

Also to help secure his power, the Shah maintained a CIA-trained secret police, SAVAK, a force notorious for its savagery: torture "equal to the worst ever devised," the murder of an estimated 10,000 Iranians, long-term imprisonment without trial, the ubiquitous monitoring of innocents—including dissident Iranian students studying in the United States, where its agents seemed to operate openly—these were the stock in trade of SAVAK's reign of terror (Rubin 1980, pp. 177–178).

Not surprisingly, the Shah's brutality, together with the carnival of corruption that marked his government, made him immensely unpopular. Finally, in 1979, a broadly popular revolution—supported by students, intellectuals, religious leaders, and industrial workers—overthrew the Shah and captured the embassy and staff of the "Great Satan" Americans who had supported him (Afary and Anderson 2007).

By promising a complete "break with Western imperialism—cultural and political," the Fundamentalist Islamic cleric Ayatollah Khomeini took power. He established the repressive theocracy that continues to govern Iran[7] (Afary and Anderson 2007).

This history was a classic instance of "blowback"—the intelligence term for the tendency of American empire building to produce hostile reactions that imperil U.S. goals. The term is a synonym for the biblical adage that "as you sow, so shall you reap." Now Iran and its formidable, U.S.-provided arsenal were in the hands of an avowed archenemy of the United States.

Iraq: Ally, Enemy, Tool, Archenemy

This, of course, did not mean that the United States was willing to surrender its hegemony in the region. What it was willing to do was get into bed with Saddam Hussein, despite knowing full well that the Iraqi dictator was a ruthless thug.

Prior to the U.S. alliance with Hussein, the CIA had actually brought his dreaded Ba'ath Party to power in a violent coup in 1963 and then helped the Ba'athists to push out their coalition partners in 1968, leaving a Ba'ath regime "unquestionably midwifed by the United States" (Johnson 2004, p. 223). Once Saddam Hussein emerged as the Ba'athist leader in 1979, it was not long before his penchant for mass murder became evident. In the summer of 1980, for example, Hussein "detained" 5,000 Kurdish-Iraqi dissidents, who were never seen again, and may well have been victims of poison gas and chemical weapons experiments (Fisk 2002, p. 15).

Nevertheless, when Hussein launched an attack on Iran's oil fields later that year, he qualified himself to be the United States' designated hitter in the region. Then-President Reagan ordered the Pentagon and CIA to provide Hussein with military intelligence and weapons. By November 1983, Hussein was using chemical weapons against the Iranians "almost daily," and the United States knew it (Prestowitz 2003, p. 188).

But that knowledge did not deter Reagan from dispatching special envoy Donald Rumsfeld to Baghdad to resume diplomatic relations with Iraq, in December 1983. Subsequently, the United States provided

---

[7]In 1997, a very hopeful liberalization movement resulted in the election of pro-reform President Mohammad Khatami. Unfortunately, when George W. Bush designated Iran a member of the "axis of evil" and warned of possible military action in 2002, hardliners used the occasion to quash the reformers and elect arch-conservative Mahmoud Ahmadinejad as president (Afary and Anderson 2007).

Hussein with "a veritable witch's brew" of chemical and biological agents (Blum 2000, p. 121) along with computer parts for ballistic missiles, technology for biochemical weapons research, and the Bell helicopters used to spray deadly toxins on Iraqi Kurds in March 1988, killing an estimated 5,000 of them in the village of Halabja. Throughout this mayhem, the United States remained Hussein's staunch ally. When asked about the gassing of the Kurds, Assistant Secretary of State Richard Murphy replied, "The U.S.-Iraqi relationship is important to our long-term political and economic objectives" (Blum 2000, p. 121; Prestowitz 2003, p. 189).

This partnership might well have persisted indefinitely if it weren't for Hussein's own imperial ambitions in the Mideast, together with one of the most colossal miscommunications in the history of diplomacy.

From Ally to Enemy

Iraq had long laid claim to territory inside its oil-rich neighbor, Kuwait. "Before moving [against Kuwait,] however, [Hussein] first tried to determine how the United States would react. On July 25, 1990, he met with U.S. Ambassador April Glaspie, who assured him that President Bush 'wanted better and deeper relations, and that we have no opinion on the Arab-Arab conflict like your border dispute with Kuwait'" (Prestowitz 2003, p. 189).

On August 2, Iraqi troops stormed into Kuwait. Although the United States had overlooked or condoned other, similar invasions, this one, upending a crucial, oil-rich ally and the stability of a crucial, oil-rich region, was unacceptable (Exoo 1994, p. 6).

So when Hussein proved intransigent, he quickly went from the friend with whom the United States wanted "deeper relations," to, in the elder President Bush's words, Adolf Hitler.

By the following January, it was U.S. troops who "Desert Stormed" into Iraq. Total Iraqi casualties, many of them civilian, were estimated in the hundreds of thousands (Harbrecht 2003).

Then, when the newly dubbed "Butcher of Baghdad" was expelled from Kuwait and his army routed, American forces withdrew—though not without adding an armoire full of new jewels to the crown of American empire. These included the first major foreign military installation ever sited in Saudi Arabia—the huge Prince Sultan air force and surveillance base; the relocation of the Navy's 5th Fleet, with its 4,200 personnel, to Bahrain; the $1.4 million Al-Udeid air base and Camp As Sayliyah in Qatar, the latter being "the largest locale of pre-positioned war material in the world" (Johnson 2004, p. 249). This military necklace draped around the Persian Gulf also added new bases in

Kuwait, Oman, the United Arab Emirates, and Djibouti (Johnson 2004, p. 242). Together, these new installations are a giant U.S. military footprint, planted firmly in the heart of the world's energy supply.

The "Stability" of Tyranny

The American withdrawal from Iraq left Hussein free to crush the Kurdish and Shiite rebellions that President Bush had explicitly encouraged the Iraqi people to undertake. The Butcher of Baghdad was back in business, and soon, an estimated 2 million Kurds were refugees (Cowell 1991). White House officials explained the seeming contradiction this way: "Whatever the sins of the Iraqi leader, he offered the West . . . a better hope for stability than did those who have suffered under his repression" (Cowell 1991, p. 1).

Likewise, after all the talk of ending "brutality and lawlessness," the pro-democracy and human rights groups in Kuwait had reason to hope for help from the American government. They would have reason to be disappointed. As Kuwait rounded up thousands of its imported workers suspected of supporting Saddam, and tortured, beat, and sometimes murdered them, President Bush said there was "little he could do" (Rosenthal 1991, p. D1) to urge democratic reform on the ruling Emir (Whitley 1991, p. 19). This, after crushing the invader who had crushed the Emir.

White House officials further explained that while they would not encourage democratic reforms that might "destabilize" Kuwait's oligarchy, they would exercise another kind of influence. "By virtue of the military victory, the United States is likely to have more influence" on the Emirates and Princes now under American protection "than any industrial nation has ever exercised." They explained "how they might use their new franchise" for the benefit of American business, at a cost to the American consumer: "If crude oil prices plunged, Washington might lean on Saudi Arabia to push prices back up high enough to allow American energy companies to make profits" (Uchitelle 1991, p. D1).

Once again, the "stability" in which American corporations could conduct business as usual had proven to be the paramount value of U.S. foreign policy. Just as it had in overthrowing Mossadegh, installing the Shah, supporting Saddam, then attacking and finally tolerating him, the "stability" of American corporate hegemony had trumped all other values.

This is where, for now, our story of American ventures in the Persian Gulf ends and begins again in Chapter 3, when a foreign policy team calling themselves the Vulcans will begin the next episode in the tragic history of America and this battle-scarred land.

❖ OUR MANICHAEAN MEDIA

Again, the point of telling this story—the story of an American foreign policy designed to make the world safe for capitalism—is not to argue that it is the only plausible story of America abroad. The point is rather to tell a well-documented story the press seems phobically averse to.

For example, to another observer, it might seem that the first Gulf War was a morally ambiguous situation: a situation in which a nation went to war against a nation it had just supported, causing hundreds of thousands of deaths, on behalf of another regime with a poor human rights record, over an invasion like many others it had tolerated or condoned, and refusing in the aftermath to urge democracy or human rights on the defeated/rescued regimes.

But not to the American press. To the American media, the 1991 Gulf War was, unambiguously, "a just message on behalf of honorable goals," a message sent to "messianic tyrants and madmen." A war fought by the "majesty and utter menace" of the American military, "a star-spangled display of threatening force," unleashing "the full fury of modern warfare" in assaults both "spectacular and terrifying." The war was "a moral victory," which defeated "not just the Iraqi army, but also any . . . self doubt, fear of power, divisiveness and uncertainty about America's purpose in the world" (Exoo 1994, pp. 4–17).

But this is not surprising. Indeed, a fundamental tendency of American mass media is to view the world in "Manichaean" terms. Just as the medieval followers of Manes conceived of the world as a struggle between light and darkness, good and evil, so, in their own way, do our mass media.

In the media's Manichaean world, conflict arises when bad guys make mischief and have to be dealt with by good guys. Conflict could, of course, be seen in other ways. It could be seen as a result of social inequality, or injustice, or ignorance. But the mass media tend to see conflict in black and white, good and evil.

In the film and TV business's most valuable genre, "action-adventure," bad guys are not bad as a function of social forces or of human weakness common to us all. No, say these modern melodramas, the bad, to paraphrase Fitzgerald, are different from you and me. They are bad for the sheer hell of it; they are evil incarnate.

These villains being the subhuman psychotics that they are, violence is a necessity. Nonviolence is a non-option. Having watched *Shane* and John Wayne, *Dirty Harry,* Eliot Ness, *Batman, Darkman, Spider-Man, Dick Tracy,* multiple semesters of *The Terminator, Lethal Weapon,* and *Die Hard,* we have learned their relentless lesson: the imperative of violence, so succinctly formulated by Stallone's *Cobra:* "You're a disease. I'm the cure."

George Gerbner's 30-year study of television has found that one of TV's main effects is the creation of a "Mean World Syndrome." The average viewer, Gerbner notes, is exposed to six to eight acts of violence per hour on prime-time TV—some by villains making problems, some by heroes solving them. Not surprisingly, heavy viewers see the world as more dangerous than it actually is: They feel "more insecure, more threatened, more dependent on people who claim they'll protect you. You'll even approve repression, in the country or in the world, if that is presented to you as a way of enhancing your security" (Gerbner, in Jhally 1994).

These viewers are ripe, says Gerbner, for political exploitation. Previously, we've seen that a goal of American foreign policy is, at least sometimes, protecting U.S. corporate interests, even at the expense of democracy and human rights. Ordinarily, such a policy would be a hard sell. But it becomes easier when politicians, with the cooperation of the press, can put the breastplate of righteousness on themselves and the mask of the bad guy on those foreign leaders who don't cooperate: the "Evil Empire," the "little dictator in designer sunglasses," the "Mad Dog of the Middle East," the "drug-dealing dictator." Such appeals to our Manichaean beliefs have justified recent interventions in Nicaragua, Libya, Panama, Grenada, and the Persian Gulf.

The Utility of Fear

Polls showed that the number of Americans suffering from "Mean World Syndrome" increased markedly after 9/11 (*Newsweek* 8/6/05). To some extent, of course, these fears are warranted: The 9/11 assaults brought home a terrorism threat that had not previously been much on Americans' minds.

But is it also possible that Americans' fears were stoked beyond reason, by politicians and media who understood Gerbner's dictum that fearful people are "exploitable" people—who understood that, like sex, fear sells? (Jhally 1994).

A-level Republican strategist Frank Luntz certainly understood the possibilities of 9/11. His 2004 memo to Republican candidates advised that "no speech about homeland security or Iraq should begin without a reference to 9/11," and every such speech should pound home the theme that "9/11 changed everything" (Lustick 2006, p. 104).

Luntz's strategy was applied with a vengeance by the George W. Bush White House. In a typical rendering of its message of threat, a 2002 presidential statement said:

> The threat of terrorism is an inescapable reality of life in the 21st century. It is a permanent condition to which America and the entire

world must adjust. The need for homeland security . . . is tied to the underlying vulnerability of American society and the fact that we can never be sure when or where the next terrorist conspiracy against us will emerge. The events of September 11 were a harsh wake-up call to all citizens, revealing to us the danger we face. Not since World War II have our American values and our way of life been so threatened. The country is now at war, and securing the homeland is a national priority. (Bush 2002b)

Between 2002 and 2006, the president's five State of the Union addresses mentioned education 11 times, unemployment 3 times, and terrorism 122 times.

"Terrorism," said the president's director of national intelligence, "is the preeminent threat to our citizens. The War on Terror is our first priority and driving concern" (Negroponte 2006).

For its part, the mass media also understood the potential of fear. Just as it could sell a candidate, so could it sell movies and newspapers. "The relationship between the War on Terror and the news media," says international relations scholar Ian Lustick, "is particularly robust. It is probably not too strong to say that the lifeblood of the War on Terror is the attention of the media to scary questions about disasters that terrorists could visit upon us." The media "revel in headlines that maintain the image of a constant state of semi-emergency. For the national media, it is as if, for a local news outlet, a gigantic blizzard or hurricane were permanently identified as 'possibly about to strike our city'" (2006, pp. 90–91).

With headlines like that, there is no need to add, "Stay tuned." Viewers will. In the two years following 9/11, MSNBC, CNN, and FOX News all enjoyed soaring viewership and revenues (Journalism.org 2005). Between the news' horror stories—and the ones ladled out by the entertainment divisions of the same companies, who also understood that fear sells—it became difficult for Americans to avoid "repeated depictions of their country as living beneath a sword of Damocles" (Lustick 2006, p. 26).

The American people, for their part, took these fears to heart. At one point, 94% of Americans believed that "there are terrorists inside the United States planning attacks" (CBS 7/15/05). There were 82% who thought it "likely" or "very likely" that "Islamic extremists will carry out major terrorist attacks against U.S. cities, buildings or national landmarks in the near future" (*Newsweek* 8/6/05). In addition, 40% were "somewhat" or "very worried" that "someone in your family might become the victim of a terrorist attack" (CBS 7/15/05).

But we still haven't answered the question that began this section. Yes, politicians and media alike advised us to be afraid after 9/11, and Americans took their advice. But wasn't that fear justified—a rational response to a very real threat? Or was the specter created—of a hyper-potent, omnipresent, evil enemy—amped up, hyped beyond reason in pursuit of ratings and votes?

Terror: A Reality Check

It is exactly this question that political scientist Ian Lustick seeks to answer in his exhaustive, meticulous survey of the first five years of the War on Terror. He begins by documenting the "enormous scale of resources devoted to the search for terrorists, the virtual nonexistence of restraint on the conduct of investigations and the gathering of evidence, and the disposition of authorities to err on the side of arresting the innocent so as to maximize the probability of discovering the guilty" (2006, p. 46).

Such conditions, he reasons, maximize the chances that we will know something about the magnitude of the threat. "The truth is that in the four and a half years since 9/11, the government has assiduously investigated virtually any Middle Easterner in the United States who could in any way have been suspected of being associated with terrorism" (p. 46).

And the results?

> Of the 80,000 Arabs and Muslim foreign nationals who were required to register after September 11, the 8,000 called in for FBI interviews and more than 5,000 locked up in preventive detention, not one stands convicted of a terrorist crime today. In what has surely been the most aggressive campaign of ethnic profiling since World War II, the government's record is 0 for 93,000. (Lustick 2006, pp. 44, 46)

In those few terrorism cases the government has actually pursued, "the record reveals a string of false arrests followed by de-escalated indictments, failed prosecutions, and sometimes what appear to be rather desperate attempts to trumpet some sort of accomplishment in the War on Terror" (Lustick 2006, p. 44).

Yes, Lustick concludes, "there is and will continue to be a terrorist threat." But the "undisciplined, spiraling, hysterical War on Terror" our politicians and press have conjured

> is itself more damaging and dangerous than the terrorist threats it is supposedly combating. . . . The effort to master the unlimited catastrophes we can imagine with the scarce resources we have will drain our economy, divert and distort our military, intelligence and law enforcement resources, undermine our faith in our institutions and fundamentally disturb our way of life. In this way, the terrorists who struck us so hard on September 11, 2001, can use our own defensive efforts to do us much greater harm than they could ever do themselves." (pp. ix–x)

For our purposes, the inference to be drawn from this study is not that Lustick is right and the terror hawks are wrong about the size of the threat we face. The point is simply that Lustick's not unreasonable point of view is absent—curiously, conspicuously, completely absent from the news.

❖ AMERICANS AND AMERICAN EMPIRE

This book argues that the press's default option is to boost American foreign policy, even though that policy often seems to be serving U.S. corporate interests, at a high cost in Third World human suffering.

This press support would be more understandable if serving corporate interests abroad also served the interests of most Americans. But does it? Is what's good for GM good for America?

To answer that question, let's return to the moment when the economies wrecked by World War II—the European and Japanese—had not only recovered but were often beating American companies at their own game. Suddenly, in the 1960s and 1970s, this foreign competition produced a "crisis of profitability" for American business. To maintain profit levels, the corporate community realized it would need to take a bigger piece of what was now a smaller pie—including a piece of what had been American workers' slice. In a 1974 editorial, *Business Week* sounded the call to arms:

> It will be a hard pill for many Americans to swallow—the idea of doing with less so that big business can have more. . . . Nothing that this nation, or any other nation, has done in modern economic history compares in difficulty with the selling job that now must be done to make people accept this new reality. (in Dreier 1987, p. 65)

To reduce labor costs, business massively "restructured." Abandoning the American worker, corporations decided that the land of opportunity was, in fact, Sri Lanka, South Korea, Mexico, or Brazil—places where wage rates are a tenth or a fifth of the American average. In other cases, the land of opportunity was out of the realm of production altogether and in the realm of "paper entrepreneurialism," where goods and services are bought and sold instead of made (Harrison and Bluestone 1988, p. 32).

Either way, American workplaces were padlocked. Often enough, their failure was not that they weren't profitable, but that they weren't *profitable enough* to suit corporations whose only interest was in profit maximization. For a period during the 1980s, nearly a million jobs were lost each year. Most of them were in the unionized, well-paid manufacturing sector (Harrison and Bluestone 1988, p. 37).

As another kind of profit-maximizing strategy, business began creating other kinds of American jobs. Most of them were in the low-paying, nonunionized service sector.

Even expressed statistically, the consequences of this "deindustrialization" have been startling. By the late 1980s, the proportion of "middle wage" American workers had dropped from nearly 90% to less than 50% of all year-round, full-time workers. At the same time, the proportion of "low-wage" workers increased from less than 20% to about 35% of the total (Harrison and Bluestone 1988, p. 127).

By the 1990s, "globalization" was in full stride, but it carried a two-edged sword: global opportunities for corporations and investors, global threats to American workers (Freeman 2007). Between 1977 and 1999, the income of America's richest 1% increased by 100%, while that of the poorest fifth of Americans declined by 10% (Katznelson et al. 2002, p. 57; percentage changes represent constant dollars).

"Moreover, there appears to have been a sea change in economic patterns during the 90s. Periods of full employment usually empower labor to demand higher wages. Yet despite steady productivity growth and [what the Clinton White House enjoyed boasting of as] the longest economic expansion in history, with record levels of employment and an intense demand for labor—wages barely inched upward. Intensified global competition" has cowed workers: Ask for "too much," and you may have nothing, as your factory relocates to the Third World (Katznelson et al. 2002, pp. 57–58).

As this two-edged sword of globalization hacks away, indices of inequality have gone, literally, off the charts: Graphs comparing nations' inequality cannot contain the U.S. line; those showing U.S. inequality over time cannot hold the most recent lines. In 1980, the ratio of CEO to average worker pay in the United States was 42 to 1. By 1990, it was 107 to 1—a startling increase but nothing compared to the inequality yet to come. By the mid-2000s, the gap was 431 to 1 (Jackson 2006).

No other industrialized nation comes close to matching these U.S. inequalities. Our closest "competitors" in the inequality contest, historical oligarchies such as Argentina and Brazil, sport CEO to worker pay ratios of between 40 and 50 to 1. More developed democracies, including Western Europe, Japan, and Canada, have ratios of between 10 and 20 to 1. In the world's second and third largest economies, Japan and Germany, the ratios are 11 and 13 to 1 (Katznelson et al. 2002, p. 47).

By 2006, Forbes 400 *millionaires* were a thing of the past. In that year, the magazine's list of the richest Americans was "billionaires only." Even in the anemic recovery of the mid-2000s, corporate profits burgeoned by 72% between 2003 and 2007, largely because "almost all of the benefits from productivity improvements are flowing to the owners of capital rather than to the workers" (Sklar 2006). So it was that in 2006, the combined wealth of the Forbes 400 was $1.25 trillion— about the same amount held by half the U.S. population, numbering 57 million households (Sklar 2006).

And while the rich got richer, the poor, with their minimum wage, service sector jobs, got poorer: By 2007, four years into an economic expansion, the percentage of Americans defined as poor was higher than at the bottom of the last recession (*New York Times* 4/17/07). At the same time, the percentage of Americans living in "severe poverty," defined as half or less of the federally defined poverty level, reached a 32-year high, growing by 26% from 2000 to 2005, to include 16 million Americans. Once again, this trend showed "how hard it is for low-skilled workers to earn their way out of poverty" in the new, global job market (McClatchey 2/25/07).

Finally, these stark inequalities became a major contributor to the economic crisis of 2008. As the newly superrich maintained their portfolios of safe investments, but then had oodles of cash to spare, they used it to gamble and, for a long time, win on the superhigh return of risky subprime mortgage-based investments. When this gamble eventually came up snake eyes, everyone lost. But even as bailed out financial firms were again showering their executives with bonuses, many working and lower-class Americans were losing the basics: house, job, college fund, retirement income (Collins 2008).

❖ CONCLUSION

No, America is not El Dorado. The Lone Superpower is not the Lone Ranger, righting wrongs wherever it goes. Capitalist hegemony and its monotonous story have not made ours "the best of all possible worlds." And yet, somehow, the alchemy of our mass media has made it seem so: It has made the land of inequality, the land of opportunity; the stench of belligerence, the bouquet of idealism; cupidity and rapacity, the American Way. This book is a case study in one such metamorphosis: the transformation of 21st-century American imperialism into the story of a benevolent America, trying its best to defend the world from tyrants and terrorists. If George Gerbner is correct, and we "live in a world created by the stories we tell," then we need to get our stories right (Jhally 1997). And there is no more important story than this one—of America's role in the world in our time.

September 11, 2001, 10:00 a.m. Tower 2 of New York's World Trade Center collapses. With this "blood-dimmed tide" now flowing, "what rough beast, its hour come round at last, slouches toward Bethlehem to be born?"

2

Night Falls

9/11 and the Afghan War

Our story of America at war in the 21st century begins, as it must, on September 11, 2001. We'll meet the horror of that day head-on, stepping back into the ghastly hours that unleashed the fury of war.

We'll see that, just after the tragedy, there was a moment of debate, but quite quickly this "multilogue" was replaced by an insistent monologue: One voice, one message soon dominated the media conversation that would decide America's future. Its four-part message was classic Manichaeism:

1. *Our enemies are deranged and evil. Hatred and war are the only possible responses to them.* This mask of the bad guy was affixed to the faces, not just of the al-Qaeda perpetrators of 9/11 but also to our erstwhile partners, the Taliban, and eventually to anyone who challenged the U.S. writ. Our world was on its way to becoming a very "Mean World" indeed.

2. *President Bush and his White House team are the heroes of a struggle between good and evil and are to be revered.* We'll see that as it lionized

the president, the press abdicated its watchdog function, an act that would have far-reaching consequences.

3. *Those who disagree with the New Orthodoxy are to be condemned, derided, and marginalized.* Before the press was through with its branding of dissidents as traitors, the marketplace of ideas would have only one hegemonic idea left.

4. *See no evil; inconvenient facts are to be forgotten.* Another reverse content analysis will lift up the rug to see what was not there in the mainstream media's version of the Afghan war. Here we'll see that U.S. covert action was "the rib from which" the Taliban and, indeed, bin Laden himself were fashioned as U.S. proxies in Afghanistan's 1980s war with the Soviet Union (quotation from Roy 2001). But you wouldn't learn that from the mainstream press. Nor would you learn much about civilian casualties, which were inconsistent with the story of a good war and perhaps for that reason were deemed "not news." Apparently, such casualties were also on the list of "Dig here, *not there* [italics added]!" (Bagdikian 2004).

In this chapter, we'll also see the entertainment media, corporate first cousins of the news, enlist in the war effort to create a seamless unity of message about the justice of the battle for Afghanistan.

As the bombing begins, we'll see that even war can be made into infotainment. The battle is rendered as the dramatic story of a fierce and formidable enemy bested by the grit and know-how of American GIs and their marvelous machines.

Of course, the most infotaining stories have Hollywood endings, and as the conclusion to this war, the press gave us the happy tableaux of celebration and liberation from the oppressive Taliban.

But meanwhile, in the forgotten ghetto of untold stories, the end of the war left an Afghanistan that had suffered thousands of civilian casualties, six months of starvation, and a half million refugees—an Afghanistan that now faced provincial rule by brutal, opium-growing warlords, and the return of the Taliban. And all of this carnage, it would turn out, was only the beginning.

❖ "ALL CHANGED, CHANGED UTTERLY"

It was a crisp September morning, and there wasn't a cloud in the sky when, out of the blue, the first plane struck. As refugees from Tower 1 poured into the street and the crowd stared up at the fire spewing like dragon's breath from the building's gaping wounds, a second plane hit Tower 2. Soon, up and down the avenues surrounding the towers, onlookers could hear the screams of people plunging from the inferno. One couple, witnesses said, held hands as they fell. "I guess they couldn't see any hope," said a man in the crowd.

Within minutes, a third plane tore into the western face of the Pentagon. Shortly afterward, tourists were stunned by the sight of workers fleeing the White House in terror.

Back in New York, a real estate broker working on the 86th floor of Tower 2 called his wife, she said, "several times until 10:00" then nothing.

> He sounded calm, except for when he told me he loved me. He said, "I don't know if I'll make it." He sounded like he knew it would be one of the last times he would say he loved me.

At 10:00 a.m., as rescue workers continued to rush into the building and up its many flights of stairs, Tower 2 collapsed. At 10:29 a.m., Tower 1 dissolved.

Eleven minutes later, a fourth plane—and all its passengers and crew—fell to Earth in a Pennsylvania field.

All over the East Coast, overloaded phone circuits shut down; survivors dialed loved ones in vain. New York's television stations, their antennae fallen with Tower 1, went dark. The White House switchboard asked callers to wait for an operator then went dead. For the first time in aviation history, the whole country was grounded.

As the fallen Towers billowed up from the ground as black clouds—a million tons of dust, said the EPA—a kind of night fell over Lower Manhattan and, indeed, across the whole country.

Through this Stygian darkness and, through the thick slush of memos, computer disks, and—witnesses said—body parts, an exodus of survivors, covered in white ash and plaster dust, staggered like ghostly refugees from a war zone across the bridges to Brooklyn. "This is America," one of them said. "How can it happen in America?"

Indeed, how could it? But it did. And in those few minutes on that day, the most lethal on American soil since the Civil War, all was "changed, changed utterly." And now, with the "blood dimmed tide" loosed upon the nation, "what rough beast, its hour come round at last, slouches toward Bethlehem to be born?" (Yeats 1974, pp. 152, 158).

A Moment of Debate

In the media, in the days that followed, the dead were mourned. Heroes were praised. Shock, horror, dismay, fear, and anger were given vent. But as a nation, what was our response to be?

As is perhaps inevitable and proper in a democratic society, opinions differed. Some writers were critical of the administration on grounds small or large. They wondered, for example, why the President spent much of 9/11 hunkered down in a bunker in Nebraska, at a moment when the nation needed its leaders, and there was no sign that the president had been a terrorist target (Apple 2001, p. A24).[1]

More important, others wondered how such a massive failure of the nation's intelligence and security systems could have been allowed to happen (Elliott et al. 2001). Some called for us to wage war on the Afghan government that harbored bin Laden. Others argued that this attack was not an act of war—not an aggression by Afghanistan against the United States—but a monstrous crime that should be treated as such, with the al-Qaeda perpetrators rounded up and tried in an international court (Howard 2001).

These advocates for an international law resolution to the attack added that a war brought by the world's richest and most powerful nation against one of the world's poorest would further immiserate a starving and war-weary Afghan people. They worried, too, that such a war would only fan the flames of the Islamic world's animosity toward the United States, producing "a further cycle of terrorist attacks, American casualties and escalation" (Chalmers Johnson, in Bernstein 2001, p. A13). "If our goal is to reduce the number of people in the world who want to kill us," said author Barbara Kingsolver, "this is not the way to go about it" (Gates 2001, p. 2).

Nicholas Lemann, dean of Columbia's School of Journalism, wanted to know what the experts thought. He interviewed a group of the country's most respected foreign policy mavens—focusing on scholars from the "realist," as opposed to the liberal or leftist, school

---

[1]On the morning of 9/11, Bush was attending a Sarasota, Florida, photo opportunity, reading to schoolchildren to promote his education initiative. Curiously, he remained in the classroom posing for cameras for a full 50 minutes after the first plane struck and long after the Federal Aviation Administration, White House, and Secret Service became aware that three commercial jetliners had been hijacked. From there, 30 minutes after the second attack, Bush was, in his own words, "trying to get out of harm's way." Air Force One then flew to an air force base in Louisiana, where Bush made brief remarks to the nation, then to an underground bunker at the U.S. Strategic Command (USSTRATCOM) in Offutt, Nebraska. Stung by suggestions, including some from Republican lawmakers and conservative commentators, that the president's movements that day did not show the strength needed from the nation's leader, the White House insisted they were reacting to "hard evidence" that Air Force One had been a target of the terrorists. After several media accounts challenged that assertion, White House spokesman Ari Fleischer refused further comment. Eventually, White House officials explained that, despite the earlier claims of "hard evidence," the fear for Bush's safety on 9/11 occurred because White House telephone operators "apparently misunderstood comments made by their security detail" (Alterman and Green 2004, pp. 225–230).

of thought. These scholars' assumption is that the United States should focus exclusively on its own interests. Lemann's interviews revealed a remarkably consistent and, in retrospect, insightful set of analyses. "Military power is not necessary to wiping out al Qaeda," said Stephen Walt of Harvard's Department of Government.

> It's a crude instrument, and it almost always has effects you can't anticipate. . . . This is ultimately a battle for the hearts and minds of people around the world. When your village just got leveled by an American mistake, the conclusions you draw will be rather different from what we'd want them to be. (Lemann 2002)

Statistical evidence for this concern about the "hearts and minds" of Muslims "around the world" was not long in coming. A Gallup poll conducted in nine Muslim countries in February 2002 found that 77% of respondents deemed the U.S. war in Afghanistan "unjustifiable." Only 9% expressed support (Green 2002).

In the wake of the attack, we also asked ourselves, "Why?" The Bush administration argued that attacks by Muslims on the United States were motivated by "evil." "They can't stand the thought of a free society. They hate freedom," said Bush. "They love terror. They love to try to create fear and chaos" (Associated Press [AP] 2003).

Others contended that Bush's explanation was simplistic—that it ignored the grievous suffering that U.S. policies had, in fact, imposed on Islamic people. They pointed, for example, to U.S.-led sanctions against Iraq, imposed after the 1991 Gulf War, which denied not just weapons to the Iraqi regime but food, water, sanitation, and medicine to the Iraqi people, causing the deaths of an estimated 500,000 Iraqi children.[2] While these writers were at pains to point out that such grievances did not justify attacks on American civilians, they maintained that we ignore U.S. misconduct at our peril. "Let's by all means grieve together," wrote novelist Susan Sontag, "but let's not be stupid together" (2001, p. 32).

Not surprisingly, this complex debate helped produce a complex public opinion. At this early stage, 15% of Americans thought the United States should declare war on Afghanistan. Sixty-one percent were "not sure" whom to declare war against (Elliott et al. 2001, p. 5).

---

[2]This number is somewhat controversial, due to the difficulty of assigning numbers to the various causes of Iraq's very high childhood mortality rate during the sanctions regime. What does seem clear is that a very large number of Iraqi children died as a result of the sanctions and that the United States was the prime mover behind those sanctions (Gordon 2002; Welch 2002). For an unblinking report on other grievances the Islamic world may justifiably harbor against U.S. foreign policy, see Pintak (2006, chap. 1).

❖ FROM MULTILOGUE TO MONOLOGUE

But quite quickly, this multilogue among many voices faded from the mass media, leaving only monologue; one voice, one message, soon dominated the conversation that would decide America's future. The tenets of the new orthodoxy were as follows:

1. Our enemies are deranged and evil. Hatred and war are the only possible responses to them.

The media delivered this Manichaean message first, by quoting President Bush often and at length on the subject. A study of 15 major speeches by the president during this period found that the "themes of evil, security and peril were present in at least one of every ten presidential paragraphs, and often much more" (Pintak 2006, p. 91). Here is a sample of the presidential language that permeated the media in the fall of 2001:

> The great purpose of our great land . . . is to rid this world of evil and terror. . . . The evil ones have roused a mighty nation, a mighty land. And I am determined that we will prevail. . . . [In this] war between good and evil [our nation] was targeted because we're the brightest beacon for freedom and opportunity in the world. . . . These are people [who] hate freedom. . . . [Together] with all those who want peace and security in the world [America will now] go forward to defend freedom and all that is good and just in our world. (Pintak 2006, pp. 89–91)[3]

But the press was not content just to quote the president and his spokesmen on the subject of evil. The news would also echo and amplify the president's Manichaean views. A special 9/11 issue of the nation's leading newsmagazine set the tone for the new orthodoxy in an editorial entitled "The Case for Rage and Retribution":

> What's needed is a unified, unifying . . . purple American Fury—a ruthless indignation that doesn't leak away. . . . Let America explore the rich reciprocal possibilities of the fatwa . . . America needs to relearn why human nature has equipped us all with a weapon . . . called hatred. The worst times . . . separate the civilized of the world from the uncivilized. This is the moment of clarity. Let the civilized

---

[3]This language, argued Bruce Lincoln (2003), Caroline E. Haskell Professor of the History of Religions in the Divinity School at the University of Chicago, was an "eerie echo" of bin Laden's words: "Both men constructed a Manichaean struggle, where Sons of Light confront Sons of Darkness, and all must enlist against one side or another, without possibility of neutrality, hesitation or middle ground" (p. 20).

toughen up, and let the uncivilized take their chances in the game they started. (Morrow 2001)

The editor in chief of *U.S. News & World Report* added another note to this hymn of hatred, a note that would become common in the months ahead: Not only are our attackers' motives not rational, but they are despicably petty—they are jealous of us:

> The extreme fundamentalists who carried out these attacks . . . are trapped in a medieval mindset. . . . These fanatics resent our cornucopia. They resent our moral values. . . . There is no deal we can ever make with such people. None. (Zuckerman 2001, p. 76)

A good deal of the coverage during this period seemed designed to emphasize the otherness, the alienness of Muslims who opposed the U.S. writ. Again and again, their beliefs and behaviors are presented as irrational and incomprehensible to civilized people. A *Chicago Tribune* editorialist specifically dismissed the motive suggested by Taliban and al-Qaeda spokesmen ("a result of the U.S. government's wrong policies"). Instead, he declared, "The bin Ladens of the world hate us simply because we are Americans." This is "a form of odium as intense as it is irrational," he said, and we find ourselves "under a Kafkaesque indictment for unspecified crimes" (Grossman 1998). A *San Francisco Chronicle* article laid out the weird beliefs that explain "Why Suicide Terrorists Embrace the Unthinkable," including a faith that "he will get permission to send to heaven 70 members of his family" and that "the martyr will find 72 virgins waiting for him in heaven" (Asimov 2001). A *New York Times* account of a protest against the United States in Kabul described a "frenzied . . . mob" beset by "passions that spiraled out of control. . . ." While "a group of turbaned black-clad Taliban men" pulled the seal of the United States from a former embassy, the crowd "danced ecstatically and shouted 'Long Live Osama' and 'Death to America'" (9/27/01). Subsequent demonstrations around the Islamic world were described in a second *New York Times* piece as "feverish protests" and "fevered chants." This article concludes that "the world these militants want to create" is based on such "hollow" grievances as the taking of the Palestinian homeland and the punitive sanctions imposed on the Iraqis after 1991 (Crossette 2001a, p. B4).

Many of these references to "frenzied . . . out of control" Arabs were classic examples of what one writer calls "raiding the Orientalist cupboard . . . picking up old prejudices" (Ahmed 1992, p. 186). Jack Shaheen's classic study of the media's biases against Islam identifies two of the recurring media prejudices as basic: seeing Muslims as "barbaric and uncultivated" and "reveling in acts of terrorism" (1984, p. 4). As a result, Arabs have been "dehumanized," leading Americans "to think in 'us versus them' dichotomies," according to Muslim scholar Edward Said (1997, p. 109).

Likewise, the notion that Muslims "hate our values" is a false and pernicious stereotype. The U.S. official who knew bin Laden best, the CIA officer who headed the bin Laden task force in the 1990s, explains why bin Laden's words (though not necessarily, as we shall see, his deeds) had resonance in the Muslim world:

> Bin Laden's genius has been to focus the Muslim world on specific U.S. policies. He's not, as the Ayatollah did, ranting about women who wear knee-length dresses. He's not against Budweiser or democracy. The shibboleth that he opposes our freedoms is completely false, and it leads us into a situation where we will never perceive the threat. (Scheuer 2004)

A 2004 survey of attitudes in six Arab countries confirmed that "there appears to be no empirical evidence to support the claim that Arabs have a negative view of the United States because 'they hate American values'" (Pintak 2004). Likewise, a 2002 survey of public opinion in eight Muslim countries found that, while there was overwhelming resentment of U.S. policies among the respondents, substantial majorities had a favorable view of American freedom and democracy and even of U.S. television and movies (Zogby 2002). "Those who hate America love its freedoms," said a columnist for Pakistan's *Nation* magazine. "They hate America because America's hypocritical policies deny them those freedoms" (Pintak 2006, p. 105).

Lawrence Pintak, a decorated journalist who has spent most of his career living in Muslim countries, argues persuasively that the Islamic world reacted to 9/11 in two main ways:

1. First, with a huge outpouring of outrage and sympathy for the loss of innocent life: "brutal," "insane," "inhumane," "cowardly," "crimes against humanity whose ugliness and barbarism exceed all imagination," "un-Islamic and immoral." These are just a few of the reactions Pintak cites from Muslim editorialists and political leaders around the world (2006, p. 77).

2. And secondly, "Arab and Muslim leaders and the region's media" implored the United States to use the tragedy as an "opportunity for Americans to reassess their relationship with the Muslim world" (p. 84).

This suggestion was seconded by the National Commission on Terrorism, which sensibly admonished, "An astute American foreign policy must take into account the reasons people turn to terror, and, where appropriate and feasible, address them" (Bremer 2000, p. 2).

Unfortunately, in the climate of rage and fear created after 9/11, any news story exploring the "reasons people turn to terror" was attacked "as if somehow we were not explaining a reality but justifying the 9/11 attacks," according to *Los Angeles Times* editor Simon Li. "And . . . that sort of superpatriotism does cause us to hesitate" ("Report on International News Coverage in America" 2003).

So instead of stories that opened Americans' minds to Muslim opinion, the news was filled with stories that closed minds, fostered ignorance, and stoked the fires of fear and hatred. Perhaps the single most damaging decision made by television news during this period was to air, incessantly, footage of a group of Palestinians dancing, cheering, and passing out chocolates in celebration of the 9/11 attacks. Given the frequency of the airings and the inflammatory nature of such an outrageous celebration, this was bound to be, "for many Americans," their enduring image of the Muslim world's attitude toward 9/11 (Pintak 2006, p. 78).

Unfortunately, that impression was terribly wrong; it was, in fact, the opposite of the truth. A Gallup poll conducted in December 2001 found that only 5% of those surveyed in seven predominantly Muslim countries believed the 9/11 attacks were "morally justified" (Morin and Deane 2002). Yet 54% of Americans surveyed believed that "all or most people in the Muslim world admire Osama bin Laden" (CNN 5/4/02).

Why wouldn't they, when no cameras "caught the spontaneous sorrow, despair, tears, and heartache of the vast majority of the Palestinian people," said Reverend Sandra Olewine, Jerusalem liaison for the United Methodist Church. "My phone rang and rang," she added, "as Palestinians from around the West Bank called to offer their horror and their condolences" (Olewine 2001, p. 16). And so, steeped in ignorance and primed by fear, Americans marched in lockstep with their president and press, toward the inexorable conclusion.

War Is So the Answer

And what, according to the news, is the appropriate foreign policy response to enemies who are deranged and evil? In the nation's leading newspapers, the *New York Times* and the *Washington Post*, a total of 46 op-ed pieces discussed responses to 9/11 in the three weeks after the attacks. Forty-four of those urged a military response while two sought nonmilitary solutions (Rendall 2001). On television, the move from shock to fury to war was quick and decisive. On September 12, CNN's logo for 9/11 coverage was "America Under Attack." Two days later, it was "America at War" followed the next week by "America's New War." These declarations of war were well in front of the U.S. government, which did not begin the bombing of Afghanistan until October 7.

Over the next few months, TV network commentators approved of George W. Bush's military answers to 9/11 almost 80% of the time (*Human Events* 2001). This is not surprising, given the "experts" TV chose to lead their discussions. One survey showed that conservative, or right-leaning think tanks, outnumbered progressive, or left-leaning, ones by more than 3.5 to 1 in post-9/11/2001 (Dolny 2002). Another survey found that in the week after 9/11, "alternative perspectives" from activist or advocacy groups were represented only 2% of the time on network news—and even this 2% consisted entirely of advocates for firefighters, airline pilots, and Arab Americans, with the latter "simply urging tolerance and explaining that most Arab Americans do not support terrorism" (Ackerman 2001).

During this period, network television reporters and anchors would refer to Afghan soldiers as "rats," "terror goons," "psycho Arabs," "terrorist thugs," "diabolical," and "henchmen" (Hart and Naureckas 2002). Fox News' chief war correspondent said, among other things, "[If I find bin Laden] I'll kick his head in, then bring it home and bronze it." And

> We want to be there when they bring Osama bin Laden to justice. . . . I've got a New York City fire department hat I want to put on—on the body of his—you know, the head of his corpse. It's deeply personal on the one hand. On the other hand, it is my professional calling. (Rutenberg 2001)

2. President Bush and his White House team are the heroes of a struggle between good and evil, and are to be revered.

The media might, at this moment, have adopted Mark Twain's definition of patriotism: It means, he said, "loving your country all the time, and loving your government when it deserves it." But they didn't. Instead, George W. Bush in particular, as head of state, was unconditionally lionized by the media as few presidents have ever been.

"War Has Made Bush a First-Rate Commander in Chief," pronounced *Hearst Newspapers* (11/25/01). "Global Spotlight Falls on Bush, and He Shines," trumpeted the *Los Angeles Times* (10/23/01). "Surer Voice, Wider Vision," proclaimed the *New York Times* article, redolent with praise: "forceful ... plain speaking ... eloquence ... engaged and activist ... full throated ... strode into the ... House ... as one of the most popular presidents in modern history ... sustained applause ... the tableau was that of a celebration of a war hero" (1/30/02). "George W. Bush has found his mission and his moment," effused *U.S. News & World Report* (10/1/01). "A President Finds His Voice," exulted *Time* (9/24/01). *Newsweek* declared, "Succeeding When It Matters Most: George Bush has always risen to the occasion ... [now he has] inspired the nation, rallied the allies, and impressed even his critics ... calm and commanding in private, warm and dignified in public ... 'Our George:' the designated dragon slayer, a boyish knight in a helmet of graying hair" (9/24/01; 9/27/01).

These characterizations—of a president we've since come to see as mortal after all—might seem amusing in retrospect. But they helped set the stage for the uncritical acceptance, by press and public alike, of President Bush's message as he led the nation down the path to dubious battle.

This aura of greatness attached to Bush was, in fact, large enough to include the entire "Bush Team." "It's hard to imagine a more tested lot than the group that gathers with Bush ... to make decisions in the new, worldwide campaign against terrorism," said *Newsweek* (9/27/01). *Vanity Fair* added a

> reverent spread ... which lionized the presidential team with solemn head shots and TV wrestlers' nicknames—Cheney was "The Rock," Ashcroft was "The Heat," while ranking [Bush] with Demosthenes: "It's been a while since presidential rhetoric could raise the hairs on your arm"

whispered the awestruck author (Miller 2002).

One measure of the Bush team's preeminence in the media was the team's sheer ubiquity; according to one study, CNN carried 157 live events featuring administration officials during this period, while elected Democratic officials were featured seven times.

Perhaps Dan Rather summed up the attitude of the news media generally when he said, "George Bush is the president. He makes the decisions, and you know ... wherever he wants me to line up, just tell me where, and he'll make the call" (Hart and Ackerman 2001, p. 6).

The valorizing of George W. Bush is doubly remarkable when we contrast it with the press's view of Bush prior to 9/11. Back then, only 38% of Bush's evaluations on network news were favorable—nowhere near the 77% positive evaluations of his post-9/11 role as Terror Buster (*Human Events* 2001). Until 9/11, Bush was the accidental president who hadn't won the popular vote, the president of the deer in the headlights misspeech, of the budget-busting tax cuts for the rich, of the "screw you foreign policy," the "slash and burn environmental policy." What a difference a day makes (Miller 2002).

3. Those who disagree with the New Orthodoxy are to be condemned, derided, and marginalized.

The process of purging dissenters began almost immediately. Columnists who had criticized Bush's 9/11 hopscotch around the country were summarily fired (Hart and Ackerman 2001).

Veteran progressive radio host and frequent Bush critic Peter Werbe was dropped by radio station KOMY-AM in Santa Cruz, California. The station's owners explained that "partisanship is out. We cannot afford the luxury of political divisiveness." Meanwhile, the station continued to air six hours a day of right-wing talk show host Michael Savage. Apparently, his accusations that peace marchers were committing "treason" were not divisive (Hart and Ackerman 2001, p. 6).

When asked whether their coverage had included any antiwar voices, TV networks came up short. A CBS spokesman pointed to a segment on *The Early Show* in which a reporter interviewed former 1960s war protestors who turned hawkish after 9/11. MSNBC's president said his network had trouble finding "anyone credible" opposed to the war. But this claim was disputed by the seemingly credible Phil Donahue, who argued that "opportunities were few" for antiwar voices to be heard on TV: "You cannot say that people willing to speak up are not in existence," he said. "There is just not a lot of enthusiasm for this in the programs" (Stanley 2001, p. B4).

In the post-9/11 climate, any deviation from the new orthodoxy, no matter how minor, was swiftly and surely condemned. Speaking to a class of Columbia University students, ABC News President David Westin was asked whether the Pentagon was a legitimate target for America's enemies. "As a journalist," he said, "I feel strongly that's something I should not be taking a position on." But after his comment was attacked on Fox News' *Special Report*, in the *New York Post*, the Drudge Report, and on Rush Limbaugh's radio show, Westin recanted. With Limbaugh's hour-long attack on him still in progress, Westin e-mailed this abject retraction: "I was wrong. Under any interpretation the attack on the Pentagon was criminal and entirely without justification" (Alterman 2003, p. 203).

Comedian and then-ABC talk show host Bill Maher made the fatal mistake of agreeing with his conservative guest, who had warned against stereotyping the terrorists as cowards, because "people willing to die for their cause are not cowards." Maher added, "We have been the cowards, lobbing cruise missiles from 2,000 miles away. That's cowardly" (9/24/01). For this comment, Maher was publicly reprimanded by White House Press Secretary Ari Fleischer, who denounced Maher personally and also issued a more general warning: "The reminder is to all Americans to watch what they say and that this is not a time for remarks like that" (*New York Times* 9/30/01). Maher's program was quickly dropped by 19 ABC affiliates and two major sponsors. Shortly thereafter, the network cancelled Maher's program, the ironically titled *Politically Incorrect.*

In several cases, writers deemed too close to the boundaries of political heresy were pushed over the line by shameless media distortions of their words. Author Barbara Kingsolver, winner of a National Humanities Medal, made the mistake of pointing out that patriotism had been used to justify death threats against an antiwar congresswoman and the murder of a Sikh man. She asked, rhetorically, whether the perpetrators thought the American flag stood for intimidation and violence. Taken out of its actual context and placed in a false one, her question was used to imply that Kingsolver thought the answer was "yes." (For the record, she believes the flag is "an emblem of peace, generosity, courage, and kindness.") Kingsolver then watched, "amazed, as some ultraconservative journalists ignited an attack on my patriotism with a stunning prevarication that blazed like a grass fire through the Internet and countless newspapers, including the *Wall Street Journal*" (Kingsolver 2002).

A few months later, the media's patriotism police were busy planting evidence again—this time on the National Education Association (NEA), a teacher's union. *The Washington Times'* Ellen Sorokin began the frame-up with a story charging that the NEA's Web site was about to offer lesson plans that would "take a decidedly blame-America approach" to 9/11. She quoted the site as advising teachers to avoid "suggesting that any group was responsible" for the attacks (Somerby 2002, p. 3).

An actual visit to the NEA's site revealed that the source of the quotation was an obscure link to an essay by the National Association of School Psychologists (NASP). (Sorokin did not mention that the site also sported much more prominent links to speeches by George W. Bush.) The psychologists' message was quite clear: "Explain that all Arab-Americans are not guilty by association or racial membership." In an act of startling intellectual dishonesty, Sorokin turned this perfectly unobjectionable suggestion into perfidy: the claim that the NEA was telling teachers not to blame al-Qaeda for the crimes of 9/11.

Despite the fact that Sorokin's hatchet job was immediately exposed by alternative press writer Robert Kuttner (2002) as a "completely trumped-up hoax," it continued to pong through the media pinball machine: "The liberal hold on our education system amounts to a kind of moral disarmament," wailed Mona Charen. The NEA is "a national menace," announced *Washington Post* columnist George Will (8/5/02). "The folly of the NEA is staggering," declared Jon Leo (*U.S. News & World Report* 9/9/02). Sorokin herself wrote two follow-up articles, both featured on page one by the *Washington Times* (8/20/02; 8/24/02). "Each promoted the absurd idea that the NEA was a shill for Al Qaeda" (Somerby 2002, p. 3). Lillian Helman once called an earlier moment of such fear and falsity, the McCarthy era, a "scoundrel time." Were we now, in the wake of 9/11, entering another?

Even after a year had passed, the pro-war, pro-Bush climate had not cooled, and dissenters were scorched. When in September 2002, Al Gore dared to deliver a "calm and soberly delivered" speech echoing the concerns raised by several four-star generals about the direction of the war on terror, he was met with an "astonishing explosion of invective" from the media. Fox News contributor Charles Krauthammer called the speech "a disgrace—a series of cheap shots strung together without logic or coherence." And Michael Kelly, not mincing words in the *Washington Post,* called the speech "dishonest, cheap, low, hollow . . . wretched . . . vile . . . contemptible . . . a lie . . . a disgrace . . . equal parts mendacity, viciousness, and smarm" (Alterman 2003, p. 210).

Right to Assemble?

But perhaps the media's sharpest invective was reserved for those Americans who took to the streets to protest the bombing of Afghanistan. The editor of the *New Republic* demanded that demonstrators explain themselves: "This nation is now at war. And in such an environment, domestic political dissent is immoral without a prior statement of national solidarity, a choosing of sides" (9/24/01).

A *Los Angeles Times* guest columnist warned demonstrators that blood would be on their hands, just as it was on the hands of earlier antiwar demonstrators:

> The blood of hundreds of thousands of Vietnamese and tens of thousands of Americans is on the hands of the anti-war activists who prolonged the struggle and gave victory to the Communists. . . . This country was too tolerant toward the treason of its enemies within. (Hart 2001, p. 18)

A *Washington Times* columnist took this last point a step further and made a suggestion about how to deal with the protestors' "treason": "Why are we sending aircraft carriers halfway around the world to look for enemies, when our nation's worst enemies—Communists proclaiming an anti-American jihad—will be right there in front of the Washington Monument on Saturday" (Hart 2001, p. 18).

This threatening tone was common in attacks on the protestors, as when *Newsweek* warned protestors, "Blame America at Your Peril": "A sizable chunk of what passes for the left is already knee-deep in ignorant and dangerous appeasement of the terrorism of Sept. 11. . . . Peace won't be with you, brother. It's kill or be killed" (Alter 2001).

Even news reports about the protests could not conceal the media's contempt for them. After thousands gathered in Washington, D.C., on September 29 to call for a nonmilitary response to terrorism, the *New York Times* covered the event in a 10-sentence story that vastly underreported the size of the crowd and, in a gross distortion of the protestors' message, was headlined "Protestors in Washington Urge Peace with Terrorists."[4]

4. See no evil; inconvenient facts are to be forgotten.

"The greatest triumphs of propaganda have been accomplished, not by doing something, but by refraining from doing," Aldous Huxley once wrote. "Great is truth, but still greater . . . is silence about truth." In Afghanistan, the silences were sometimes deafening.

When Freedom Fighters Go Bad

The basic tenets of the New Orthodoxy were simple: United States good, Taliban bad. Unfortunately, this catechism would require a vow of silence about a very inconvenient truth: The United States had helped create the Taliban and, indeed, al-Qaeda, all with the dutiful support of the U.S. press.

After a Soviet-backed government came into power in Afghanistan in 1978, U.S. officials decided to back its opponents, hoping to "lure the Soviets into a Vietnamese quagmire." "It was July 3, 1979, that President Carter signed the first directive for secret aid to the opponents of the pro-Soviet regime in Kabul. And that very day, I wrote a note to the President in which I explained to him that this aid was going to induce a Soviet military intervention," said Carter's National Security Advisor, Zbigniew Brzezinski (*Extra!* 2001, p. 1).

---

[4]The *New York Times* reported that "a few hundred protestors," etc., were on hand. The official police estimate was 7,000; organizers estimated 25,000 (Hart 2001).

After the Soviets took the bait, invading Afghanistan in 1979, the United States mounted "the largest covert operation in the history of the CIA." From 1979 to 1992, the United States funneled at least $3 billion to the factions fighting the Russians (Parenti 2001).

And who were these U.S.-backed "Mujahadeen," as they called themselves, or "freedom-fighters," as the U.S. press liked to call them? "In general, the most radically Islamic groups always received the bulk of the funding" (Parenti 2001). Among the beneficiaries was Mohammed Omar, who would later be known as the leader of the Taliban. Other senior members of the Taliban also fought with the Mujahadeen. Many of the Taliban members who were too young to fight the Soviets were trained in Mujahadeen-controlled refugee camps in Pakistan.

Worse yet, the appalling human rights record of the Taliban—so rightly condemned by the media after 2001—was there in the Taliban's incubator, the Mujahadeen, as the press looked on in silence. Fully one third of U.S. aid, for example, went to a group headed by Gulbuddin Hekmatyar, who directed his compatriots to throw acid in the faces of unveiled women (Gibbs 2002, p. 13; Parenti 2001). By 1985, the Mujahadeen had prohibited aid agencies from bringing women doctors to rebel-controlled areas—"this in a society where no male doctors are allowed to examine female patients" (London's *Guardian*, in Gibbs 2002, p. 14).

To reinforce the ranks of the Mujahadeen, the U.S. CIA also facilitated the influx into Afghanistan of some 35,000 fervent young Muslim men from 40 Islamic countries between 1982 and 1992. Tens of thousands more, inspired by the Mujahadeen, came to study in radical Islamic madrasas in Pakistan. "Eventually, more than 100,000 foreign Muslim radicals were directly influenced by the Afghan jihad" (Rashid 1999). One of the first of these imported fighters, "recruited by the CIA," was a wealthy young Saudi Arabian named Osama bin Laden. One of bin Laden's duties was to maintain identity and contact information about the international recruits. "From this little black book would emerge Al Qaeda" (Parenti 2001).

To help fund their rebellion, the Mujahadeen also expanded Afghanistan's opium-growing sector from a local and regional business into a major supplier for the world's heroin trade (Gibbs 2002, p. 14). Between 1982 and 1983, opium production near the Afghan–Pakistan border doubled. By the end of the decade, production had reached 800 tons and accounted for 50% of European and North American heroin sales (Prashad 2001).

Not surprisingly, this increase in Afghan production was related to a sudden surge in U.S. heroin consumption. A congressional investigation reported that overdose deaths in the United States increased by 93% between 1979 and 1983 (Robison 1985). During this period, the CIA sought to block investigations into the "Afghan connection" (Gibbs 2002).

This dark profile of the Afghan guerillas—the intolerance, the extremism, the torture, the executions for violations of religious rules, the massacres, and the drug trafficking—was well known to American reporters, but somehow did not, for the most part, become part of their reports. Instead,

> there was near unanimous agreement that the guerillas were . . ."fighting the good fight," [that] a "heroic struggle [was being] waged by the Afghan freedom fighters," [that] "The Afghan guerillas have earned the admiration of the American people for their courageous struggle," [that] "the rebels deserve unstinting American political support and . . . military hardware," [and that] "The fight for freedom in Afghanistan is an awesome spectacle and deserves generous tribute." [Furthermore], "Heroes come in many shapes and sizes. . . . the civil rights leaders who led American blacks to equality . . . [and] the Afghan freedom fighters." (from *New Republic, Wall Street Journal, Los Angeles Times, Washington Post,* and *Christian Science Monitor,* quoted in Gibbs 2002, p. 15)

Perhaps surprisingly, this U.S. government and press support for Islamic extremism in Afghanistan did not end with the Soviet occupation. By 1992, the USSR was history and so was Kabul's Communist government. "With no external enemy, the Mujahadeen coalition soon tore itself, and the cities of Afghanistan, to pieces" (Parenti 2001). It was from this melee that the Taliban emerged victorious in 1996. Immediately, their Mujahadeen-trained Mullah announced that adulterers would be stoned, drinkers hung, women veiled, and that "education would cease to be available to women." Nonetheless, "Washington extended a warm hand towards Mullah Omar and the Taliban," hoping to seal a deal for the Unocal Corporation to build a $4.5 billion oil pipeline through Afghanistan (*Extra!* 2001, p. 3; Parenti 2001).

In May 2001, the Bush administration again extended a warm hand, this one delivering a $43 million check to the Taliban. The grant, said Secretary of State Colin Powell, was intended to support "those farmers who have felt the impact of the ban on poppy cultivation, a decision by the Taliban that we welcome" (Crossette 2001b, p. A7).

In other words, the opium trade expanded by Afghan Muslim extremists with the complicity of the United States was now being contracted by the Muslim extremists, with a $43 million incentive from the United States. Without hinting at the history or the irony of the situation, the *New York Times* extolled the virtues of this new U.S.–Taliban war on drugs. The Taliban, said the *New York Times*, urged the ban "in very religious terms, citing Islamic prohibitions against drugs, and that made it hard to defy" (Crossette 2001b, p. A7).

A few months later, when the Taliban suddenly became evil personified, the earlier encomiums to their U.S.-backed origins as "freedom fighters" and their more recent status as U.S.-supported devout drug busters, became inconvenient. And so, they were mostly forgotten. In their stead, the media paraded the Taliban's history of thuggery and drug dealing, with scant mention of U.S. support for it all. If George Orwell had been alive, he might have said "I told you so":

> To tell deliberate lies while genuinely believing in them, to forget any part that has become inconvenient, and then, when it becomes necessary again, to draw it back from oblivion for just so long as it is needed . . . all this is indispensably necessary. (Orwell 1992, p. 214)

See No Evil: Civilian Casualties Are "Not News"

By the media's lights, this was a good war. But in a good war, what becomes of bad facts such as the civilian casualties that will inevitably occur? In one sense, those bad facts were simply ignored. While human rights groups and the European press tried to measure the cost of the war in innocent lives, the U.S. networks offered almost no estimates of the number of civilians killed, except to assure us in general terms that there were few (Coen 2002b, p. 6).

Consider the contrast in coverage of the bombing of Kandahar. France's leading wire service, *Agence France Presse,* saw it this way: "Two months of relentless bombardment have reduced the city of Kandahar to a shattered ghost town," bereft of water, electricity, and food, "housing only the famished who were too poor to leave. . . . [Refugees from Kandahar] spoke of horrendous civilian casualties as wave after wave of American bombers" targeted their city (12/6/01).

The Washington Post's version, on the other hand, was headlined "Civilian Deaths Not Evident in Kandahar":

> The campaign in Kandahar was conducted mostly from the air, with US warplanes conducting more than two months of strikes against the city and its environs. Despite repeated reports of civilian casualties . . . a trip around the city indicated that, for the most part, the bombs hit their targets and there were relatively few civilian injuries. . . ."We were scared because of the explosions, but they didn't hit us in the end," said a resident. (12/12/01)

This was more than just a matter of perception. The U.S. press said quite explicitly that, for them, civilian deaths were (a) unimportant, (b) the necessary price to be paid for the lives of the 9/11 victims, or (c) a propaganda tool of the Taliban. So while the British *Independent* reported

> After viewing the pulverized homes of Karam, what was apparent was that dozens, and perhaps as many as 200, civilians had been killed by American bombing. From all over the countryside, there came stories of villages crushed by American bombs; an entire hamlet destroyed by B-52's at Kili Sarnad, 50 dead near Tora Bora, eight civilians killed in cars bombed by U.S. jets on the road to Kandahar, another 46 in Lashkargah, 12 more in Bibi Mahru. (12/4/01)

Thomas Friedman of the *New York Times* fumed:

> Think of all the nonsense written in the . . . European media about the concern for "civilian casualties." It turns out that many of those Afghan "civilians" were praying for another dose of B-52's to liberate them from the Taliban, casualties or not. (11/23/01)

Brit Hume, of Fox News, also wondered whether civilian casualties were important news: "The question I have is civilian casualties are, historically, by definition, a part of war, really. Should they be as big news as they've been?" Fox commentator and *U.S. News & World Report* columnist Michael Barone answered Hume's question: "I think the real problem here is that this is poor news judgment on the part of some of these news organizations. Civilian casualties are not . . . news. The fact is that they accompany wars" (11/5/01). This is a somewhat curious logic. The fact is that almost all aspects of the Afghan war—battles, enemy casualties, U.S. casualties, strategies, victories—"accompany wars." Are they also "not news"?

CNN's chairman, Walter Isaacson, instructed reporters that they were not "to focus too much on the casualties or hardship[5] in Afghanistan." Furthermore, any mention of civilian casualties, CNN's head of Standards & Practices said, should also include this rationale for those deaths:

> We must also keep in mind, after seeing reports like this . . . that the Taliban regime continues to harbor terrorists who are connected to the

---

[5]This is probably a reference to increases in malnutrition. The UN and other relief agencies argued that while U.S. bombing interrupted famine relief efforts, starvation would rise sharply.

Sept. 11 attacks that claimed thousands of innocent lives in the United States. Even though it may start sounding rote, it is important that we make this point each time. (*Washington Post* 10/31/01)

CBS reporter Jim Martin cast his own aspersion on casualty stories by arguing that "the Taliban's chief weapon seems to be pictures they say are innocent civilians killed or injured by the bombing" (10/23/01). In another story that touched on the issue of civilian casualties, Martin reminded viewers that "according to the Pentagon, the Taliban is likely to try anything to win the propaganda war" (11/24/01). NBC's Jim Miklaszewski joined the chorus of reporters equating civilian casualties with Taliban propaganda, ruing the fact that the United States is "on the defensive today" because "the Taliban took foreign journalists on a guided tour of the village of Karam, where they claim U.S. bombs killed 200 civilians" (10/15/01).

Because their focus was on America's battle "to protect its image as a compassionate nation" (NBC 11/4/01) against the Taliban "propaganda machine" (CBS 10/24/01), these stories did not try to determine whether, or how many, civilians had actually been killed or wounded.

❖ THE ENTERTAINMENT MEDIA ENLIST

The monolithic message of a righteous U.S. war against the evil Taliban was not confined to the news media. The non-news media also enlisted in the PR campaign, creating a seamless unity of message about the justice of the "war on terror."

Advertisers were among the first to get into the game. Their ads seemed designed to be inoffensive to antiwar consumers while implicitly endorsing the use of force. In one full page ad, placed in the *New York Times* just 10 days after the attack, the Statue of Liberty, looking angry and determined, strides off her pedestal, rolling up her robe sleeves. Clearly, Lady Liberty is opening up a can of whup-ass. The text says simply, "We will roll up our sleeves. We will move forward together. We will overcome. We will never forget. A message from G.E." Another full page ad, filled by an American flag, quoted a few words from JFK—words that echoed George W. Bush's own warning:

Let every nation know, whether it wishes us well or ill, that we shall pay any price, bear any burden, meet any hardship, support any friend, oppose any foe to ensure the survival and the sources of liberty—from the 130,000 men and women of Lockheed.

GM warned, "The American Dream: We refuse to let anyone take it away." Chevrolet announced its intention to "keep America rolling," in an homage to Flight 93 hero Todd Beamer, whose last words, heard on a cell phone before a struggle with hijackers, were, "Are you guys ready? Let's roll."

While Madison Avenue led the way, Hollywood was not far behind. In November, President Bush's chief campaign operative Karl Rove flew to Los Angeles to meet with more than 40 Hollywood executives, asking them to "make films showing the heroism of American armed forces" (Stephen 2002). He promised producers making "patriotic" films the equipment, personnel, and full cooperation of the U.S. military. Fox Studios quickly took up the challenge, rushing *Behind Enemy Lines*, a "rock and roll driven celebration of the American can-do spirit," into theaters. Other studios followed quickly with such titles as *We Were Soldiers*, *Black Hawk Down*, and *Hart's War* (Ansen 2001).

Before the year was out, CBS had begun taping *AFP: American Fighter Pilot*, a "Top Gun-like reality series" following the lives of American pilots from training to their exploits in the "U.S. anti-terrorist war," according to the networks (AP 12/12/01). A&E, "the arts and entertainment network," quickly produced flattering biographies of 9/11 good guys George W. Bush, Tony Blair, and Rudy Giuliani.

Time Warner's Showtime network followed with *DC 9/11: Time of Crisis*, a reverent tribute to George W. Bush's leadership in the days following the tragedy. In it, Bush (played by actor Timothy Bottoms) is seen heroically resolving to return to the White House on 9/11, despite warnings of a threat against it; a "composed but tough-talking" Bush refuses "to cede to his staff decisions on key passages of an oval office speech"; a charismatic and inspirational Bush rallies rescue workers—and the nation—through a bullhorn at Ground Zero; and so on. "Yes, it is a flattering portrait of the President," declared the film's writer–producer, Lionel Chetwynd, who is also a Bush supporter, campaign-donor, and Bush appointee to the President's Committee on the Arts and Humanities.

> [Chetwynd] does not deny [that the film is,] as one observer put it, a shot across the bow of Democrats seeking to replace Bush. That characterization initially bothered him, but no longer. "Let him (Bush) and his administration's handling of those nine days be the standard by which we judge our leaders because they rose to the occasion." (CNN.com 9/7/03)

Or at least, that was the message broadcast by Showtime via Chetwynd's movie.

Meanwhile pop radio's addition to the national conversation was actually a subtraction. The Clear Channel Corporation, owner of over 1,200 radio stations, including over 60% of all rock stations in 2001, compiled a list of "questionable" songs after 9/11—songs that were to be "steered clear of" by its stations. This long list included Bruce Springsteen's "War," John Lennon's "Imagine," and Cat Stevens' "Peace Train," as well as tunes by System of a Down, and "all songs" by Rage Against the Machine, a band that made no secret of its left-wing, antiestablishment politics (Morello 2001).

Also during this period, live-action video games popped up "all over the internet that let you punch, shoot, and basically torture in every way imaginable the bearded likeness" of bin Laden. Some sites allowed "wrathful gamers to enlist images of 'good guys'" such as George W. Bush, Dick Cheney, or Colin Powell to administer the beat-down. One game had players shooting bin Laden as he hid in a mosque. Its bloody conclusion, in which bin Laden's head explodes, had been seen over 300,000 times within three weeks of 9/11. Even in the popular and previously pacific game *The Sims*, thousands of players were starving or poisoning the bin Laden character to death—"or worse"—while also enjoying "good guy" characters such as Bush, Tony Blair, and Arnold Schwarzenegger (Cox News Service 10/6/01).

When its turn came, the nation's ultimate media extravaganza, the Super Bowl, also did its part for the pro-war effort. During pregame festivities, Barry Manilow and other performers sang his composition "Let Freedom Ring," while a field of cheerleaders pranced about in Statue of Liberty costumes and children in military fatigues ringed around a "Liberty Bell." Once the game began, statistics were presented "by a frequently repeated little series of automated logos starting with what appeared to be a U.S. soldier pressing a button" (Stephen 2002). This game's advertising also waxed patriotic. Budweiser, for example, aired a commercial during the game that featured the Clydesdales traveling to Ground Zero, where they bowed in tribute to the fallen. This Bud's for you, 9/11 victims.

And so, in ways sometimes subtle and sometimes not, the entertainment media joined the news media in producing a Phil Spector–like "wall of sound" in favor of war. And this was not politically unimportant in an era when 79% of Americans under 30 "sometimes or regularly" get their political information from the entertainment media (Williams and Delli Carpini 2002, p. B14).

❖ THE BOMBING BEGINS

On October 7, less than a month after the hijackers' attack, the rush to war became war. President Bush's announcement that the bombing of Afghanistan had begun was met in the press with unequivocal enthusiasm:

> George W. Bush had promised the war on terrorism would be a war like no other, and on Sunday, he delivered. Striking a blow for the hearts and minds of Muslims at the same time he struck Afghanistan, the president fired the opening salvos of Operation Enduring Freedom at midday. (*Newsweek* 10/7/01)

"The American people, despite their grief and anger, have been patient as they waited for action. Now that it has begun, they will support whatever efforts it takes to carry out this mission properly" (*New York Times* 10/8/01).

Immediately and unanimously the five major TV news networks dubbed their coverage of the war "America Strikes Back" or "America Fights Back"—thus giving linguistic victory to the pro-war position by ending the argument, before it began, about whether attacking the cities, roads, bridges, sanitation and water treatment facilities, food storage units, and so on that sustained the impoverished people of Afghanistan was, in fact, "fighting back" against those who had attacked us.

Right Makes Might

Once again, the media left no doubt that this was not merely a just war but, indeed, a war of good against evil:

> If the prior campaign in Araby had been a war of choice, this one is a war of necessity. A brutal band of merciless men, bereft of all scruples and as convinced of their righteousness as Nazi leaders were six decades ago, brought the war to our shores. There are no half truths in this kind of war. It is order versus malignance. (*U.S. News & World Report* 10/12/01)

Often the evil we were up against was personified in the form of Taliban leader Mullah Mohammed Omar or, of course, Osama bin Laden. Like many a good Hollywood villain, Omar was marked, we were told, by his physical repulsiveness as well as by his supposedly characteristic Middle Eastern lunacy: "Mullah Omar Mohammed, the Taliban's one-eyed leader, is, we are often told, insane. A twitching, convulsing Cyclops in a turban, this lunatic clergyman is, apparently, a standout kook even in a region known for its delusional and psychotic despots" (Struttaford 2001).

At the same time, hatred of bin Laden was stoked, not in the name of justice but in the name of a more volatile and dangerous satisfaction—revenge:

> It must be one of the most repulsive home movies ever made. Osama bin Laden chuckles contentedly over slaughtering his own men along with several thousand Americans. . . . In the hearts of wary Americans, bin Laden's smirking and gloating, at once cruel and feral, inspired an overwhelming desire for revenge. They may get it soon enough. (*Newsweek* 12/24/01)

"Powerful Beyond Comprehension"

The press couched the story of combat in Afghanistan in dramatic terms: a fierce and formidable enemy would be beaten by the wonders of American technology, and by the resourceful courage of American GIs and their cohorts, the Northern Alliance.

Intuitively, it might seem that the ragtag "army" of impoverished Afghanistan would not prove much of an obstacle to the armies of the world's only superpower. But that was not the picture provided in the American media. Instead, the press warned of the "brutal terrain and brutal fighters" that had sent first the British and then the Soviets into ignominious retreat.

> Afghanistan is a land of fierce tribal fighters, rugged terrain and no obvious targets. (Knight Ridder 9/29/01)

> They are the ultimate fighters in their own terrain . . . a super tough breed of warriors . . . their basic military skills honed by the intertribal feuding and a ruthless culture of vendetta. (Underhill 2001)

> For centuries it has been known as the place where great powers go to die. The terrain was a nightmare for Soviet and British troops, who were ambushed from the hills, massacred in the passes, cornered on the steep, treeless mountainsides. (Hirsh and Barry 2001)

Fortunately, the U.S. military was up to the daunting challenge, boasting technological marvels undreamed of by the Soviets, much less the medieval-minded Taliban:

Over the last seven weeks in Afghanistan, the US military has shown the world . . . the new American way of war, one built around weapons operating at extremely long ranges, hitting targets with unprecedented precision, and relying as never before on gigabytes of targeting information gathered on the ground, in the air, and from space. (*Washington Post Weekly Edition* 12/10/01)

This dazzling technology, said the press, struck fear in the hearts of our once-fearsome foes:

To many Taliban, the Americans must have seemed like creatures from another planet: out there somewhere, in the sky or across the horizon, powerful beyond comprehension. . . . The Taliban are the first victims of a revolution in military affairs . . . which results largely from astounding leaps in information technology, [and] will eventually be as important as the introduction of gun powder. (Barry 2001)

The specs of this arsenal were rendered in gee-whiz detail in the news, like some super-video gamers' powers:

Super Stallion helicopters . . . refueled in midair . . . zigzagged like rabbits to confuse the enemy . . . Super Cobra attack helicopters scanned the perimeter. "We surprised the hell out of the enemy." A Predator "painted" a house, and an F/A-18 from a carrier then dropped a thousand-pound laser-guided bomb (Barry 2001).

Tomahawk cruise missiles, launched from submarines hundreds of miles away, evade radar by skimming low. . . . satellite guidance enables missiles to slam 1,000-pound warheads into a target with pinpoint accuracy . . . Preludes . . . Gnats . . . Global Hawks . . . JDAMS—a guidance kit attached to a 2,000-pound gravity bomb converts it into a satellite-guided smart bomb. (Newman, Mazzetti, and Whitelaw 2001)

The Right Stuff

Another common theme, in this story of good battling evil, celebrated the bravery, patriotism, and resourcefulness of the American warrior. On the first day of bombing, said Fox News reporter Brett Baier,

Some of those pilots . . . described those bombing runs. . . . They talked about the pride, the adrenaline and the precision of this first night of strikes. . . . They did say they took some anti-aircraft fire, but they were trained to deal with it. (10/7/01)

Another dramatic report came from a *Newsweek* reporter "on the ground with the Special Forces who turned the tide—and just lost one of their own":

> They were a tight-knit group, each man trusting the others with his life. Yet it wasn't until the chopper faded from view and the vastness of the landscape came into focus that they realized how far they were from home, and how alone: 90 miles behind enemy lines, in the heart of Taliban territory. . . . The mission ahead sounded almost impossible . . . storm a key Taliban stronghold, Mazar-e Sharif. . . . After wresting control from the enemy . . . restor[ing] order and help[ing] local leaders begin rebuilding . . . in the harrowing, heroic days that followed, they did just that. (Lorch 2002)

This penumbra of virtue and courage also covered the U.S. allies in Afghanistan, the Northern Alliance. One Fox News reporter described them this way:

> And these are great fighters by the way. . . . They don't have sleeping bags or uniforms, but they got courage, and they've been fighting these bad guys for years all on their own without any help from the rest of the world. Now they are truly the enemy of our enemy, so they're our friends. (12/6/01)

Few of these reports mentioned our allies' human rights record, which was awful. General Rashid Dostum's forces had a long record of raping, killing, and looting, for example, in Mazar-e-Sharif, which Dostum controlled from 1992 to 1997. Now he was retaking the city in the "harrowing, heroic" Special Forces mission just referred to.

In fact, the widely respected Revolutionary Association of the Women of Afghanistan (RAWA), referring to actions documented by Amnesty International and Human Rights Watch, called life under the Northern Alliance's previous rule "a living hell." "From 1992 to 1996," their statement read, "these forces waged a brutal war against women using rape, torture, abduction, and forced marriage as their weapons. Many women committed suicide as their only escape" (Ireland 2001).

RAWA's heroic struggle against the Taliban was often justly praised in the press, but their concerns about the Northern Alliance were not often mentioned. Indeed, when RAWA spokeswoman Saha Saba reported that "people are very worried" about the Northern Alliance, she was quickly "corrected" by CNN host Zain Vergee: "You have harshly criticized the Northern Alliance, but I just want to make a distinction here. Within the Northern Alliance there is a liberal wing.... Today it's the liberal wing that's running the show" (4/20/01). This must have come as a surprise to Ms. Saba, who knew that at that moment, the Northern Alliance forces of Berhannudin Rabbani were entering Kabul. It was Rabbani who had just banned women from schools in Afghanistan, and it was Rabbani's military commander, Ahmad Shah Maasoud, who had ordered mass rape in Kabul in 1995, according to human rights groups (Flanders 2002, pp. 10–12).

❖ HAPPY DAYS ARE HERE AGAIN: BURKAS OFF, MUSIC ON!

The media story of the war's aftermath was a story of liberation and joy at the rout of the oppressive Taliban.

> Residents of Mazar-e Sharif were rejoicing at the retreat of the Taliban military ..."There is music, there is dancing—these all had been banned under the Taliban," said ... a spokesman for General Rashid Dostum, one of three Northern alliance generals to spearhead the takeover. "Men are shaving their beards. Women are burning their burhkas. All of these things are happening." (*Newsweek* 11/12/01)

And, according to the news, the U.S. victory meant more than just freedom from burkas; it meant freedom from hunger and disease. "A Win Over Famine Too," exalted the *Los Angeles Times* (1/6/02). "Massive Food Delivery Averts Afghan Famine," said the *Washington Post*'s front page story (12/31/01). "New Year's Good Message is that Famine Averted," chimed in the *Houston Chronicle* (1/7/02). These stories arrived just in time to bolster George W. Bush's State of the Union Address, which opened by declaring that America "had saved a people from starvation."

Unfortunately, this jubilant story of liberation from repression and starvation had several drawbacks. First, it was the U.S. attack on Afghanistan that had created the threat of widespread famine in the first place. "It's not like there was a famine and we averted it," said Roger Normand, who led a UN-sponsored humanitarian assessment of postwar Afghanistan. "Had we not bombed there never would have been a famine in the first place. ... There's no question that the military campaign disrupted the food supply networks" (Ackerman 2002, p. 8).

Second, it was not clear that the postwar effort had, in fact, averted famine. Because the war had disrupted supply networks and unleashed roving bands of rival warlords' gangs, especially in the hinterlands, "there's much more looting and problems with food supply than there were under the Taliban," said Normand. Indeed, not until months after Bush and the media proclaimed victory over hunger were relief agencies able to return to isolated Afghan villages. In April 2002, for example, aid workers reached villages in western Afghanistan that had not received food aid since September 2001, before the U.S. bombing began. They found children "on the verge of dying from hunger." Arriving in the province of Ghor in March 2002, doctors with Action Against Hunger found 40 people had died of malnutrition in one small district. Doctors Without Borders reported a doubling of the mortality rate in Faryah province. And in Zareh, another group reported that half the children under 5 were malnourished. These reports, not in keeping with the story of the good war, "attracted little attention" from the U.S. press (Ackerman 2002, p. 8).

Promises, Promises

As the war "ended," President Bush promised that we would soon see "an Afghanistan that is prosperous, democratic, self-governing . . . respectful of human rights." But at this writing, years after the dancing in the streets, with the American-backed government still in place, Afghanistan remains desperately poor. Life expectancy is 42; yearly per capita income is $700; and literacy is under 40% (Price 2005). Afghanistan's new, U.S.-backed government is ranked as the third most corrupt out of 30 countries surveyed by Freedom House, a Washington-based research group (Stockman 2005a). In 2005, a UN report ranked Afghanistan 173rd out of 178 countries in quality of life (Price 2005).

And all this would be much worse if not for the mainstay of the Afghan economy: opium production, which doubled between 2003 and 2004, to a level 36 times higher than in the last year of the Taliban's rule (National Public Radio [NPR] 8/23/05). Today, opium in Afghanistan is estimated to be a $2.8 billion a year industry, comprising more than 60% of the country's GDP and 50% of the U.S. heroin problem (Prashad 2001; Price 2005).

Nor is it clear that Afghanistan has progressed in the area of human security and rights. After George W. Bush declared victory in Afghanistan and redirected U.S. attention toward Iraq, the United States decided not to provide a peace-keeping force. Instead, a small 5,000-troop International Security Assistance Force (ISAF) mobilized to support the new U.S.-backed government of Hamid Karzai.

ISAF's writ, and therefore the government's, did not extend much beyond the country's capital, Kabul. Meanwhile, in the countryside, former Mujahadeen warlords were back in business. Although the national "Loya Jirga," or grand tribal council, had harshly criticized these warlords, Washington dubbed them "regional leaders," "giving them a legitimacy that Afghans themselves are unwilling to bestow" (Rashid 2002).

Under these circumstances,

> it is not surprising that very few women have discarded the burhka . . . because they fear for their safety. Recent reports of gang rapes by armed Afghan factions echo the indiscriminate sexual violence of the four-year civil war of 1992–96. . . . Human Rights Watch now reports a "wave of killing, rape and widespread ethnic persecution. . . . We have found case after case of gang-raping of women, and even children," says [Human Rights Watch] senior researcher Peter Bouckaert.

"We felt safe under the Taliban," said a UNICEF project officer. "We could sleep with our doors open at night, but no longer" (Goodwin 2002, p. 20).

Even such a seemingly joyous occasion as Afghanistan's first postwar parliamentary election was tainted by the power of these warlords. The media's headlines touted this election as a triumph for democracy: "War-Ravaged People Embrace Chance to Choose"; "Afghans Go to Polls in Historic Vote" (Stockman 2005b, p. A1; *Atlanta Journal-Constitution* 9/18/05).

But the reality was a triumph for intimidation. While many Afghans complained that the warlords responsible for decades of strife and carnage should not be able to run for election, run they did—roughshod over the democratic process. Topping the ballot in Nangarhar was a "24 carat warlord [Hazrat Ali] with alleged narcotics links and a dubious human rights record" (*Economist* 2005). In one Kabul neighborhood,

> residents . . . cringe at the sight of posters of Abdul Sayyaf, the commander they say destroyed their homes and murdered their families [in the early 1990s]. Sayyaf's militia is tied to mass rapes and the disappearance of hundreds of people. (Stockman 2005b, p. A1)

These gangsters joined local strongmen "in many provinces . . . offering nothing but the promise of patronage or the threat of retribution" (*Economist* 2005).

On election day, "complaints [of fraud and intimidation] were heard in almost all regions of the country" (Wiseman 2005). In Mazar-e-Sharif, long since liberated by heroic U.S. Special Forces, "about 100 women" were seen arriving at polling stations, but returning without casting their votes when they saw warlords' militia-men acting as polling station workers (*Financial Times* 9/18/05).

When the smoke cleared, "almost all" the militia leaders had won seats, including Sayyaf and Ali (*The Advertiser* 2005; *St. Petersburg Times* 2005). The win conferred "unprecedented legitimacy and political power" on mass murderers and rapists (Stockman 2005b, p. A1). "It's not," said Shukria Barakzai, a women's rights activist, "good news for Afghanistan" (*The Advertiser* 2005).

❖ RETURN OF THE TALIBAN

As we shall see in Chapter 3, the Bush administration has envisioned a world dominated by its only superpower. To achieve that goal, the United States would need to be able to impose serial military punishments on rebellious nations and movements. This policy of "preemptive war" against nations said to be potentially threatening became known as the "Bush Doctrine" of foreign policy (Scheer, Scheer, and Chandry 2004, p. 23). This doctrine, in turn, meant two things:

1. In order to be ready for subsequent conflicts, the military could not be bogged down in a previous one, such as Afghanistan, for too long.

2. Casualties would have to be limited, so that the American people, whose support would be necessary to sustain serial warfare, would not suffer battle fatigue.

The first principle meant, as we've already seen, that the United States would drastically reduce its commitment in Afghanistan once the Taliban had fled from office. The second principle, limiting U.S. casualties, meant that the United States was willing to rely largely on Afghan warlords' forces as its proxies on the ground, augmented by a few Special Forces troops calling in air support.

This strategy actually worked well until the war's climactic battle. When Taliban and al-Qaeda forces retreated from the American-led onslaught, they holed up in a redoubt of cave-riddled mountains at a place called Tora Bora. Here, military analysts have since concluded, was the United States' last and best chance to post a decisive victory and capture or kill the mastermind of 9/11 (Gellman and Ricks 2002).

As U.S. bombing over the area intensified and flushed al-Qaeda fighters from their caves, warlords (including Hazrat Ali) were assigned to mop up the region behind the bombing and guard the escape routes out of Tora Bora.

Unfortunately, the warlords proved reluctant to engage their "Muslim brothers" and eager to accept payment from them for safe passage to Pakistan. When the last of the caves had been taken, only 21 exhausted al-Qaeda soldiers of no rank or importance were left out of an estimated force of 2,000 (Smucker 2002).

Subsequent "after-action reviews" of Tora Bora, conducted by the Bush administration, concluded that the escapees did include bin Laden, as well as his chief deputy, Ayman al-Zawahiri. These reviews deemed the battle a "significant defeat for the U.S." (Gellman and Ricks 2002, p. A1). Press coverage at the time of the battle, however, saw it quite differently. Despite witnesses' accounts saying that bin Laden had escaped Tora Bora by November 30, and that his followers were gone by December 12 (Walker 2001, p. A25), most U.S. press accounts continued to suggest that the battle was a victory and that the "noose" was "tightening":

"Afghans Mop Up, Hunt bin Laden"; "It's Just a Matter of Time, Bush Vows" (*Atlanta Journal-Constitution* 12/18/01)

"Al-Qaeda Holdouts Trapped" (*Atlanta Journal-Constitution* 12/15/01)

"Heavy Fire Crippling al Qaeda" (*Boston Globe* 12/16/01)

"Taliban's Omar Reportedly Trapped" (*San Francisco Chronicle* 12/17/01)

"Afghan Fighters Declare Victory; Al Qaeda Force Is Routed Near Tora Bora" (*St. Louis Post Dispatch* 12/17/01)

"Mullah Omar 'Held'" (*New York Post* 12/8/01)

"Enemy Routed in Search for Leader" (*New York Daily News* 12/9/01)

"Al Qaeda Crumbling Under Massive Attack" (*New York Daily News* 12/12/01)

"Allied Forces Say They've Cornered Osama bin Laden" (*New York Times* 12/14/01)

These celebratory headlines lasted well into January and then, following the administration's lead, gradually dissolved into a story of the United States "shifting forces" away from the caves and toward "rebuilding" Afghanistan. Few of these stories acknowledged the magnitude of the failure at Tora Bora:

"US Blasts Suspected Al Qaeda Cave Hideouts" (*Daily News* 1/13/02)

"Bin Laden Hunt to Turn From Caves" (*Boston Globe* 1/9/02)

"New Leads in Manhunt as US Smashes Caves" (*New York Post* 1/15/02)

"US Shifts Focus, Troops from Tora Bora" (*Wall Street Journal* 1/9/02)

The escape at Tora Bora, together with the withdrawal of most of the U.S. forces from Afghanistan, probably meant that it was just a matter of time before Taliban forces would return—and not much time at that. Within a year, our old friend Gulbuddin Hekmatyar, the main beneficiary of CIA largesse in the 1980s, had "joined forces with al Qaeda and Taliban remnants to destabilize the Karzai regime" (Rashid 2002). Since then, the number of insurgent attacks has "steadily increased each year," as fresh troops, training, and funds—Muslim blowback against the U.S. war in Iraq—replenished the Taliban (Jones 2005, p. A19). In just the first nine months of 2005, 1,200 Afghans and 82 U.S. soldiers—six times as many troops as were lost in the war itself—were killed by Taliban attacks (Baldauf and Khan 2005). In each year since 2003, the death toll for coalition soldiers has increased. In 2008, there were 3,276 improvised explosive device (IED) attacks, a 45% increase over 2007; and in just the first two months of 2009, IED attacks had already killed 36 foreign troops, triple the number for the same period in 2008. The untold stories of Afghanistan had returned to haunt us, as we shall see in Chapter 5.

❖ CONCLUSION

In the winter of 2001, a war was fought in Afghanistan. Or perhaps there were two wars. The first was the one we saw and heard about in our mass media. Then there was another war—one we didn't see or hear much of.

The first war was a fight for freedom and against "evil." The other was a mistaken and cruel use of military force against a defenseless Afghanistan in retaliation for a crime—monstrous indeed—but committed by a small cabal of al-Qaeda men—none of whom were Afghans.

The media war was heroic—a thrilling show, a high stakes game—and took no toll. The other war was not an epic tale, or a fireworks display, or a game. It was pain and death and displacement on a massive scale: thousands of civilian casualties, six months of starvation, a half million refugees (Conetta 2002). The media's war ended as a great victory, with the promise, as the president put it, of "an Afghanistan that is prosperous, democratic, self governing . . . respectful of human rights." But the other war handed a new lease on power to Afghanistan's brutal warlords, sowed the seeds of a resurgent al-Qaeda, roiled up a tsunami of worldwide Muslim anti-Americanism, boosted a heroin trade more murderous to Americans than terrorists could ever be, and left a forgotten Afghanistan immersed in poverty and violence.

The conclusion to be drawn from this is not that the other war was the real war and the media's was spurious, but that both wars happened. The facts of the unreported war occurred. Its critics spoke. Its inferences were drawn. And yet, this other war was curiously, almost completely absent from the mass media.

Then again, perhaps this absence was not so curious. Perhaps, in fact, it was neither an aberration nor an accident. Perhaps it was just business as usual—a possibility that suggested itself anew as the next chapter of American history began to unfold in Iraq.

February 15, 2003. Hundreds of thousands of protestors rally against the looming war with Iraq. The media's long-standing practice of ignoring, undercounting, and disparaging protestors continues. After months of telling Americans that protestors "hate America," "align themselves with terrorists," and "want to cause anarchy," the media were able to report polls showing that most Americans had an "unfavorable view" of demonstrators.

3

Iraq

War Comes to the "City of Peace"

In this chapter, we'll meet the Bush foreign policy team that led the nation to war with Iraq. They nicknamed themselves the "Vulcans" to show that they were tough, and so they were. But we'll also see that their policies were firmly rooted in the American elite consensus on global strategy. They were firmly pro-business, deeply committed to a Manichaean worldview, and to that worldview's corollaries—the necessity of violence and an American "right to invade." Indeed, they looked forward to and planned for a world dominated, militarily and economically, by the world's only superpower. They were especially ardent on the need for American power to assert itself in the oil-rich Middle East.

But when it came time to sell war with Iraq to the public, the White House sales team chose neither American empire nor oil as its campaign theme. Instead, Iraq's "weapons of mass destruction" and its ties with "international terrorism," both charges that would prove to be untrue, became the sales pitch. As the White House avoided a rationale that wouldn't sell, and sold one that wasn't true, would the people's watchdog sound an alarm?

Content analysis, we'll discover, shows that despite ample reasons for skepticism, the press parroted and even amplified the White House's fearsome claims without question or qualification. We'll see this sad spectacle at work as we examine the following:

- How aluminum tubes that were "only really suited" for nuclear centrifuges were actually unsuited for that purpose

- How Iraqi defectors with "no credibility at all" somehow continued to make "heavy-breathing headlines"

- How "sixteen words" the White House, and soon the press, knew to be false somehow ended up in a State of the Union address that the press embraced

- How one of the ringing phrases in Secretary of State Colin Powell's UN presentation, "web of lies," applied to his own speech, which the press called "unassailable"

But we'll also discover that this tendency of the press to be more lapdog than watchdog was not a certain tendency. There were reporters during this period—just a courageous few—who went against the grain and got the story right. Unfortunately, we'll see that these isolated stories were voices in the wilderness, without much effect on the national conversation.

Once again, we'll see that, in the campaign for a "good war," bad news (i.e., antiwar news) is minimized, marginalized, and disparaged. For example, we'll learn about these issues:

- How the only credible evidence about weapons of mass destruction (WMD) actually coming from within Iraq—the reports issued by UN weapons inspectors—was either ignored, minimized, or berated by the press

- How the press told Americans exercising their constitutional right to assemble that they "hate America," are "agents of evil," and are "leftist stooges for anti-American causes"

- How the failure to persuade the UN of the case for war became a story of "French treachery"

- How those who spoke against the march toward war were accused by the press of "drinking Saddam's Kool-Aid"

Once again, we'll see that the entertainment media are quick to report for duty in the campaign for war: for example, hiring hawks and firing doves as talk show hosts, boycotting the Dixie Chicks, and airing a TV movie based on a "true story" that was a fabrication.

In these ways, whether intentionally or not, the media did work with the White House to bring us to this chapter's conclusion, at the threshold of war.

❖ VULCANIZED

When George Bush took office in 2001, so did a foreign policy team that had dubbed itself "the Vulcans," after the Roman god of fire, the forge, and metalwork. The name was meant to connote power and toughness, and the policies the Vulcans wrought would live up to that billing.

While the foreign policy they forged has sometimes been characterized as extreme, it was actually rooted in what we've already identified as the American elite consensus on global politics. In accord with that consensus, the Bush team was firmly pro-business, deeply committed to a Manichaean worldview, and deeply committed to that worldview's corollary, the necessity of violence (Mann 2004, pp. 276–284). To the extent that the Bush foreign policy differed from past practice, the difference was one of degree, not of kind. So it was that, in the aftermath of 9/11, the Vulcans "began turning to . . . Harry Truman, George Kennan and Dean Acheson." After all, these were the authors of the Truman Doctrine that had posited an immoral enemy and therefore a right of the United States, at its discretion, to intervene, militarily, in other countries. Quite naturally, the Bush Doctrine of preemptive war was seen by its proponents as a new Truman Doctrine, with terrorism now replacing Soviet communism in the role of America's enemy (Mann 2004, pp. 313–316).

The outspoken Vulcans had staked out public positions on many global issues before coming to the White House, and the Middle East was no exception. One of their early, defining documents "envisioned a US that took advantage of its lone-superpower status to consolidate American control of the world both militarily and economically" (Scheer et al. 2004, p. 23). As part of this larger project, members of the Bush team had, for a decade, argued that Iraq's Saddam Hussein should be removed from office. Interestingly, their concern was not that Hussein represented a threat to the United States or to his own people. Instead, they argued, "While the unresolved conflict with Iraq provides the immediate justification, the *need for a substantial American force presence in the Gulf* [italics added] transcends the issue of Saddam Hussein" (Project for the New American Century [PNAC] 2000).

This "substantial American force presence" would provide several benefits, according to this logic. First, it would strike fear in the hearts of those who would oppose U.S. policy. Not only would the U.S. military be in Iraq, but they would be there *as a result of the United States' willingness to wage war.* "Can you imagine what our enemies think of us right now?" asked Under Secretary of State Douglas Feith, after Hussein had fallen. "The deterrent value of what we've accomplished far overshadows the direct results" (McManus 2003). The American-led overthrow of Saddam Hussein, wrote Bush speechwriter David Frum, "would put America more wholly in charge of the region than any power since the Ottomans, or maybe the Romans" (Alterman and Green 2004, pp. 299–303).

Of course, the matter that made this particular region and this country so important was, as a founding Vulcan document referred to it, the need to ensure "access to vital raw material, primarily Persian Gulf oil" (Muwakki 2003). Paul Wolfowitz, "the administration official most closely identified with the invasion of Iraq," had, since the late 1970s, "feared that some regime hostile to U.S. interests might come to dominate the oil reserves of the Persian Gulf. These same strategic concerns continued to affect Wolfowitz's thinking over the following quarter century" (Mann 2004, p. 368). Conquering Iraq, on the other hand, would put a friendly regime in control of the world's second-largest oil reserves, at a time when the United States is becoming steadily more dependent on foreign oil.

Former Federal Reserve Board Chairman Alan Greenspan "spent more time at the White House [after 9/11] than ever before in my Fed career." While there, he met often with "Dick Cheney, Condoleezza Rice, Andy Card . . . and, of course, the president." At the top of his agenda were the issues of "international economics" and "the global dynamics of energy and oil" (Greenspan 2007, p. 241). Here is what he said, in his autobiography, about those meetings:

> Whatever their publicized angst over Saddam Hussein's "weapons of mass destruction," American and British authorities were also concerned about violence in an area that harbors a resource indispensable for the functioning of the world economy. I am saddened by the fact that it is politically inconvenient to acknowledge what everyone knows: the Iraq war is largely about oil. (2007, p. 463)

So it was that when the 9/11 attack took place, White House hawks immediately urged war against Iraq—whether or not it was linked to al-Qaeda and 9/11. Secretary of State Colin Powell disagreed, arguing that there was no direct link between Iraq and al-Qaeda, and that using 9/11 as a pretext for attacking Iraq would be seen as, in his words, "bait and switch" (Scheer et al. 2004, p. 15).

President Bush responded by telling advisers that al-Qaeda and the Taliban in Afghanistan would be his first target—but that planning for a war against Iraq should continue. By November 21, 2001, with Taliban resistance beginning to crumble, Bush instructed his secretary of defense to begin planning an Iraq offensive "in earnest" (Western 2005, p. 192).

By the following year, other reasons to open a new front in the popular "War on Terror" had emerged: The glow of a popular Afghan war was fading. The stock market was free-falling to its lowest level in four years (Western 2005, p. 208). The nation was in economic recession—almost inevitably ballot box poison for the party in power. As if that weren't enough, some of George W. Bush's biggest backers were now being unmasked as corporate crooks whose avarice had left their employees and shareholders in the lurch with sleight of hand accounting that resembled maneuvers Bush himself had used back in 1990, making nearly $1 million from a rapidly failing oil company (Alterman and Green 2004, pp. 70–73). Worst of all, this perfect storm of bad news for Republicans was rolling in during an election year.

These considerations did not affect the decision about *whether* to invade Iraq. That decision, the Downing Street Memo would later reveal, had probably already been made (see Chapter 5). But electoral considerations did affect the *timing* of the campaign for war, as the White House itself admitted (Bagdikian 2004, p. 83). "They are using the War on Terror politically," said Bush's own counterterrorism czar about the campaign for war in Iraq. "They are doing *Wag the Dog!*" (Randy Beers, cited in Clarke 2004, pp. 241–242).[1]

So it was in July 2002 that the seasoned White House public relations team began planning one of its elaborate campaigns. This particular one was designed to sell, not a candidate, but a war. Not surprisingly, the Vulcans' quest to extend American empire was not one of the campaign's selling points: Whatever its merits, it sounded rather like Dr. Evil's quest for world domination. Nor was the need to ensure "access to . . . Persian Gulf oil," which sounded too much like the protestors' charge that the war was a ruthless exchange of "blood for oil."

Instead, said Wolfowitz, the newly formed White House Iraq Group (WHIG) "settled on . . . weapons of mass destruction as the core reason" (Fritz, Keefer, and Nyhan 2004, p. 152). In fact, as a rationale for war, WMD had only one drawback: Saddam Hussein had no WMD, and so, of course, available intelligence did not prove that he had them. Nevertheless, once this rationale was chosen, the team "pressed for dramatic material to make its case to the public" (Fritz et al. 2004,

---

[1]*Wag the Dog* is a Hollywood movie that depicts the politically ingenious use of a nonexistent, but White House and media-promoted, "war."

p. 152). Three administration officials later explained that the WHIG team "wanted gripping images and stories not available in the hedged and austere language of intelligence." And so the PR campaign took what one senior intelligence official called "literary license" in describing the threat from Iraq (Gellman and Pincus 2003).

In retrospect, "literary license" is a charitable way of describing what the White House did to sell the war. Other observers have used the terms *cherry-picking, distorting, suppressing,* and *lying* to describe the campaign tactics.

As the White House went about avoiding a rationale that the public would not buy and selling a rationale that was not true, would "the watchdog of people" sound an alarm? How would the press respond to the campaign for war?

❖ WAR DRUMS: FALL 2002

The kickoff of the White House PR campaign began on September 8: "From a marketing point of view," explained Chief of Staff Andrew Card, "you don't introduce new products in August" (Western 2005, p. 202). The product, in this case, was war, and it didn't take White House salespeople long to introduce the product's slogan: Be afraid. Be very afraid.

What White House officials openly described as a "meticulously planned strategy to persuade the public . . . of the need to confront Saddam Hussein" began with these assertions (Bumiller 2002):

1. That Hussein had WMD and was, in fact, close to having nuclear weapons

2. That Hussein had links to "international terrorism," and to al-Qaeda in particular

3. That Iraq, along with al-Qaeda, was intent on seeing the United States attacked

Down the Tubes

"Simply stated, there is no doubt that Saddam Hussein now has weapons of mass destruction," said Vice President Dick Cheney. "There is no doubt that he is amassing them to use against our friends, against our allies, and against us" (Address to VFW 8/26/02). "Imagine a September 11 with weapons of mass destruction," warned Donald Rumsfeld on *Face the Nation.* "It's not 3,000. It's tens of thousands of innocent men, women and children" (9/8/02).

Hussein had acquired aluminum tubes that were "only really suited" for nuclear weapons development, said Condoleezza Rice on CNN's *Late Edition,* adding, "We don't want the smoking gun to be a mushroom cloud" (9/8/02). The United States had "irrefutable evidence," added Cheney on *Meet the Press,* that the tubes were to be used for centrifuges (9/8/02). As evidence for his claim, Cheney cited a *New York Times* story on the tubes—a story, *American Journalism Review* later reported, that Cheney himself had leaked to the paper (Layton 2002a, p. 29). "It's pretty obvious what happened here," said reporter Jonathan Landay, one of the few who would question the case for war. "It's what happened with most of the *New York Times* reporting, which is that they were fed stuff to bolster the administration's case. They were used" (Borjesson 2005, p. 375).

Even at this early juncture, the press had reason to be skeptical of such claims. For one thing, the White House advance team had offered no supporting evidence for their assertions. For another, a 1998 UN Report concluded that Hussein's nuclear weapons program had been dismantled. And reporters who covered the Iraq beat knew that after 1998, the year UN weapons inspectors withdrew from Iraq, intelligence about Hussein's weapons was notoriously sketchy (Fritz et al., 2004, p. 153).

But if reporters were skeptical, they didn't show it. For example, the *Washington Post* and *New York Times* reported the alarms sounded by the White House without question, without reference to the UN's report, or to the dearth of reliable information about Iraq's weapons. When President Bush reiterated the White House message in a speech to the UN on September 12, newspaper editorials across the country endorsed his position (Western 2005, p. 203).

Soon afterward, further cause for skepticism would step forward. David Albright, a former weapons inspector and physicist who headed the Institute for Science and International Security, had been asked to consult on the matter of the aluminum tubes. In doing so, he'd discovered that "many experts" in the U.S. Department of Energy and the UN's International Atomic Energy Agency believed that the tubes were to be used not for nuclear centrifuges, but for conventional artillery rockets—relatively, weapons of minimal destruction.

Having heard and read the administration's stark words in the news, Albright felt strongly that the public should know about the scientists' doubts, and in several "long conversations," he alerted the nation's newspaper of record, the *New York Times,* to this important aspect of the story. But when the *Times* story appeared, Albright was dismayed. The article began, once again, by summarizing the White House's case against Iraq. After six paragraphs of this, the article acknowledged that "there have been debates among intelligence experts" about the tubes. But the *New*

York Times quickly added, "the dominant view" of "other more senior officials" had "wide support, particularly among the country's top technical experts and nuclear scientists." "This is a footnote, not a split," a senior administration official said. "The *Times*," said Albright, "made a decision to ice out the critics and insult them on top of it." At that point, Albright issued his own report on the tubes, and he approached *Washington Post* reporter Joby Warrick with his information. Warrick knew that this was an important story. He wrote a hard-hitting piece about the "independent experts" who were challenging administration claims and about the White House's efforts to "quiet dissent among its own analysts." The article "was one of the first public mentions of the administration's possible misuse of the data on Iraq." Amazingly, however, the *Washington Post* buried this groundbreaking story on page 18, and also surprisingly, it attracted little attention or follow-up from other journalists (Massing 2004, pp. 36–40).

Swimming Against the Tide

Proof that the media could have been more vigilant during this time came from at least one brave news source, Knight Ridder's Washington bureau. "Almost alone among national news organizations, Knight Ridder had decided to take a hard look at the administration's claims for war" (Massing 2004, p. 41). The speech that Knight Ridder editor John Walcott gave to his reporters was, in one sense, just "Watchdog 101." But because Walcott was, apparently, one of very few editors to convey such a message, the speech was also a profile in courage: "This is a really important story," he said. "They're putting together a case for war, and as journalists we have an obligation to question, or at least to look into what the Administration is telling the American people and whether or not it's right. . . . We have a special obligation to the people who read our papers to explain to them why their loved ones are being sent into harm's way" (Knight Ridder reporter Jonathan Landay, in Borjesson 2005, p. 370).

Walcott's reporters quickly found that many experts within the military, the intelligence bureaus, and the Foreign Service, as well as the UN and private think tanks, were alarmed at the claims being made by "political appointees" on the Bush team (Landay and Strobel 2002).

Then, in October, the CIA released its National Intelligence Estimate (NIE), a summary of the best available intelligence about Iraq. This document, according to Knight Ridder, "exposed a sharp dispute among US intelligence experts" over Iraq's weapons. Knight Ridder made it plain in a series of articles that "a growing number" of government experts "privately have deep misgivings about the administration's double-time march toward war." These officials "charge that administration hawks have exaggerated evidence of the threat" from Iraq (Landay, Strobel, and Walcott 2002). Unfortunately, these important articles, raising serious doubts about the administration's case for war, attracted little attention or follow-up from other journalists.

Among the "threats" scrutinized by Knight Ridder—and few others—was the alleged alliance between Saddam Hussein and al-Qaeda. The fact that the secular Hussein and the religious fundamentalist bin Laden had long despised and denounced each other was common knowledge among journalists in 2002. Asked about Hussein in a 1997 CNN interview, for example, bin Laden said, "He is a bad Muslim. He took Kuwait for his own self-aggrandizement" (Alterman and Green 2004, p. 277). But the reddest red flag about these claims came from the crucial NIE. The document expressed "low confidence" about "whether Saddam in desperation would share chemical or biological weapons with al Qaeda, fearing that exposure of Iraqi involvement would provide Washington a strong case for making war" ("Key Judgments" 2002). This skepticism about a Saddam–al-Qaeda connection would prove to be warranted: After Saddam's capture, "Documents were found in his possession ordering Iraqi resistance fighters to refuse to cooperate with any Islamic fundamentalists who entered Iraq" (Bennett, Lawrence, and Livingstone 2007, p. 22).

Nevertheless, Bush and his team frequently repeated the Iraq–al-Qaeda allegation. "We've learned," said Bush, citing no evidence, "that Iraq has trained al Qaeda members in bomb-making and poisons and deadly gases." But by then, many U.S. intelligence experts had concluded that Hussein had no plans to "sacrifice his own life and his country to go on stupid adventures with terrorists who had completely antithetical goals to his," as one CIA analyst put it (Greenwald 2004).

Despite Knight Ridder's articles and despite the "many sources available to journalists interested in scrutinizing the administration's statements about Iraq," the rest of the press corps chose not to do so. A survey of coverage during this period shows that few articles even touched on the debate within the intelligence community (Massing 2004, pp. 43–45).

Our Survey Says: "Heavy-Breathing Headlines"

Instead, a seemingly endless parade of news articles and TV commentators simply parroted the White House's fearsome claims without question or qualification. News analyst Andrew Tyndall reported that of 414 Iraq stories aired by the three major networks from September 14, 2002, to February 7, 2003, "the vast majority" originated from the White House, Pentagon, and State Department. And a review of newspaper stories during the same period revealed a similar pattern (Johnson 2003).

Another survey of newspapers and television networks showed that the lion's share (47%) of source citations went to conservative, pro-war think tanks in 2002. "Centrist" sources, most of which were pro-war, received 41% of citations, and progressives 12%—the lowest number garnered by the left since 1998. The two progressive organizations most involved in international issues declined precipitously in media exposure—by 39%, in the case of the Center for Defense Information (CDI). This included a 28% drop in newspaper citations of the CDI and a 59% drop in the organization's TV and radio presence (Dolny 2003)!

The quality of these sources sometimes suggested that while few antiwar voices were welcome in news stories, almost any pro-war voice would do. For example, the *Washington Post* front-paged an article asserting that Iraq had supplied nerve gas to al-Qaeda. The story's evidence was so evidently "shaky" that readers complained to the *Post*'s ombudsman, who agreed with readers' frustration, asking, "What, after all is the use of this story that practically begs you not to put much credence in it" (Massing 2004, p. 45).

War, INC: The "Iraqi National Congress"

Also during this period, *New York Times* reporter Judith Miller wrote a series of page-one articles bolstering the administration's claims about WMD. On September 18, 2002, for example, Miller quoted Khidir Hamza, who "led part of Iraq's nuclear bomb program until he defected in 1994." Hamza warned that Iraq was "now at the 'pilot plant' stage of nuclear production" and "now excelled" in hiding nuclear and biochemical weapons.

But experts outside the PR campaign were dismayed by Hamza's confident, sweeping pronouncements. "Hamza had no credibility at all," said an International Atomic Energy Agency (IAEA) representative. "Journalists who called us and asked for an assessment of these people—we'd certainly tell them." In fact, contrary to Miller's description, Hamza had left Iraq's nuclear program in 1990 and had no first-hand knowledge of it after that. Subsequently, he had gone to work for David Albright's Institute for Science and International Security, but the unverified claims he made while there about Iraq's weapons were so incredible that he was asked to leave. "Judy [Miller] should have known about this," Albright said. "This is her area" (Massing 2004, p. 51).

But Miller's stories continued to rely heavily on Iraqi defectors with a personal stake in the overthrow of Hussein, often supplied by the White House's paid broker of anti-Saddam information, convicted embezzler Ahmed Chalabi, through his "Iraqi National Congress" (INC) (Alterman and Green 2004, p. 273). Miller persisted in spite of the fact that a publicly reported Defense Intelligence Agency paper had concluded that Chalabi's defectors' information was of "little or no value," coming as it did from sources who "invented or exaggerated their credentials as people with direct knowledge of [Iraq's] weapons program" (Massing 2004, p. 26).

A year and a half later, the *New York Times* itself confessed that Miller's stories were often "inappropriately italicized by lavish front-page display and heavy-breathing headlines," while "several fine articles that challenged information in the faulty stories were played as quietly as a lullaby" (*New York Times* 5/26/04).

But Miller was by no means the only reporter "played" by the INC. Even though "veteran reporters knew the CIA and State Department were skeptical of INC-produced information," Chalabi's organization was able to point to 108 INC-inspired news stories published between October 2001 and May 2002—three months before the White House began its own PR campaign. A review of these stories found that they "advanced almost every claim that would become the backbone of the Bush administration's case for war." The credulous news outlets giving these stories prominent play included "nearly every blue-blooded news outfit in America," including the *New York Times,* the *Washington Post,* the *Wall Street Journal, Vanity Fair, Time, Newsweek, 60 Minutes,* and Fox News (McCollam 2004, p. 32).

Skepticism as Treason

Meanwhile, the Sunday morning talk shows continued to offer a steady diet of White House apologists. "They'd take Rice, Powell, or Rumsfeld every week if they could," said Adam Levine, assistant White House press secretary, who was in charge of placing Bush officials on TV. "And of course, the Vice President is sort of the Sunday matinee idol" (Cox 2002).

When David Albright appeared as a commentator on TV news during this period, he "felt a lot of pressure" from his TV hosts to "stick to the subject, which was Iraq's bad behavior" (Massing 2004, p. 47). Those commentators who failed to heed this advice often found themselves reprimanded by their talk show hosts. On CNN, Representative Mike Thompson (D-CA) dared to suggest that there was no evidence of collusion between Iraq and al-Qaeda. Connie Chung replied, "Well let's listen to something President Bush said tonight, and you tell me if this doesn't provide you with the evidence that you want." She then aired a clip of Bush asserting that Iraq had colluded with al-Qaeda. Then Chung demanded, "Congressman, doesn't that tell you that an invasion is justified?" When Thompson began to disagree, Chung interrupted: "You mean you don't believe what President Bush just said? With all due respect . . . It sounds almost as if you're asking the American public, 'Believe Saddam Hussein, don't believe President Bush'" (10/7/02). A similar reception greeted distinguished scientist Dr. Helen Caldicott when she appeared—again on CNN. Caldicott warned that the depleted uranium used in U.S. anti-tank shells had caused a dramatic rise in birth defects in that country. Interviewer Wolf Blitzer then, appropriately, presented the Pentagon's position—that depleted uranium was not a health hazard. As Caldicott began to respond, Blitzer cut her off, pointed out that the Hussein regime used torture, and asked her, "Do you feel comfortable, in effect, going out there and defending the Iraqi regime?" (11/7/02). One of the first to propose that skepticism about war equaled support for Saddam was CNN's Paula Zahn, who told anti-war former weapons inspector Scott Ritter that he stood accused of "drinking Saddam Hussein's Kool-Aid" (9/13/02). Fox anchor Neil Cavuto called an antiwar college professor "a self-absorbed, condescending imbecile," an "Ivy League intellectual Lilliputian," and to make sure that his comments were "fair and balanced," he added, "an obnoxious, pontificating jerk" (Rampton and Stauber 2003c, p. 176).

The (Too) Loyal (Non) Opposition

During this period, most Democrats in Congress went AWOL from their own obligation to scrutinize and, because the evidence warranted it, to critique the opposing party's war plans. But there were notable exceptions. Senior Democrats Robert Byrd, Edward Kennedy, and John Conyers all gave major speeches attacking the White House case for war. Kennedy, for example, "laid out what was arguably the most comprehensive case yet offered to the public questioning the Bush administration's policy and timing on Iraq," according to the *Washington Post*'s ombudsman. The next day, the *Post* devoted one sentence to the speech. In vain, the *Post*'s ombudsman protested, "Whatever one thinks about the wisdom of a new war, once it starts it is too late to air arguments that should have been aired before" (10/6/02).

By November 2002, the White House message, with the press as its compliant megaphone, had gotten through: 81% of Americans believed that Saddam Hussein "posed a threat to the United States" and 59% supported an invasion of Iraq (Judis and Ackerman 2003).

❖ FINAL STRETCH

In early 2003, the United States, led by its president and its press, took the next lockstep toward war. On January 28, George W. Bush delivered a

State of the Union speech in which all of the now-familiar bogeymen reappeared: "Saddam Hussein aids and protects . . . members of al Qaeda," he said. Repeating that Iraq's attempt to acquire aluminum tubes was evidence of a nuclear weapons program, he also added the now infamous "sixteen words": "The British government has learned that Saddam Hussein recently sought significant quantities of uranium from Niger." Then he concluded, "If this threat is permitted to fully and suddenly emerge, all actions, all words and all recriminations would come too late."

Of all the questionable claims the president made that day, the Niger allegation would prove to be the most dubious. The documents on which the claim was based had come from an Italian newspaper— which hadn't run the story because the documents seemed phony (Isikoff and Thomas 2003). Within weeks of Bush's speech, the IAEA labeled the Niger story an easy-to-spot fraud (Corn 2003, p. 229). One of the documents, for example, was "signed" by a Niger minister who had been out of office for a decade prior to the "signing." Other inaccuracies were so obvious that the counterfeit could have been spotted "by someone using Google," said an IAEA official (Hersh 2003).

Nonetheless, the CIA dispatched former U.S. diplomat Joseph C. Wilson to Niger to investigate. Wilson reported back in February 2002 that, indeed, no such transaction had occurred. For these reasons, the CIA had removed the Niger allegation from an earlier Bush speech. But somehow it was resurrected for this, the State of the Union address that explained the momentous decision to proceed to war.

"Web of Lies": The Powell Speech

Then, on February 5, Secretary of State Colin Powell delivered the case for war to the United Nations. Brimming with declassified satellite images, communications intercepts, artists' renderings of "mobile bioweapons labs," vials of white powder, and scarifying scenarios, the speech was a masterful performance with but one serious flaw: None of it, we would later discover, was true.

Despite its bells and whistles, journalists had reason to be skeptical of the speech from the start. For one thing, Powell had cited almost no verifiable sources. Many of his assertions were unattributed. The speech had more than 40 vague references, such as "human sources," "an eyewitness," "intelligence sources," and the like (Cranberg 2003).

What's more, there was plenty of existing evidence that cast doubt on Powell's claims. For example:

- Just two years before the speech, Powell himself had publicly proclaimed that ongoing sanctions against Hussein had worked: "He has not developed any significant capability with respect to weapons of mass destruction. He is unable to project conventional power against his neighbors," said Powell, in a February 2001 statement available to reporters in February 2003 (MSNBC 9/24/03).

- Powell showed satellite photos of trucks he labeled "decontamination vehicles" associated with chemical weapons. He also showed drawings of "mobile bio-weapons labs" and videotape of an Iraqi plane spraying "simulated anthrax." But former weapons inspector Scott Ritter knew immediately that the "decontamination trucks" were just fire trucks, the "mobile labs" were harmless hydrogen generators, and the plane in question had been destroyed in 1991 (Greenwald 2004).

- In fact, the sites Powell showed had very recently been inspected by the UN teams that had gone into Iraq in November 2002. Chief weapons inspector Hans Blix had stated the day before Powell's speech that "no contraband was found and that no signs that anything had been moved were detectable" (Alterman and Green 2004, p. 258).

- Powell asserted that Iraq had created four tons of the nerve agent VX. "A single drop of VX on the skin will kill in minutes." What Powell forgot to add, but the press should have remembered, was that most of the VX Powell was referring to had been destroyed in the 1990s under UN supervision. Any of the remaining "four tons" would have degraded, according to the International Institute of Strategic Studies (Alterman and Green 2004, p. 259).

- Powell also warned, "Our conservative estimate is that Iraq today has a stockpile of between one hundred and five hundred tons of chemical weapons agents." This, too, was a curious claim, given that a September 2002 report of the Defense Intelligence Agency had concluded "There is *no reliable information* [italics added] on whether Iraq is producing and stockpiling chemical weapons, or whether Iraq has—or will establish—[*sic*] its chemical warfare agent facilities" (*Los Angeles Times* 6/7/03).

- Powell suggested that chemical warheads found by UN inspectors the previous month were "the tip of an iceberg." Again, he neglected to add that the warheads were empty and that UN inspectors had called them "debris from the past" (Alterman and Green 2004, p. 260).

- Powell declared that "Saddam Hussein is determined to get his hands on a nuclear bomb. He is so determined that he made repeated covert attempts to acquire high-specification aluminum tubes from 11 countries" (*Guardian* 2/5/02).

By this time, even more reasons to be chary of this claim had emerged. In addition to the doubts expressed by David Albright, by many other experts cited in the Knight Ridder stories, and even by the NIE, there were now the doubts supplied by the only non-Iraqis in a position to view Iraq's weapons firsthand. After being withdrawn from Iraq in 1998, UN weapons inspectors returned in November 2002. Based on information provided by U.S. intelligence agencies as well as other sources, inspectors immediately set out to visit more than 100 sites of interest. They found no suspicious activity. They also investigated the case of the aluminum tubes, and officially reported on January 9, 2003, that indeed the tubes were "consistent with" use in conventional rockets—not in nuclear centrifuges (Massing 2004, pp. 53–54).

Although their investigations were ongoing, the inspectors' preliminary report, based on almost two months of surprise visits across Iraq to sites identified as "major facilities of concern" by intelligence agencies, concluded, "To date, no evidence of ongoing nuclear or nuclear-related activities has been detected" (www.un.org/News/press/docs/2003/sc7682.doc.htm).

Finally, there was the skepticism of Powell's audience, the Security Council, which, despite Powell's exhortations, refused to back the resolution he sought authorizing military force against Iraq.

In spite of all these reasons for skepticism, the press reaction to Powell's speech was anything but skeptical. A survey of 40 newspapers from all parts of the country found the following encomiums to the speech:

"a massive array of evidence," "a detailed and persuasive case," "a powerful case," "a sober, factual case," "an overwhelming case," "a compelling case," "the strong, credible, and persuasive case," "a persuasive, detailed accumulation of information," "the core of his argument was unassailable," "a smoking fusillade . . . a persuasive case for anyone who is still persuadable," "an accumulation of painstakingly gathered and analyzed evidence," "only the most gullible and wishful thinking souls can now deny that Iraq is harboring and hiding weapons of mass destruction," "the skeptics asked for proof; they now have it," "a much more detailed and convincing argument than any that has previously been told," "Powell's evidence . . . was overwhelming," "an ironclad case . . . incontrovertible evidence," "succinct and damning evidence . . . the case is closed," "Colin Powell delivered the goods on Saddam Hussein," "masterful," "If there was any doubt that Hussein . . . needs to be . . . stripped of his chemical and biological capabilities, Powell put it to rest." (cited in Cranberg 2003)

❖ YOU DON'T SAY

For the next six weeks, a steady torrent of pro-war allegations, assumptions, and experts continued to pour from the mainstream media. After an Iraqi spokesman offered a point by point rebuttal of Powell's charges, for example, CNN's Paula Zahn asked a former State Department official this question: "You've got to understand that most Americans watching this were either laughing out loud or got sick to their stomach. Which was it for you?" (Rendall 2003).

But the media didn't need to deride antiwar opinions very often, because such opinions simply didn't appear very often. For example, a survey of all 393 on-camera sources appearing on the major TV networks' nightly news programs in the weeks before and after Powell's speech found that 76% were current or former government officials. Only 6% of U.S. sources in the sample questioned the need for war. Of the four networks combined, only 3 of the 393 sources were identified with antiwar activism (Rendall 2003).

Meanwhile, however, some decidedly antiwar events, facts, and experts emerged. But for some reason, these were deemed "not newsworthy" or, at best, "not very newsworthy." The media-studies pioneer Warren Breed once suggested that a great deal can be learned from a "reverse content analysis" of what *might* be deemed news, but is in fact *absent* from the news. And so we turn to the question: On the eve of war, what was *not* news?

Weapons Inspectors: No WMD = No News

When UN weapons inspectors, under the auspices of the IAEA (which later received the Nobel Prize for its work), reported on January 9 that they had found "no evidence" of any nuclear weapons program in Iraq, the story was largely ignored by the U.S. press (El Baradei 2003). The *New York Times,* which had run the administration's claims about aluminum tubes under page-1 banner headlines, buried the IAEA's debunking of those claims on page 10. A spokesperson for the IAEA said that "reporters showed little interest" in the agency's report on the aluminum tubes. "Nobody wanted to challenge the President. Nobody wanted to believe inspections had anything of value to bring to the table. The press bought into that," he said (Massing 2004, p. 55).

In fact, press reaction ranged from ignoring to berating weapons inspectors' reports. When Iraq declared that it had no WMD, the *Wall Street Journal* sneered, "If you believe that, you are probably a Swedish weapons inspector" (Mooney 2004, p. 31).

On March 7, the IAEA made a second report to the UN, again stating that inspectors had found no evidence of any Iraqi nuclear program. This time IAEA Director General Mohammed El Baredei directly assailed the Niger and the aluminum tubes stories as fabrications. Here was "the most important rebuttal to U.S. intelligence claims . . . , dismantling the central tenet of the U.S. case for war, and the press either ignored or dismissed it" (Mooney 2004, p. 32). The *Chicago Tribune* didn't even mention El Baredei's report. The *Washington Post* called it a "diversion"; the *Wall Street Journal* called it "a public fuss" about "peripheral" issues. *USA Today* gave the report three sentences, chiding the United States and, inexplicably, its critics for using questionable intelligence (Mooney 2004, p. 32).

Watchdogs on a Short Leash

Meanwhile, at three of the nation's leading news outlets, enterprising reporters had unearthed information that gave the lie to crucial White House claims about Iraq. In all three cases, the stories were, once again, buried in small, out-of-the-way places, as pro-war stories continued to receive front-page, code-red headlines.

In the first case, *Newsweek*'s John Barry learned that the White House had been prevaricating about a very important matter. Since August 2002, the White House had stated that much of its information about Iraq's WMD came, in Vice President Cheney's words, "from the firsthand testimony of defectors—including Saddam's own son-in-law," General Hussein Kamel. This was impressive documentation, because Kamel had directed Iraq's weapons program until his defection in 1995. Kamel's detailed accounts of an Iraqi nuclear and biochemical weapons buildup were cited often by White House representatives as evidence of their charges. Most recently, Colin Powell's "irrefutable" UN speech had cited Kamel as proof that Iraq "had produced four tons of the deadly nerve agent VX. A single drop of VX on the skin will kill in minutes. Four tons. The admission only came out as a result of the defection of Hussein Kamel, Saddam Hussein's late son-in-law."

What Barry discovered was that the White House version of Kamel's testimony was a half-truth that amounted to a big lie. Kamel had indeed described an Iraqi weapons buildup. But the rest of his testimony, which the White House neglected to mention, was that this buildup had occurred in the pre-1991 Gulf War period—and that after the 1991 war, "All weapons—biological, chemical, missile, nuclear—were destroyed" (Hersh 2003). In short, Kamel had said the opposite of what the White House claimed he said.

Given the fact that Kamel's information "had been cited as central evidence and a key reason for attacking Iraq," Barry's revelation might have been regarded as big news (Baker 2003). But it wasn't. *Newsweek* ran the story as a brief, 500-word item in its "Periscope" section—a breezy

mélange of short pieces on such light subjects as a corporate guru advising execs to watch *Lost* on TV, or the process of picking the Washington,
D.C., subway system's "door closing" voice. The rest of the media followed suit, doing little or nothing with Barry's momentous story.

At about the time that Barry was unearthing his potential bombshell, C. J. Chivers of the *New York Times* was also doing some digging
(Chivers 2003). At issue this time was another pillar of the White House
case for war: the supposed Iraq–al-Qaeda connection. "We've learned,"
Bush had said in an October 7, 2002, speech, "that Iraq has trained al
Qaeda members in bomb making, poisons and deadly gases." This
"alliance with terrorists," Bush warned, "could allow the Iraqi regime
to attack America without leaving any fingerprints." Again playing the
fear violin like a maestro, Bush later added, "Imagine those nineteen
hijackers with other weapons and other plans, this time armed by
Saddam Hussein. It would take one vial, one canister, one crate slipped
into this country to bring a day of horror like none we have ever
known" (2003 State of the Union address).

This connection became a constant mantra of White House officials, culminating in Colin Powell's famous declaration that there is a
"sinister nexus between Iraq and the al Qaeda terrorist network, a
nexus that combines classic terrorist organizations and modern
methods of murder . . . Iraq today harbors a deadly terrorist network,"
which had established a "poison and explosive training center camp,
and this camp is located in northeastern Iraq" (un.org/news/
press/docs/2003sc7682.doc.htm).

This claim was suspect on several grounds. For one thing, Osama
bin Laden released a taped message shortly after Powell's speech in
which he exhorted Muslims in Iraq to resist an American invasion.
Powell declared the tape proof that bin Laden was "in partnership with
Iraq," but that was a stretch. A very long stretch, given the fact that bin
Laden also reaffirmed his contempt for Hussein and his cronies in the
taped message, labeling them "hypocrites," "apostates," and "infi-
dels." Muslims, he said, should fight the "crusaders" for the "cause of
Allah not for Hussein." These words, perfectly consistent with bin
Laden's past references to Hussein, were not the language of partner-
ship (Corn 2003, p. 236). Another cause for doubt about the
Hussein–bin Laden connection was that the area of "northeastern Iraq"
Powell mentioned had not been under Saddam Hussein's control since
the 1991 Gulf War. And finally, Chivers learned that the Kurdish
authorities who did control this area were mystified by Powell's claim.
Visiting the "camp" a few days later, Chivers learned why. It was, he
reported, a "wholly unimpressive place" that lacked even plumbing,

much less poison-making facilities. His story was relegated to page 29 of the *New York Times*, which carried three front-page stories on the Powell speech, all of them gushing with praise for Powell's "well documented . . . intelligence breakthrough" (2/6/03).

Also during this period, veteran investigative reporter Walter Pincus of the *Washington Post* began to have his own doubts about the case for war. He began by reviewing UN inspectors' reports from 1998 to 1999 and was struck by how much of Iraq's weapons stock had been destroyed during the inspections process of the 1990s. He also learned from former U.S. Central Command head General Anthony Zinni that hundreds of the remaining suspected weapons sites had been destroyed in a 1998 bombing ordered by Bill Clinton after weapons inspectors were withdrawn.

This research, Pincus said, "Made me go back and read Powell's speech closely. And you could see that it was all inferential. If you analyzed all the intercepted conversations he discussed, you could see that they really didn't prove anything" (Massing 2004, p. 59).

But when Pincus proposed an article interrogating the White House's case, his editors rejected the idea. Only when the *Post*'s Bigfoot reporter, Bob Woodward, weighed in on Pincus's side did his article finally appear—on page A17. One more follow-up article, by Pincus and Dana Milbank, began with this seemingly momentous charge: "As the Bush administration prepares to attack Iraq this week, it is doing so on the basis of a number of allegations against Iraqi President Saddam Hussein that have been challenged—in some cases disproved—by the United Nations, European governments and even U.S. intelligence reports." This story, clearly one of the utmost urgency, appeared on page C1 (Pincus 2003; Pincus and Milbank 2003).

Did the placement, far from the front page, of these skeptical stories make a difference? Newspeople think it did. The *New York Times* (2004), for example, would later apologize to its readers for these "buried" stories, "which might well have appeared on p. A1."

"The front pages of *The New York Times*, *The Washington Post*, and the *Los Angeles Times*," lamented Pincus, "are very important in shaping what other people think. They're like writing a memo to the White House." But the *Post*, he said, "went through a whole phase in which they didn't put things on the front page that would make a difference" (Massing 2004, p. 60).

Voices of Protest: Crying in the Wilderness

The media's longstanding practice of ignoring, undercounting, and disparaging protestors continued as Iraq came into the nation's crosshairs. At a September 2002 "Mobilization for Global Justice" in Washington, D.C., speakers condemned the coming war as D.C. police "penned in" a crowd of about 600 people in (ironically) Freedom Plaza. According to on-site reporters for alternet.org and the University of Maryland's newspaper, the *Diamondback*, these demonstrators began chanting, "We want to leave peacefully." They were then clubbed, arrested, and many of them were detained—along with the journalists— for 24 hours, and denied food and access to attorneys, "while lying on the floor of a gymnasium with their right wrists shackled to their left ankles" (Coen 2002a, p. 12).[2]

But mainstream news reporters did not see, in these events, a gross violation of civil liberties. Instead Fox News' Brian Wilson explained that "in a post 9–11 world," police "were in no mood to be challenged" (9/27/02). While Wilson conceded that "violence was not on the agenda" of the D.C. demonstrators, he nonetheless insisted, "Still, anti-Americanism is in the air. . . . Critics of the protestors argue they are motivated not by smart policy, but by misguided hate for much of what America and the West stand for."

On MSNBC's *Hardball*, reporter David Shuster introduced "another round of violent demonstrations" by asking, "Do the protestors have a legitimate gripe or are they just hooligans?" Shuster then answered his own question, labeling the protestors "the same crowd" who "broke windows, looted stores and generally incited lawless mayhem" in Seattle in 1999. Not to be outdone by his reporter, *Hardball* host Chris Matthews then turned to conservative pundit Cliff May and asked, "Those people out in the streets, do they hate America?" To which May replied, "Yes, I'm afraid a lot of them do. They hate America. They align themselves with Saddam Hussein. They align themselves with terrorists all over the world" (9/27/02).

On October 26, 2002, another rally convened in Washington to oppose the looming war. Once again, the media tended to ignore, trivialize, or denigrate the protest. Knight Ridder's story began, by now predictably, with some funny math: "Organizers, hoping for the largest anti-war protest in Washington since the Vietnam era, were expecting 100,000 participants. While no official head count was available . . . most agreed the turnout fell short of that" (10/27/02). This was a doubly odd pronouncement, because (a) the organizers had taken out a permit for only 20,000 marchers, thus contradicting Knight

---

[2]Reliable reports indicate that the violence in Seattle, as in Washington, D.C., was "overwhelmingly committed by police, not by demonstrators" (Coen 2002a, p. 13; *Extra!* 1/2/02).

Ridder's assessment of what organizers were "expecting"; (b) the *official* police estimate of the crowd size was, in fact, 100,000 (organizers themselves estimated an actual turnout of 200,000) thus making it what Knight Ridder's report said it was not—the biggest antiwar march in D.C. since the Vietnam War (Astor and Nammour 2002).

But Knight Ridder was not the only outlet whose numbers didn't add up that day. The *New York Times'* brief, page-eight story also claimed that the "thousands" of demonstrators were "fewer than organizers had hoped for" (10/27/04). NPR's Nancy Marshall chimed in that the crowd of "fewer than 10,000" was "not as large as the organizers . . . had predicted" (10/26/02).

And once again, descriptions of the protestors seemed designed to portray them as the "Birkenstock and beads set," outside the pale of normal Americans (*Newsweek* 10/1/01). Knight Ridder's story called them "a colorful mix of peace activists, Vietnam-era protestors, students, veterans groups, avowed socialists and many of their children and dogs" (10/27/02). The photos accompanying such stories often focused on hirsute young men and hemp bag–toting young women, often kissing, tossing Frisbees, or otherwise cavorting and generally connoting frivolous ignorance about the "menace" of Iraq.

Then, in January 2003, a tsunami of protest spread across the globe. A British newspaper described it this way in an article titled "The World Against the War": "In the biggest day of protest the world has yet seen against a war in Iraq, hundreds of thousands of demonstrators across four continents took to the streets yesterday" (*Independent* 9/19/03).

While these demonstrations would seem to be a meaningful expression of the heartfelt beliefs of many people, *Chicago Sun Times* reporter Neil Steinberg could muster only contempt for the protestors. In an article headlined "War Protestors' Worst Enemy Is Logic, Not Spies," he observed:

> There were perhaps 300 people at the rally, well salted with young green-fatigued anarchist types selling "The Daily Socialist" and gray-haired NPR radicals. Half the group seemed like the brand of bone-deep activists who would show up to protest a kindergarten picnic.
>
> A woman narrowed her eyes and asked me if I support the war. "Yes," I said. "I do." I didn't add there isn't yet a war to support or oppose, that right now all that was being done was pressuring Iraq. War might still be avoided, and then wouldn't these people look silly?
>
> But that would confuse the issue. The peace movement is proceeding, on autopilot, as if we were already fighting. Their logic, I suppose, is: Why wait? ("Logic," I realize, might be too strong a term.)
>
> Sadly, there were few ideas on display at the rally, only fierce, reflexive anger and suspicion. Looking around at the peace

protestors, at how angry they are over a war that has not yet started, how much hate they have for their country, it was hard not to see them as the very agents of evil itself. The devil, when he comes, of course, will come cloaked in disguise, as a man of peace.

A white-haired man, with a colorful scarf around his neck, came over and touched my arm. "It is an exercise in irrelevance. It is masturbation." That seemed to sum it up nicely, and I closed my notebook and left. (Steinberg 2003)

And finally, as the war began, the protests flared up again. When more than 100,000 people surged into New York's streets on March 22, the *New York Times,* whose offices were two blocks from the march's starting point, placed the story on page B11.

Over the next 10 days, as opposition spread throughout the country like the "wave" through a stadium, television news turned a similarly blind eye toward the demonstrators. From March 20, the day after the bombing of Baghdad began, through March 30, as protests raged throughout the nation and the world, CNN, in its 264 hours of air time, found room for three stories on the demonstrations.

The Fox News Network managed two brief references to dissent during the 10-day period. The first described "a very few . . . pro-Saddam anti-American protests" in the Middle East that looked "angry and violent," but "within days . . . had for the most part fizzled" (3/26/03).[3]

But once again, some in the media were not content just to ignore the protestors. The only other reference to them on Fox News was a tirade by Bill O'Reilly, reminding us that "they hate America. . . . they want to cause anarchy. That's who they are, and they are very good at it" (3/24/03). The host of *MSNBC Reports,* Joe Scarborough, demanded that "these leftist stooges for anti-American causes" be made to "stand up and be counted for their views, which could hurt American troop morale" (4/10/03).

Another MSNBC talk show host, Michael Savage, called for the arrest of antiwar activists and the repassage of the Sedition Act to silence them: "Then we can stop some of these maniacs who are encouraging our enemies, weakening our troops' resolve and confusing the American people" (3/8/03).

A talk show host for Citadel Communications, one of the largest radio conglomerates in the United States, admonished his listeners to go outside, heckle the demonstrators, and "put these goofballs in their

---

[3]When antiwar demonstrators appeared outside Fox's Manhattan studio, the network's electronic billboard, usually flashing news headlines, instead taunted demonstrators: "Attention protestors: The Michael Moore Fan Club meets Thursday at a phone booth." And, in a jape that caught the spirit of TV news coverage generally, "How do you keep a war protestor in suspense? Ignore them [sic]" (Hart 2003).

place," adding that they "deserve a bullet in the head" (Associated Press [AP] 3/30/03).

Not to be outdone by its competitor, Clear Channel Communications, the nation's largest radio conglomerate, financed a series of pro-war demonstrations during this period under the banner of "Rally for America." These were hosted by radio talk show host Glenn Beck, whose show has since ascended to a prime-time spot on CNN, and then another on Fox News.

After months of ignoring, belittling, and berating antiwar protestors, the media were able to report polls that showed 63% of Americans harboring an "unfavorable" view of demonstrators (Fox News 3/27/03).

❖ THE ENTERTAINMENT MEDIA REENLIST

As they had been in the Afghan War, the entertainment media were willing volunteers in the Iraq War effort.

MSNBC, the 24-hour news channel co-owned by Microsoft and General Electric/NBC, promised its viewers a "wide range of strong, opinionated voices" as war loomed in early 2003. Unfortunately, the station "honored" this pledge by canceling its highest-rated show, hosted by Phil Donahue, one of the very few antiwar voices on television. An internal network memo explained, "[Donahue is] a tired, left-wing liberal out of touch with the current marketplace," who would be a "difficult public face for NBC in a time of war . . . he seems to delight in presenting guests who are anti-war, anti-Bush and skeptical of the administration's motives" (Naureckas 2003). While it might seem that having one lone voice "skeptical of the administration's motives" was the least a station committed to "a wide range of voices" could do, MSNBC thought otherwise.

As a better "public face" for MSNBC, the network hired Michael Savage in early 2003. Savage is a rabid, pro-war, racist, anti-Semitic, homophobic misogynist, who, on his radio show, had dispensed these pearls of wisdom:

- On what he frequently refers to as "turd-world immigrants" from "turd-world nations": "You open the door to them, the next thing you know they are defecating on your country and breeding out of control."

- "We need racist stereotypes right now of our enemy in order to encourage our warriors to kill the enemy."

- Referring to American children killed by guns: "They're not kids, they're ghetto slime. . . . They're the same kids that are in Sierra Leone toting AK-47's."

- On women: "Today in America we have a 'she-ocracy' where a minority of feminist Zealots rule the country" and have "feminized and homosexualized much of America."
- In case of war: "Arrest the leaders of the anti-war movement."
- On critics of his hiring by MSNBC: "Stinking rats who hide in sewers. . . . I'll put you in jail! We have a Republican president, we have a Republican attorney general. I have millions of people who vote. . . . I'm going to ask for a trade in favor. If they keep it up, my favor is going to be I want these groups investigated" (Naureckas 2003).

MSNBC staunchly defended its hiring of Savage, calling it "a legitimate attempt to expand the marketplace of ideas" (Naureckas 2003). At about the same time, MSNBC also brought conservative Republicans Joe Scarborough and Dick Armey to its expanding marketplace of ideas.

On the eve of war, Natalie Maines, of the chart-topping country music trio Dixie Chicks, told a London concert audience: "Just so you know, we're ashamed that the president of the United States is from Texas," the group's home state. Cumulus Media, which at the time owned 262 U.S. radio stations, ordered its 42 country format stations to stop playing Dixie Chicks records. Cumulus then sponsored a pro-war rally in Shreveport, Louisiana, that featured a bulldozer crushing a pile of Dixie Chicks CDs. Many of the 1,225 radio stations owned by Clear Channel Communications also banned the group from their airwaves (Cooper 2004, p. 58).

During this same period, antiwar activists Martin Sheen and Sean Penn were fired, respectively, from an ad campaign for Visa and a film produced by Steve Bing. Appearances by war opponents Tim Robbins and Susan Sarandon were canceled, respectively, by the Baseball Hall of Fame (marking the anniversary of Robbins's baseball film *Bull Durham*) and by the United Way. Peace groups trying to buy airtime for antiwar ads were refused by all the major networks. CBS President Martin Franks explained, "We think that informed discussion comes from our news programming" (*New York Times* 3/13/03).

At the midpoint of the White House's campaign for war, HBO aired *Live From Baghdad*, a TV movie purporting to tell the "behind-the-scenes true story" of how the 1991 Persian Gulf War was covered by CNN (which, like HBO, is owned by AOL Time Warner). The film told the tale of intrepid CNN reporters investigating one of the Gulf War's most horrifying stories: Invading Iraqi soldiers had reportedly entered Kuwaiti hospitals and torn babies from their incubators, leaving them on the floor to die. This story had been Exhibit A in the case against Saddam Hussein in 1991: No fewer than six U.S. senators cited the story as an influence on their vote for a Gulf War resolution that passed by five votes.

In HBO's version, CNN reporters are outraged by Iraqi officials who compound the atrocity by trying to dupe the network into reporting that it hadn't happened. *Washington Post* TV critic Tom Shales probably spoke for viewers generally when he praised the film: "The horror wreaked on Kuwait is brought back vividly during a sequence in which [CNN crew members] travel to Kuwait to investigate allegations that Iraqi troops had ripped babies out of incubators as part of their plundering—remember?" (12/7/02).

Unfortunately, what HBO helped viewers "remember" was not an Iraqi atrocity but a propaganda hoax made in the USA. The main source for the incubator story was a 15-year-old Kuwaiti girl who testified in front of the Congressional Human Rights Caucus under the pseudonym "Nayireh." Nayireh turned out to be the daughter of Kuwait's ambassador to Washington. Her testimony was coached by the public relations firm of Hill & Knowlton, which had been paid over $10 million by the Kuwaiti government to drum up support for the Gulf War. Postwar investigations, including one conducted by Amnesty International, found no evidence to support any of Nayireh's claims. CNN's Robert Weiner, whose story was the basis for HBO's movie, acknowledged to Wolf Blitzer that "that [incubator] story turned out to be false" (11/21/02).

So in the end, HBO's "behind-the-scenes true story" wasn't true. But for those who wanted war with Iraq, it was, like the "centrifuge tubes," "poison training camps," the "Niger uranium," and so many other stories, a useful fiction.

❖ ENDGAME

Two events immediately preceded the outbreak of war. In each case, the media spun the stories in ways the White House must have appreciated. The first was the story of White House efforts to secure UN backing for the imminent invasion. Despite the administration's efforts to cajole, bully, and buy Security Council votes, 10 of the 15 members continued to resist the war (Solomon and Erlich 2003, pp. 68–69).

It is possible that some or all of the 10 balky nations honestly believed that the case for war had not been made. But apparently, the media could not conceive of this possibility. So instead, the failure at the UN became a story of French (or German) treachery, born of greed or jealousy that somehow managed to outbully the United States and secure a *non* vote:

So the French have been running around Africa urging tiny nations on the UN Security Council to help humiliate America and frustrate the war in Iraq. . . . More American soldiers may die as a result of France's dubious diplomacy. (*U.S. News & World Report* 3/24/03)

And what would motivate the French to do this? "There, one sees a visceral and irrational anti-Americanism, connected, one must guess to the decline of France as a world power and the rise of the US as a hyper-power" (*U.S. News & World Report* 4/7/03).

Et tu, Germany? "What began as a desperate ploy to save [Gerhard Schröder's] sinking electoral campaign has now escalated into barely masked antagonism toward the US" (*Time* 3/3/03).

Soon, the theme of European treachery had trickled down to late night comedians' routines, and "freedom fries" were on the menu.

And the UN? "We don't need their permission," said White House Chief of Staff Andrew Card (Solomon and Erlich 2003, p. 70). Indeed not, now that UN members had been cast in the roles of knaves and dupes.

The other endgame story was President Bush's dramatic "ultimatum," delivered in a televised speech on March 17: "Saddam Hussein and his sons must leave Iraq in 48 hours. Their refusal to do so will result in military conflict, commenced at a time of our choosing."

The press dutifully relayed the seemingly urgent message: "President Tells Hussein to Leave Iraq Within 48 Hours or Face Invasion" was the *Washington Post's* headline, typical of hundreds of others. Implicitly, these stories suggested that President Bush, who had always maintained that he sought a "peaceful solution" to the Iraq question, was now pursuing one last peaceful solution. The choice of war, these stories suggested, would be Baghdad's, not Washington's. What almost no one reported, though the White House made no effort to hide it, was the fact that the "choice" being offered was no choice at all: Iraq was going to be invaded, whether Hussein and his sons left or not. As Colin Powell stated on ultimatum day, Hussein's departure would be followed by the "peaceful entry of [American] force" into Iraq, that is, an uninvited military incursion, also called an invasion, which was not at all likely to be "peaceful." Other White House sources also admitted the truth to the *New York Times'* Michael Gordon on the day of Bush's speech: "Even if Saddam Hussein leaves Iraq within 48 hours . . . allied forces plan to move north into Iraqi territory, American officials said today" (3/17/03). Gordon's story was placed on page 16, while the *Times'* own front-page headlines blared, "War Imminent as Hussein Rejects Ultimatum." "The White House said today," the story began, "that Saddam Hussein was making his 'final mistake' by rejecting an ultimatum ordering him to leave Iraq or face war" (3/17/03). At this point, it was almost fitting that the press should present things the White House way, one final time before the war. Or perhaps it was the press that made a "final mistake" before the battle, with one last pro-war prevarication.

❖ CONCLUSION

Surely the few months between September 2002 and March 2003 were among the most fateful in modern American history. During this time, the country contemplated a war that would consume its national energy for years to come.

At this most crucial moment, the nation's media failed, tragically, in their capacity as watchdog of the people and marketplace of ideas. A debate that should have been robust and included the full spectrum of opinion was reduced to a drab monopoly: one voice, in the service of one goal.

Content analysis of this period shows that "the vast majority" of Iraq stories originated from the White House, while dissident think tanks all but disappeared from the news. Independent experts challenging White House claims about WMD were "iced out and insulted," called "a footnote, not a split," while Iraqi defectors with "no credibility at all" commanded the front pages of the nation's elite press.

Colin Powell's UN speech, based so largely on the testimony of one such defector, the aptly named "Curveball," was called "incontrovertible," while the UN inspectors visiting the very sites Powell had referred to were ignored or ridiculed for contradicting his testimony.

The few courageous reporters who bucked the trend and got the story right were usually relegated to their papers' back pages, where their important revelations were easily ignored by the rest of the mainstream press.

During this period, news commentators referred to antiwar protestors as "leftist stooges for anti-American causes," "maniacs who are encouraging our enemies," and "the very agents of evil itself," who "deserve a bullet in the head." Those few antiwar commentators who were actually invited to appear on the news probably wished they hadn't been, because their hosts accused them of "defending the Iraqi regime" and "asking the American public, 'believe Saddam Hussein, don't believe President Bush.'"

In the end, thanks in part to the media, the tsunami of half-truths and untruths—the "centrifuge tubes," "poison training camps," "Niger uranium," "testimony of Hussein Kamel," the "mobile weapons labs," the "four tons of VX"—this tidal wave of misinformation and disinformation became the "reality" of Iraq for most Americans. Now the war was at hand, and sure enough, its first casualty had been the truth.

Firdos Square, April 9, 2003. "If you don't have goose bumps now, you will never have them in your life," exclaimed one reporter as U.S. Marines, together with a group of Iraqis, tear down the statue of Saddam Hussein. Unfortunately, there was another side to this story, and it was not told.

4

"And the Lord Did Shock and Awe Them That Blasphemed Him"

Coverage of the war itself was, among other things, a hymn to the thrilling power of America and an entertaining fascination with the techniques and technologies of battle: war as football, war as PlayStation—a "ballet of machines," as one news story called it.

Content analysis shows not only that the news presented us with the "official" story, but that, in this case, the particular officials chosen to explain the war were a strangely truncated group. Only 3% of the news sources during this period opposed the war, and most of them were allowed only single-sentence sound bites.

A brief history of the press at war since Vietnam will show us that the Pentagon's mistrust of the press had left journalists "frustrated and mutinous," and led to the "sheer genius" of embedded reporting. And what could be wrong, we'll ask, with a system praised by both press and Pentagon? Plenty, as we'll see, starting with censorship and hostage syndrome.

We'll also examine the fate of the "unilaterals"—reporters who dared to enter the battle zone without a military escort. They were ready for hostility from Iraqis but were surprised when they were attacked and arrested by American forces.

And we'll check in with reporters based at Central Command Headquarters in Doha, where briefings are given from a "Platform for Truth." It is also where a reporter who questions the information imparted from the Platform is told, "This is a f——ing war, a——hole, why don't you just go home."

We'll find that once again, inconvenient facts are met with obfuscation. For example, this was a war seemingly without wounds, without death.

And weapons of mass destruction (WMD)? Here we'll confront an amazing paradox: Despite the fact that Iraq had no WMD, the news media reported, again and again, that they had been discovered. These reports included nearly a dozen by the *New York Times'* Judith Miller, in which WMD were "just about to be found or had recently been destroyed."

Finally, we'll see how the press captured the war in a series of "Kodak Moments": media-government collaborations hyping unheroic incidents into stories of derring-do and pseudoevents into historic watersheds. These Kodak Moments include a "daring rescue" that wasn't. And the "pure emotional expression" of a toppling statue that was framed, literally and figuratively, to make it seem to be something it was not. But for the press, "This was the day the fog of war lifted, and the whole world could see the truth."

Finally, at the moment of "Mission Accomplished," the "end" of war was viewed as an unqualified triumph—for the United States, for Iraq, for democracy. And for George W. Bush, whose continued valorization by the press would generate continued support for his Iraq policy as the conflict wore on.

❖ POWER AND GLORY

On March 19, 2003, President Bush gave the orders for American forces to begin the war. The media were ready.

The cable networks' flags and war logos, announcing "Operation Iraqi Freedom," were ready to be placed in the corner of the screen, just in case anyone were to forget that this was a just war. Fox News commissioned a CD of *Liberation Iraq Music*, described by one writer as "Metallica rehearsing Wagner." Fox News' creative director called it "uplifting, but with a marching feel." As they had in many ways, the other networks followed Fox's lead, all introducing "regimental fanfares evoking military parades where we can see how powerful we are . . . able to beat our enemy" (Engstrom 2003, p. 45).

This theme of American might was picked up by reporters, where it became the first major theme of the news' war overture, an expression of aesthetic wonderment, a hymn to the thrilling power of America:

> Never in the history of the world has there been this much firepower all in one place. . . . If we're ordered to go forward, [the war] will be lightning quick. (*U.S. News & World Report* 3/24/03)

> I'm not sure people realize the size of the hammer we're lowering on Iraq. . . . (*Newsweek* 3/19/03)

> A strategy of reigning [sic] down missiles on strategic targets in Baghdad to devastating effect. A ninety-minute barrage today, between 1,000 and 1,500 precision weapons. The center of Baghdad is now smoldering and large mushroom clouds hang over the horizon. (Fox News 3/21/03)

> The U.S. appears to have assembled now an awesome display of missiles within striking range. . . . Fifteen hundred Tomahawks ready to fire . . . in all of the Gulf War 288 cruise missiles were fired . . . add the Tomahawks to hundreds of satellite guided bombs that will be dropped from B-2 Stealth Bombers and F-1–17 Stealth Fighters in the first night of a war. . . . Mankind has never seen anything like this. (Fox Special Report 3/18/03)

> Just before dawn was breaking . . . dark and heavy leaden sky, we heard jets overhead, we could see flashes of light . . . the golden snowflakes appearing in the clouds. (CBS 3/20/03)

> An absolutely fearsome display of aerial firepower . . . this constant pulsating light . . . like the center of a furnace, this tremendous incandescent light . . . death and destruction raining down on Iraqi military positions. (Fox News 3/21/03)

> U.S. forces have begun a double-barrel attack. . . . days of withering attacks . . . Republican guard . . . decimated by a relentless, week-long air assault. . . . "We're tightening the noose around Baghdad." . . . they're in serious trouble and they remain in contact now with the most powerful force on earth. (*U.S. News & World Report* 4/02/03)

Because the "why" of the war was not open to question, coverage, once combat began, focused on "how." Besides, these strategies and capacities were, in the media's hands, entertaining. And so the war became largely a matter of techniques and technologies: war as football, war as PlayStation.

TV screens and news pages were festooned with multicolored maps diagramming Hail Mary's and end arounds. "Tale of the Tape" charts gave us the specs on the bionic capacities of Tomcats, Hornets, Predators, Tomahawks, Dragon Eyes, Thunderbolts, Apaches, and a horde of other fearsome wonders.

Reporters watching this wizardry in action described the weapons as something like cyborgs, "a ballet of machines," as the *New York Times* called it (4/16/02).

> Missiles . . . guided by lasers and satellites . . . New tanks . . . with computerized mapping systems and cruise missiles that can be redirected mid-flight. . . . High-power microwave bombs. . . . Satellite-assisted munitions . . . the tactical Tomahawk . . . has the capability to "loiter" [in midair] and wait for a target assignment. (*Newsweek* 3/19/03)

A premium of this precision, said the press, was that more tonnage could be dropped on Baghdad than was visited on Hiroshima—without causing civilian deaths or damage to nonmilitary targets.

> Baghdad is the most digitized city . . . on this planet. We know the latitude and longitude to a thousandth of a degree of everything in that city. We are not getting involved in urban warfare . . . but very rapidly and very surgically going after military targets with overwhelming force. It should keep casualties, fratricide and collateral damage to a minimum . . . a very quick and decisive conflict with a minimum loss of casualties. (*Newsweek* 3/19/03)

> And the important thing is, its precision. That precision is designed to minimize the collateral damage. (Fox News 3/18/03)

> This is very pinpoint, indeed, very accurate aerial bombardment, rather than massive saturation bombing. (Fox News, "The Big Story" 3/21/03)

This kind of coverage, encouraged by the White House, was certainly useful to the neoconservative project. If war was to be a useful instrument for achieving American empire, then war would have to be palatable to the American people. To make it palatable, this prototype war would need to be quick, decisive, and antiseptic.

But there was a downside. If the campaign did not live up to the hype about American invincibility, it would be open to criticism. What's more, such criticism dovetailed with the press's own unwritten rules of engagement. Again, while the "why" of the war was not to be challenged, the press fixed on the "how." If America's military machine was invincible, any sign of American vulnerability would suggest errors in "how" that machine was deployed.

So it was that, when for a time, the Iraqi army dug in, fought back, killed, and took U.S. prisoners, questions arose. And when some in the phalanx of retired generals employed by the press—plus a few out on the battlefield—began to criticize the Pentagon's tactics, some reporters followed suit.

> Remember Little Big Horn . . . army commanders justify throwing centuries of military doctrine into the trash heap by citing a couple of fairly new and relatively untested theories. . . . Events of the first week of war challenged all of these assumptions. . . . Along what is now a nearly 300-mile long supply line . . . I've seen key choke points . . . where as few as three soldiers are standing guard. . . . As for air power being a replacement for boots on the ground: well we saw what good that did the soldiers from the 507th Maintenance Company who were killed or taken prisoner in Nasirya on Sunday. (*Newsweek* 3/27/03)

Even this criticism—not of the war itself, but of the tactics used to fight it—was too much for the conservative wing of the mainstream press, which lashed back. Once again, patriotism was the whip of choice:

> Like impatient back-seat children . . . scolds find a thousand vindicating reasons to carp an incessant stream of anti-Bush criticism . . . couched on the . . . argument that it is going badly. . . . tragically, the people who pay the price are the men and women on the front line. Make no mistake, what we say and do . . . either shortens or lengthens the war. American citizens—even newsmen—whose actions give aid and comfort to the enemy put the lives of men and women in the field at risk. (*Atlanta Journal-Constitution* 4/1/03)

And while the conservative press played tough cop with the dissenting generals, the mainstream made nice, explaining that both sides were right. When asked how to square the generals' criticisms with the Pentagon's reassurances, CNN's Jamie McIntyre said, "Well you can square them. It's true that at any particular point a commander may want more force than they actually have. But it also may be true that the overall plan is the one that is actually providing the most effective military strategy" (CNN.com Live 4/1/03).

❖ THE OFFICIAL STORY

The fact that this story's only controversy was over "how" and not "why" we went to war is easier to understand, once we look at the story's sources.

One study examined 1,617 sources appearing in three weeks of stories about Iraq on the evening newscasts of the six national TV networks, beginning the day after the invasion. Most of the U.S. sources (68%) were "officials"—current or former U.S. government employees. And most of these officials (68%) were current or former military officers.

Even among the range of available officials, some were "more equal than others": Of 840 U.S. official sources, only 4, all Democratic members of Congress, fleetingly expressed antiwar opinions.

The same bias appears among nonofficial sources. As antiwar protests raged throughout the country, and 27% of polled Americans opposed the war, only 3% of TV news's U.S. voices opposed the war. Even that tiny minority was "almost unanimously allowed one-sentence sound bites taken from interviews conducted on the street. Not a single show in the study conducted a sit down interview with a person identified as being against the war" (Rendall and Broughel 2003).

❖ EMBEDDING: A PREHISTORY

In the Pentagon, a common though probably mistaken view of the Vietnam tragedy has been that unrestricted media coverage of that conflict contributed to a U.S. "defeat" (Pritchard 2003).[1]

This mistrust of the media prompted the Pentagon to preclude the press from its next major initiative, the invasion of Grenada in 1983. After the press complained vociferously, Chairman of the Joint Chiefs of Staff John W. Vessey Jr. appointed a panel, headed by Major General Winant Sidle, to study the matter of press access to war. Vessey appointed representatives from the news business to the panel, and the resulting "Sidle Report," released in 1984, promised press access "to the maximum degree possible consistent with mission security and the safety of U.S. forces." Two key recommendations of the report involve "media pools"—a handful of representative reporters with access to the front lines, who would share their coverage with the rest of the press corps—and "security guidelines"—ground rules established by the Pentagon that reporters must abide by or face banishment from the pools.

Unfortunately, the new guidelines flunked their first test when "maximum access consistent with mission security" meant that the press was, again, completely excluded from covering the Panama invasion of 1989 until most of the operation was over.

Once again, the press complained, and the Pentagon tinkered. In the first Iraq War, "Operation Desert Storm," press pools did make it to some

---

[1]For a critique of the "media lost Vietnam" thesis, see Herman and Chomsky 1988.

combat zones, though they were barred from others. "For historic purposes . . . there were no independent eyes and ears" to document much of the war, said Frank Aukofer, former bureau chief of the *Milwaukee Journal Sentinel* (Newseum Speech 7/7/01). What's more, the pools were handpicked by the military, who showed a preference for "hometown" reporters who tended to do "softer," more "upbeat" stories than the national press reporters who were uninvited (Exoo 1994, pp. 96–97).

Pool reporters also complained about the requirement that they operate under the supervision of the Pentagon's media minders, called Public Affairs Officers (PAOs). These PAOs handpicked the soldiers reporters were allowed to interview, stood nearby during the interviews, and were known to "stretch out a hand holding a cassette recorder, and click it on in the soldier's face. This was patent intimidation" (NBC correspondent Gary Matsumoto, in Exoo 1994, p. 97).

The effect of this system, said Chris Hedges of the *New York Times*, was that "you never see any problems. You're never allowed to report. Nothing's ever wrong. The entire war has become videotape of planes always hitting their targets like giant Nintendo games and soldiers up front eating turkey and waving flags and it's all a lie" (Exoo 1994, p. 97).

Things went from bad, in Gulf War I, to worse in Afghanistan, where journalists were "denied access . . . to a greater degree than in any previous war involving US military forces," by a policy "more restrictive even than the burdensome constraints on media in the Persian Gulf." "Imagine this," said Sandy Johnson, the Associated Press Washington bureau chief. "There is a war being fought by Americans and we're not there to chronicle it. . . . We have practically zero access to American forces in the theatre." These restrictions, according to Neil Hickey, who interviewed "more than a score" of reporters, editors, and news executives, left the journalists "frustrated and mutinous" (Hickey 2002).

❖ EMBEDDED

It was against this backdrop of a "mutinous" press that Victoria Clarke, assistant secretary of defense for public affairs, proposed what one PR professional called the "sheer genius" of embedded reporting (Rampton and Stauber 2003b, p. 21). Clarke had come to the Pentagon after running the Washington, D.C., office of Hill & Knowlton, the PR firm hired by Kuwait to help sell Gulf War I. Clarke revealed to the *Wall Street Journal* that she "model(ed) her operation on the way she used to run media campaigns" (Schechter 2003, p. 121). As part of what the

White House chief of staff called the "product-marketing campaign" for the war, military briefers told journalists that "by making you a part of the unit, you will be a member of the team" (Anderson 2003, p. 6).

Here's how it worked: More than 600 journalists from around the world completed the Pentagon's "mini-boot camp," a required one-week course to familiarize them with military operations and equipment. When the troops rolled into battle, the journalists went with them, as *USA Today* enthused, "right in the thick of things, basically free and unfettered" (Pritchard 2003).

Well, not quite. Among the rules imposed by the Pentagon were the following:

- Reporters could not travel independently.

- Interviews had to be on the record, and soldiers who spoke ill of the war or its planners faced discipline (Shadid 2005).

- Officers could censor or delay reports for "operational security."

- As in Gulf War I, public affairs officers "helped manage the reporters, steering them toward stories, facilitating interviews and photo opportunities" (Rampton and Stauber 2003b, p. 20).

- Prohibited, among other things, were reports about ongoing missions (unless cleared by on-site commanders); reporting on specific results of completed missions or on future, postponed, or canceled missions; or reporting on "embargoed" stories. Reporters who violated these rules could be, and were, "disembedded" from Iraq (Burnett 2003, p. 43).

These restrictions were broad enough to prompt some reporters to wonder "just what they *will* be able to report, and *when?*" The answer provides one clue as to why embedding was such a PR success: "Specific ground rules for each unit," according to the military's media contract on embedding, "will be established when reporters get to their units. And those ground rules will change from mission to mission." In other words, individual unit commanders would have "huge leeway" to decide what reporters can and cannot report, said Charles Lewis, Washington bureau chief for Hearst Newspapers. The implication of these rules was unmistakable: Reporters who want to get their stories out unedited and with dispatch would do well to anticipate—and accommodate—the preferences of their commanding officers (Bushell and Cunningham 2003, pp. 18, 20). But the real genius of embedded reporting lay not in censorship, or even in anticipated censorship leading to self-censorship. The real genius lay in requiring that journalists be "taken under the wing of the United States military. . . . effectively becom[ing] hostages of the military," as former CNN anchor Bernard Shaw put it (Bushell and Cunningham 2003, p. 18). Embedded reporters were dependent on their military hosts for food, shelter, and, not least, their physical safety. The soldiers "have done anything and everything that we could ask of them," said an NBC embed, "and we in turn are trying to return the favor by doing anything and everything that they can ask of us" (Rampton and Stauber 2003b, p. 21). Embedded reporters also ate, slept, lived, and bonded with the soldiers, literally, "in the trenches." "The sagacity of the tactic," said public relations consultant Katie Delahaye Paine, "is that it is based on the basic tenet of public relations: It's all about relationships. The better the relationship . . . the better the chance of that journalist . . . reporting our messages" (Rampton and Stauber 2003b, p. 21).

And what a relationship it was. Here is how an embed from the *Orange County Register* described it:

> But the biggest problem I faced as an embed with the marine grunts was that I found myself doing what journalists are warned from J-school not to do: I found myself falling in love with my subject. I fell in love with "my" marines. Maybe it's understandable. When you live with the same guy for weeks, sharing the dangers and miseries, learning about their wives and girlfriends, their hopes and dreams, admiring their physical courage and strength, you start to make friends—closer friends in some ways than you'll ever have outside the war. Isolated from everyone else, you start to see your small corner of the world the same way they do . . . the point wasn't that I wasn't reporting the truth; the point was that I was reporting the marine grunt truth—which had also become my truth. (Dillow 2003, p. 33)

> Unsurprisingly, content analysis discovered that "compared to both nonembedded reporters in Operation Iraqi Freedom and overall coverage of Operation Enduring Freedom . . . embedded print coverage was more favorable in overall tone toward the military and in depiction of individual troops." (Pfau, Jackson, Wittenberg, Mehringer, Brockman, Lanier, and Hatfield 2005, p. 179)

The embeds' reports were often disarming human interest stories about the troops or stories of right-stuff GIs and their marvelous weapons dishing out well-deserved beat-downs to a shocked and awed enemy, as in this dispatch from *Newsweek:*

> Major Frank McClary grew more and more sullen as the day's news filtered in. . . . McClary first heard a report on his short-wave radio about the American POW's and corpses shown on Iraqi

television . . . "Oh it's on now," he muttered . . . "I ain't f——king around today . . ." McClary briefed his crew on the night's mission . . . "We will dictate the rules . . . no more falling for the ruse . . . of enemy sources faking surrender. . . . If surrendering soldiers don't follow our instructions, they will face the rapture of the co-ax," said McClary, referring to the Bradley's co-axial machine gun, which spits out up to 950 7.62 mm rounds per minute. . . . Charlie Company found . . . a command and control center for the Saddam Fedayeen . . . under control of one of Saddam Hussein's sons . . . fighters clad completely in black . . . and the black flags . . . "We're taking mortar fire!" . . . Mortars continue to pound the earth dangerously close to McClary's Bradley. "We need to get some cover!" . . . immediately powered the Bradley forth on a frenetic zig-zag amid an obstacle course of serried sand dunes . . . "Take them out," ordered McClary. Torres fired about 10 25mm high explosive rounds. . . . The militiamen disappeared from view. "Got them, Sir" . . . "There you go, that's their a——. Put a little notch in your belt, Sergeant Torres. . . . these guys are Saddam Fedayeen, which means they're the scum of the earth." (3/25/03)

For television, embedding, together with advancing technology, afforded for the first time live pictures of the battle zone, pictures that fulfilled the promise TV news is most keen to offer: "eyewitness" and "action news," without actually providing much useful information. The following gee-whiz exchange, from CNN, was typical:

Embed Walter Rodgers said, "The pictures you are seeing are absolutely phenomenal. These are live pictures of the Seventh Cavalry racing across the desert. . . . If you ride inside that tank it is like riding in the bowels of the dragon. They roar, they screech. . . . What you're watching here. . . ." Anchor Aaron Brown interjected, "Wow look at that shot." Rodgers replied, "It's truly historic television" (3/20/03).

❖ THE UNEMBEDDED: AT RISK AND AT SEA

The handful of journalists who chose to enter the combat zone without embedding, called "unilaterals," found themselves facing unexpected risks. *Columbia Journalism Review* editor Michael Massing was in the region representing the Committee to Protect Journalists. Massing asked U.S. Central Command (USCENTCOM) to investigate the cases of unilaterals who had, they said, been detained by U.S. troops at gunpoint, stripped bare, handcuffed, held for more than 48 hours, denied food and water, and beaten when they attempted to speak. Massing "never heard back" from USCENTCOM (Massing 2003).

Later, when U.S. forces fired on the Palestine Hotel, base camp for unembedded journalists, killing two journalists and injuring three others, reporters asked USCENTCOM briefer General Vincent Brooks if coalition forces could be ordered not to fire on journalists' strongholds. He replied, "'We don't know every place a journalist is operating in the battlefield. We only know those journalists that are operating with us,' i.e., those who were embedded. Any other journalists on the field of battle, he added, were 'putting themselves at risk'" (Massing 2003, p. 34). The Arab news channel Al Jazeera learned Brooks's lesson the hard way, when U.S. planes bombed its "unembedded" Baghdad bureau, killing one of its reporters. The building was bombed despite the fact that, after Al Jazeera's Kabul, Afghanistan, bureau was struck by U.S. forces, the station had been careful to give the coordinates of its Baghdad bureau to the American military (*Control Room*). Other unilaterals were simply turned away at the border, "told by coalition forces that Iraq was closed to them. 'Embeds only,' their orders said" (Massing 2003, p. 35). "The bottom line is that the Americans don't want any journalists there they don't control," said Israeli TV reporter Dan Scemama, one of the detained unilaterals. "All the journalists there wear uniforms and they are all attached to military spokespeople" (*JerusalemReport.com* 4/10/03).

Seeking to add context and background to the embeds' reports, another platoon of reporters convened at Central Command Headquarters in Doha, Qatar. There, military officers provided a daily "Freedom Briefing" from what General Tommy Franks called a "platform for truth"—a set designed by a Hollywood stage crafter for a quarter million dollars. Held at 2:00 p.m. Qatar time, so that its information would be available for the U.S. morning news, each briefing began with a film and slide show taken by Department of Defense "Combat Cameras." After being screened and edited by Defense Department personnel, hundreds of Combat Camera photos and "25 to 50" video clips each day were made available to news agencies for their own use. In these images, "sleek fighter jets, rescued POW's, and smiling Iraqis cheering the arrival of U.S. troops are easy to find . . . photos of bombed-out Baghdad neighborhoods and so-called 'collateral damage' are not" (*Baltimore Sun* 4/18/03). "Every day," according to the BBC, the briefing's pictures and words conveyed the same message: "The war is on track." Aside from that, however, "Questions are rationed, follow-ups are frowned upon, full answers are not forthcoming. . . . Military successes are briefed before they happen, civilian casualties are never confirmed" (Kampfner 2003). "At the end of your stay in Doha, you would know absolutely nothing," said Michael Wolff of *New York Magazine*. Reporters burst into applause when Wolff asked what he described as "my final question, after which I was no longer allowed to ask any more questions; the question that every reporter was asking, not just every day but literally every minute, which was, "Why should we stay, what's the value to us of what we learn at this million dollar press center?" After this query, Wolff was taken aside by the White House's man in Doha, Jim Wilkinson, who told Wolff, "This is a f—— war, a——hole, don't f—— around with things you don't understand. No more questions for you. Why don't you just go home" (Kampfner 2003).

❖ KODAK MOMENTS

But if the media were concerned that the war's full story was not being told, they did not convey that concern to the public. Instead, as we are about to see, the press collaborated with the government to convey a series of carefully cultivated half-truths about the war.

The "Daring Raid" That Wasn't

Just in the nick of time, as criticism of the war's novel tactics began to swell, in like the cavalry rode the stirring story of what the press ubiquitously called "a daring raid" (e.g., ABC 4/7/03; CNN 4/8/03; NBC 4/6/03).

Jessica Lynch's odyssey began on the evening of March 23, when she and 14 other soldiers from her convoy were ambushed on or near Highway 1. After her capture, she was transferred to Saddam Hospital in Nasiriyah. While there, the "waif like" Jessica Lynch was "beaten sadistically by an Iraqi goon," according to the *Washington Post* (Hanson 2003, p. 58).

> On April 1, U.S. Special Ops forces dropped in well outside the city and sneaked up on the compound in the dark for the "snatch." It was a moonless night, but the stars were bright enough to guide the Navy SEALs who slipped into the hospital. Led to her room by a doctor on duty, the SEALs opened the door and asked for Jessica Lynch. At first, she was silent, a sheet pulled tightly over her head. "We're U.S. soldiers," said one of the SEALs. "We're here to protect you and take you home...." Lynch, who during her capture had shot several advancing Iraqi soldiers, emptying her weapon of ammunition and possibly incurring a series of gunshot wounds... said, "I'm an American soldier, too." As they rushed her out to a nearby helicopter, Lynch squeezed the hand of an Army Ranger and said, "Don't let anyone leave me." The Special Ops left "a whole lot" of dead Iraqi's... before hooking up with a convoy and taking off.... Just before 1:00 a.m. local time, word had reached Central Command... in Qatar that the rescue had been successful.

"Some brave souls put their lives on the line, loyal to a creed that they know: they will never leave a fallen comrade behind," said Brigadier General Vince Brooks as he announced the rescue.

Fortuitously, "planes outfitted with special communications gear circled overhead," and a Combat Camera team accompanied the Special Ops, so that photos and video images of the rescue could be provided to the press.

"The grainy green footage—shot with night vision equipment, showed Lynch being carried on a stretcher. It then zoomed in on her face; pretty, but stricken" (from *Newsweek* 4/2/03; *Time* 4/2/03).

The story "buoyed a nation wondering what had happened to the short, neat liberation of Iraq," said *Time* (4/14/03). In the two weeks following her rescue, Jessica Lynch's name appeared 919 times in major newspapers, according to a LexisNexis search—far more appearances than General Tommy Franks (639) who was commanding the war (Hanson 2003). Both CBS–Viacom and NBC Universal offered Lynch movie, book, and TV deals for exclusive rights to her story. It was "a story for history, Jessica comes home," said CBS (4/11/03).

"Never mind," warned press watchdog *Columbia Journalism Review*, "that Lynch was unavailable for comment (and reported to have amnesia). Never mind that reporters would have to paper over big holes to deliver a coherent narrative." Never mind that the dramatic account offered by sometimes-anonymous military sources was uncorroborated by any eyewitnesses. The story of the "innocent waif" and the "daring rescue" was "a godsend to the press corps," and they ran with it (Hanson 2003).

But if press reports are the first draft of history, this one would need major revisions. Not long after the story of the glorious rescue had been reported in every major news outlet in the country, reporters for the BBC and the *London Times* visited the Hussein Hospital in Nasiriyah. There, hospital personnel told reporters that Private Lynch had not been assaulted by any interrogator. Her rescue, said the *Times*, "was not the heroic Hollywood story told by the U.S. military, but a staged operation that terrified patients and victimized the doctors who had struggled to save her life" (4/16/03). The assault, doctors said, had met no resistance; Iraqi forces had already fled the city. Instead, they described a "terrifying assault in which [American] soldiers handcuffed and interrogated doctors and patients, one of whom was paralyzed and on an intravenous drip." Dr. Harith al-Houssona, the doctor who treated Lynch, explained that, in fact, "he had attempted to deliver Lynch to a U.S. outpost the day before the raid, but Americans had fired on the ambulance driver, making it impossible to proceed" (Anderson 2003, p. 9).

Two and a half months after breaking the page-one story that described Lynch's capture ("She Was Fighting to the Death"), the *Washington Post* acknowledged that Lynch might not have fired her M16, which jammed. Her injuries were not from a sadistic beating or gunshot wounds, but from the crash of her Humvee, and indeed, Iraqi doctors had saved her life. These corrections were consigned to the *Post*'s back pages (6/17/03).

A few other news outlets also began raising questions about the story, though "they certainly took their time," said *Columbia Journalism Review*. "Journalists are disinclined to puncture 'feel good' stories, especially those that they themselves have sent aloft. . . . [Lynch's] dramatic rescue was very likely the one memory Americans had carried away from the war with Iraq. How awkward to have to tell them she was a truck crash victim saved by the enemy and not actually rescued by the same commando unit that did not actually find those elusive weapons of mass destruction. But that's what happens when you write first and ask questions later" (Hanson 2003, p. 59).

Incident at Firdos Square: "The Whole World Could See the Truth"

"If you don't have goose bumps now, you will never have them in your life," marveled Fox News anchor David Asman as the giant statue of Saddam Hussein toppled in Firdos Square.

On that day, April 9, U.S. tanks had stormed into Baghdad, and soon, a crowd of jubilant Iraqis climbed onto the statue and tried in vain to pull it down, using rope and a sledgehammer. Then the U.S. Marines rode in with an armored vehicle and a chain.

The crowd cheered as the dictator's statue first bent and then, finally, snapped and fell. It was the perfect picture of victory—a powerful iconic "vindication," said CNN—of just what the White House had so often promised: that the U.S. invaders would be welcomed by Iraqis "as liberators" from the oppressive Hussein regime (Alterman and Green 2004, p. 289).

The image beamed from all the news channels all day and from the print press as well, in full color, front-page photos of the falling icon and the cheering crowd, and always, the pictures were attended by the stentorian prose of inspired reporters: "It's a time for rejoicing, particularly because of what television cameras clearly revealed—that many Iraqis support the coalition's mission and see the U.S. and its allies not as enemies but as friends and liberators" (*Indianapolis Star* 4/10/03). Other headlines read "Iraqis Celebrate in Baghdad" (*New York Times*) and "Liberation Day in Baghdad" (*Boston Globe*). Tom Brokaw said, it was like "all the statues of Lenin [that] came down all across the Soviet Union" (NBC).

Other reports compared the scene to protestors facing down tanks at Tiananmen Square or the fall of the Berlin Wall. *Washington Post* reporter Ceci Connelly, speaking on Fox News, gushed that the event was "just that sort of pure emotional expression, not choreographed, not stage managed, the way so many things these days seem to be. Really breathtaking" (4/9/03).

The Other Side of Firdos Square

Unfortunately, this perfect pageant of liberation, a throng of Iraqis spontaneously surging into Firdos Square to celebrate their new freedom, gave every evidence of being exactly what the press said it was not: choreographed and stage managed.

First, there is the matter of what the U.S. media's cameras "clearly reveal" about the incident, a case study in the slipperiness of the old adage "The camera never lies." Both video and still photos taken by the U.S. press that day maintained a tight focus on the statue and the crowd of 50 or 60 Iraqis immediately surrounding it—pictures hinting at a much larger crowd extending beyond the camera's eye (see photo at the beginning of this chapter).

But wider shots taken that day "clearly reveal" that the small groups at the statue's base were the only Iraqis present—in an otherwise nearly empty Firdos Square.

What's more, those Iraqis who did show up seemed somehow familiar. Several had been seen at a pro-U.S. demonstration in Nasiriyah the previous day (Anderson 2003, p. 9). One man, leader of the "down with Saddam Hussein" chants, would later pop up in other pro-U.S. Kodak Moments—for example, as one of the Iraqi "journalists" who "spontaneously" stood and cheered at the press conference announcing the capture of Hussein. And finally, this "Zelig of Baghdad" appeared again, this time in the entourage of Ahmed Chalabi, whose Iraqi National Congress (INC) had supplied so much of the misinformation that had led to war (Pein 2004, p. 32).

Then there was the fact that this spontaneous outburst happened just across the street from the Palestine Hotel—where most of the journalists covering the war were staying. And finally, there was the "fortuitous appearance" of a pre–Gulf War era Iraqi flag among the revelers. All these coincidences led the alternative press to suggest that the tumult at Firdos Square might have been a pseudoevent orchestrated by the

Wide-angle photo of Firdos Square, April 9, 2003.

Rendon Group, a secretive PR firm employed by the CIA and Department of Defense for just this sort of occasion.[2]

Months later, an internal Army memorandum seemed to confirm the speculation, describing the event as the work of an "Army psychological operations team that made it appear to be a spontaneous Iraqi undertaking" (Jackson 2004, p. 3).

Six days after the statue fell in Firdos Square, 20,000 Iraqis demonstrated against the U.S. invasion, in Nasiriyah. Three days after that, thousands more rallied in Baghdad, demanding a U.S. exit (Rampton and Stauber 2003a, p. 15). Press reports of these demonstrations were few,

---

[2]The Rendon Group had earlier helped to organize and advise Chalabi's INC, charging the CIA $23 million for the first year of the company's work with the INC. Company founder John Rendon is famously tight-lipped about his ongoing work, but he did tell an audience at the Air Force Academy this much about his efforts in the previous Persian Gulf War: "I am an information warrior and a perception manager. . . . Did you ever stop to wonder how the people of Kuwait City, after being held hostage for seven long and painful months, were able to get hand-held American flags [to wave as U.S. Marines rolled into the city]? That was one of my jobs then" (Rampton and Stauber 2003a, p. 15). About his work in George W. Bush's Iraq campaign, Rendon would only confirm this much: "Suffice it to say, we are a support function to the decision makers in the Bush administration and the implementers/warriors at the Department of Defense" (Foer 2002, p. 5).

brief, and fleeting. After all, why muddy the waters when the press had already declared, at Firdos Square, "This was the day the fog of war lifted. And the whole world could see the truth" (*Chicago Tribune* 4/10/03).

❖ MORE INCONVENIENT FACTS, MORE OBFUSCATION

In Iraq, as in Afghanistan, the U.S. press confronted a problem: In constructing the story of a "good war," what is to be done with "bad facts," such as civilian casualties?

In Iraq, as in Afghanistan, the solution was simple: minimize, rationalize, and marginalize the inconvenient facts.

A War Without Wounds

The war Americans saw and read about in the U.S. media was different from the war the rest of the world saw.

On Al Jazeera, the all-news Arabic Channel, for example, viewers saw footage of civilian casualties "several times an hour. Al Jazeera took us to hospital wards to show us screaming children, women in pain, men without limbs. . . . Doctors and nurses described how they were being overwhelmed by casualties and how they lacked the supplies to treat them" (Massing 2004, p. 19).

Michael Massing, who analyzed press coverage of this period, saw an "Islamist" bias in Al Jazeera's coverage. But he saw an equally strong and perhaps even stranger bias in the U.S. press: the tendency to be blind to casualties, "showing a war of liberation without victims" (2004, p. 21).

For example, on the day U.S. troops made their initial raid inside Baghdad, USCENTCOM reported that between 2,000 and 3,000 Iraqi soldiers died. But on TV? Massing saw "not a single one. . . . The more than five hundred reporters embedded with military units provided some unforgettable glimpses of the war, but remarkably few showed war's real-life effects, i.e., people getting killed and maimed" (2004, p. 21). A study of the embedded journalists' coverage by the Project for Excellence in Journalism confirms Massing's impression: "While dramatic, the coverage is not graphic. Not a single story examined showed pictures of people being hit by fired weapons" (Pew Research Center 2003).

The editors of *PR Watch*, Sheldon Rampton and John Stauber, measured an aspect of the media's aversion to casualties, by counting the number of times the term *cluster bombs* appeared in articles about the war. "Cluster bombs have a very bad reputation, which they deserve," says Colin Kiry, author of *Jane's Explosive Ordnance Disposal*. Each cluster bomb shoots off about 200 bomblets

> the size of a soda can, which disperse upon impact and saturate an area the size of two football fields with explosives and tiny flying shards of steel. Between 5 and 15 percent of the bomblets fail to detonate immediately, leaving behind a deadly litter of unexploded bombs that can continue killing people. (Rampton and Stauber 2003c , p. 194)

Cluster bombs have been condemned by Human Rights Watch, Amnesty International, and a host of other human rights groups. They have been banned by more than 100 nations in a treaty the United States has refused to sign.

Rampton and Stauber found that European and Australian newspapers were 10 times more likely to mention cluster bombs than their American counterparts. But as the authors show, "Numbers alone . . . do not tell the full story." Most of the mentions in the U.S. press were one of the following:

- Just that—a mere one-sentence mention. American officials "are investigating reports that cluster bombs were used against villages" (*New York Times* 4/8/03, p. B1).

- An attack on the charge that the United States was deploying cluster bombs as part of the "Iraqi government line" (*Christian Science Monitor* 4/7/03, p. 1). These attacks abated only after U.S. generals acknowledged that, indeed, cluster bombs were being used, though they declined to say how many (Rampton and Stauber 2003c, p. 196).

- References to Saddam Hussein's use of cluster bombs in past attacks on Kurds and Shiites.

While the U.S. media were thus busy minimizing and marginalizing the cluster bomb story, the International Committee of the Red Cross and Amnesty International were busy reporting the effects of cluster bombs on cities and towns across Iraq. For example:

> The scenes at al-Hilla's hospital on 1 April showed that something terrible had happened. The bodies of the men, women and children—both dead and alive—brought to the hospital were punctured with shards of shrapnel from cluster bombs. Videotape of the victims was judged by *Reuters* and *Associated Press* editors as being too awful to

show on television. *Independent* (UK) newspaper journalists reported that the pictures showed babies cut in half and children with their limbs blown off. Two lorry-loads of bodies, including women in flowered dresses, were seen outside the hospital.

Injured survivors told reporters how the explosives fell "like grapes" from the sky, and how bomblets bounced through the windows and doors of their homes before exploding. A doctor at al-Hilla's hospital said that almost all the patients were victims of cluster bombs. (Amnesty International 2003)

What the U.S. press did for cluster bombs, in particular, it did for civilian casualties in general, which were treated as (a) unlikely, (b) unverifiable, (c) a PR "problem," (d) not numerous enough, and (e) unfortunate but unavoidable.

Unlikely. "Every weapon is precision guided—deadly accuracy designed to kill only the targets, not innocent civilians" (NBC's Jim Miklaszewski 3/21/03).

Unverifiable.

- "The BBC and al Jazeera have devoted significant time to what Iraq suggested were innocent victims targeted in the bombings" (*NBC Nightly News* 3/22/03).

- When over 60 people were killed by a missile in a Baghdad market called Shuala, the *New York Times*, like the U.S. press generally, stressed that "it was impossible to determine the cause" (3/29/03). But a reporter for the British *Independent* found a missile fragment at the scene, traced it to a Raytheon Corporation HARM missile, and received confirmation from the military that, indeed, a U.S. Navy Prowler had fired a HARM in that vicinity on that day. A subsequent LexisNexis search of major American news outlets showed that none of them had reported the *Independent*'s findings (Coen and Hart 2003, p. 18).

- Or again, when 10 members of an Iraqi family were killed by U.S. forces at a checkpoint near Najaf on March 30, U.S. media generally gave the Pentagon's version of the shooting—even though that version was directly contradicted by the eyewitness account of *Washington Post* reporter William Branigin. According to Branigin, the Army captain in charge of the checkpoint ordered "nonlethal actions to stop the civilian vehicle." But when the captain "saw no action being taken," and the vehicle continued to approach, he ordered cannon fire to stop it.

When the shooting stopped, the captain shouted, "You just [expletive] killed a family because you didn't fire a warning shot soon enough" (3/31/03). Despite Branigin's reporting, the story in subsequent headlines went like this:

"Failing to Heed G.I.'s, 7 Iraqis Die at Checkpoint" (*New York Times* 4/1/03);

"Seven Iraqi women and children are killed at an army checkpoint...after they failed to hear warning shots" (*Atlanta Journal-Constitution* 4/2/03);

"U.S. troops . . . opened fire on a civilian vehicle that refused their order to halt and ignored warning shots" (*Houston Chronicle* 4/1/03).

A PR Problem. Not because civilian casualties are themselves a tragedy, but because they are "fodder" for the "anti-American" propaganda war. CNN anchor Wolf Blitzer put it this way, after the Shuala disaster: "The pictures that are going to be seen on al Jazeera and Al-Arabia and all the other Arab satellite channels are going to be further fodder for this Anti-American attitude that is clearly escalating as this war continues" (3/29/03).

Newsweek took this point further, asserting that, "In at least one respect, it doesn't matter who bombed the two markets. Either way, Iraqis are blaming the Americans, and Saddam Hussein is reinforcing his position among his people. . . . When it comes to manipulating the minds of his countrymen, Saddam Hussein is a malevolent genius" (4/7/03). In other words, the killing of fifty to a hundred civilians, most likely the work of errant U.S. missiles, somehow became a story about the "malevolent genius of Saddam Hussein." The White House itself couldn't have spun this story any better than that.

Not Numerous Enough. The *Wall Street Journal,* complaining that the United States has too many "scruples" about harming civilians, called for more intensive bombing, despite that this would mean more casualties: "While in the near term we are likely to endure some nasty TV images, in the long run the U.S. determination will save both Iraqi and American lives" (3/28/03).

Unfortunate But Unavoidable. On March 24, CBS's report on collateral damage actually showed wounded Iraqi children, but offered a comforting pro-war context. As the footage showed a GI rocking a little girl in his arms, embedded reporter Phil Ittner explained, "[Soldiers came] streaming out to give what aid they could. They are here to take down the leadership in Baghdad . . . which they see as a threat to their families back home. They wish they didn't have to do it" (3/24/03).

Of the many lacunae in the press's casualty coverage, one of the most glaring was any estimate of the mounting total number of war deaths. One estimate of Iraqi civilian fatalities during the initial invasion put the number at 10,000. "And multiply that," said a British newsman, "many times when the figure includes the killing of mostly teenage conscripts who, as a Marine colonel said, 'sure as hell didn't know what hit them.' Keep multiplying when the wounded are added; such as 1,000 children maimed, according to UNICEF, by the delayed blast of cluster bomblets" (Pilger 2003).

Within 18 months of the invasion, a team of public health researchers from Johns Hopkins University, writing in the respected British medical journal *Lancet*, would estimate the number of Iraqi civilians killed by the war at 100,000.[3]

That report, that number, would seem to be a big story, but it wasn't—not in the United States. Perhaps, in giving that number short shrift, the U.S. press was relying on the cynical aphorism attributed to Joseph Stalin, which has proven so useful to the men who make wars: "The death of one man," he said, "is a tragedy. The death of millions is a statistic."

WMD: "We Found 'Em"

Despite all the mounting evidence for skepticism about the claim that Iraq harbored WMD, much of the media had dropped even the pretense of balance on this issue by the time the war began. Dispensing with "the formality of such modifiers as 'alleged' or 'suspected,'" the press simply asserted, categorically, that this was "a confrontation over 'Iraq's banned weapons programs'" (*Washington Post* 1/27/03). They asked not whether Saddam had them, but whether he was making any effort "'to disarm Iraq's weapons of mass destruction'" (*Time* 2/3/03). They asked

---

[3]A much more conservative estimate, based only on the numbers reported in the news stories, placed the number of civilian war deaths between 14,300 and 16,500 by late 2004 (Massing 2004, p. 3).

not whether there were such weapons but rather "'what precise threat Iraq and its weapons of mass destruction pose to America'" (*NBC Nightly News* 1/27/03). Once the invasion began, it wasn't a question of *if* but *when* the WMD would be found (Ackerman 2003).

This press credulity may explain a miraculous paradox: Despite the fact that Iraq had no WMD, the news media reported again and again that they had been discovered. And the fact that each new "discovery" turned out to be a falsity did not seem to diminish the press's faith in their existence.

Fittingly, the first scoop came from the most faithful of the faithful, Fox News: "HUGE CHEMICAL WEAPONS FACTORY FOUND IN SO. IRAQ . . . REPORTS: 30 IRAQIS SURRENDER AT CHEM WEAPONS PLANT . . ." (3/23/03). But the next day, U.S. officials acknowledged that the site contained no chemicals at all and had long since been abandoned (Dow Jones Wire 3/24/03).

On April 7, embedded NPR reporter John Burnett reported "the first solid, confirmed existence of chemical weapons by the Iraqi army . . . medium-range rockets with warheads containing sarin nerve gas and mustard gas." But once again, the weapons found on this day were unfound the next, when the Pentagon said they had "seen nothing . . . that would corroborate that" (Ackerman 2003, p. 10).

And so it went. One day's banner headlines replaced by the next day's sheepish retraction, buried in the fine print of the back pages. "U.S. troops discover chemical agents, missiles and what could be a mobile laboratory in Iraq," trumpeted ABC in an "exclusive" report on April 26. By April 28, a member of the U.S. Mobile Exploration Team admitted, "The earlier reports were wrong" (*New York Times* 4/28/03).

With each new report, the media's cheerleaders for the White House chortled with vindication. "We're discovering WMD's all over Iraq," exulted Rush Limbaugh on his Web site (4/7/03). "You know it killed NPR to report that the 101st Airborne found a stockpile of up to 20 rockets tipped with sarin and mustard gas."

Senior *New York Times* reporter Judith Miller, whose INC-inspired stories of WMD had so bolstered the Bush team's claims before the war, was now embedded with a weapons inspection team. "Every few days from late April through May, in nearly a dozen stories [by Miller] such weapons were just about to be found or had recently been destroyed" (Featherstone 2003, p. 60). These stories included a now infamous story about a mysterious "Iraqi scientist." Miller was not allowed to speak with him or name the chemicals she alleged were there, but she was "permitted to see him from a distance," as he pointed to spots in the ground where he said "chemical precursors and other weapons were buried."

This, said Miller, was the "silver bullet" in the search (*New York Times* 4/21/03). Her odd story, sourced, as it were, "from a distance" was featured on the front page of the *New York Times*. Two days later, the *Times'* editorial page acknowledged that no WMD had "yet been found."

On May 11, another Miller story ran under the headline, "Trailer Is a Mobile Lab Capable of Turning out Bioweapons, a Team Says." One of her sources called this find "a smoking gun." NBC News joined the hunt, calling the trailer, "the most significant weapons of mass destruction find to date" and, running out of metaphors, "very close to that elusive smoking gun." Two days later, the *New York Times* again acknowledged that the search "has yet to turn up anything significant" (5/13/03).

In January 2004, CIA Chief Weapons Inspector David Kay ended his fruitless, nine-month search for WMD, telling the *New York Times*, "I'm personally convinced that there were not large stockpiles of newly produced weapons of mass destruction. We don't find the people, the documents, or the physical plants you would expect to find if the production was going on" (Russert 2/8/04).

❖ "MISSION ACCOMPLISHED"

In Iraq, as in Afghanistan, the "end" of the war was described by the news media as an unqualified triumph—for the United States, for Iraq, for democracy, and for the Bush White House.

"The U.S. military's stunning success in Iraq will surely produce many superlatives in the history books," promised *U.S. News & World Report*. "'The conclusion of the war,' Vice President Dick Cheney said last week, 'will mark one of the most extraordinary military campaigns ever conducted'" (4/2/03).

"The professional warrior," intoned *Newsweek*. "The citizen soldier. In two weeks . . . thousands of comrades in arms, brother soldiers and Marines . . . performed a truly remarkable feat. In a 350 mile dash across the desert, through ambushes and over the shattered remnants of Saddam's army, they arrived at the gates of Baghdad" (4/14/03).

And this was not just a military victory. According to the press, the hearts of the Iraqi people had been won over as well:

> These are U.S. Marines being greeted, if not with garlands, then at least with handshakes by residents of the town of Safwan. . . . This war is being characterized as a war of liberation, not conquest, and images of Iraqis helping Americans destroy images of Saddam will help. (*CBS News* reporter Mark Phillips 3/21/03)

In the center of Baghdad, a symbol of tyranny is toppled and people celebrate wildly. . . . Defense Secretary Donald Rumsfeld . . . said, "Anyone seeing the faces of liberated Iraqis, freed Iraqis, has to say this is a very good day." Many people are emerging into the daylight after three weeks of battle to thank the arriving troops and the politicians who sent them. (Fox News Host Brit Hume 4/9/03)

You can see some of the smiles on the faces that are here with me and the flowers that they stuck in my ear. They're sticking flowers in the vests of U.S. marines . . . thanking them for their newfound liberty and exercising their newfound liberty. (NBC News reporter Kerri Sanders 4/10/03)

Najaf had the feel of a liberated city. Smiling citizens crowded every street around the American positions. . . . American soldiers who a day before had been in close combat were now basking in the cheers and applause. . . . [Iraqis] would say the word Saddam and spit . . . or shout "George Bush good." (*Time* 4/14/03)

As we have already seen, large anti-American demonstrations also took place within days of the marines' arrival—indicating, at best, considerable ambivalence among Iraqis about the American presence. But readers would never have gathered that from these press accounts of an unqualified triumph.

The victory celebrations culminated in a presidential speech that one PR professional dubbed "the mother of all photo opportunities." Here is how the news media described it:

When the small S-3B Viking appeared on the horizon over the Pacific this afternoon, it looked for a moment like a routine flight headed for a 150 mph landing on the deck of the aircraft carrier *Abraham Lincoln*. That fiction did not last long. Sitting in a pilot's seat, fully decked out in a flight suit . . . was the President of the United States, who breezily told reporters later, "Yes, I flew it." The plane was designated Navy One, apparently a first. As it buzzed by the deck, the words, "George W. Bush, Commander in Chief" could be seen, carefully painted just below the flight canopy. . . . Mr. Bush . . . hopped out of the plane with a helmet tucked under his arm and walked across the flight deck with a swagger that seemed to suggest he had seen *Top Gun*. Clearly in his element, he was swarmed by members of the Lincoln's cheering crew. . . . "I miss flying, I can tell you that," he told reporters. (*New York Times* 5/2/03)

Bush emerged from the cockpit in a full olive flight suit and combat boots, his helmet tucked jauntily under his left arm. As he exchanged salutes with the sailors, his ejection harness hugging him tightly between the legs gave him the bowlegged swagger of a Top Gun. (*Washington Post* 5/2/03)[4]

Casting the war as a milestone in the campaign against terrorism, Bush spoke to a national TV audience. Honoring the nation's newest war veterans, he said, "Because of you, our nation is more secure. Because of you, the tyrant has fallen and Iraq is free." (*USA Today* 5/2/03)

The President also said that al-Qaeda has been wounded but not destroyed, and for the first time claimed some move toward victory in the larger war against terrorism. [President Bush said,] "The war on terror is not over, yet it is not endless. We do not know the final day of victory, but we have seen the turning of the tide." (*NBC Today* 5/2/03)

A banner strung across the bridge of the ship exclaimed, "Mission Accomplished." On the flight deck, pilots and crew mobbed the President. "Shaking his hand is one of the best experiences I'll ever have," said Commander Diego Corral. (*USA Today* 5/2/03)

Had the media been acting as a watchdog of the people, and striving for balance and critical distance at this moment, they might have raised questions such as

1. Now that the United States had been in control of Iraq for several weeks, where was the main reason for going to war? Where were the WMD? Where was the evidence for Bush's assertion that "our nation is more secure"?

2. Now that Saddam Hussein's records and papers were under U.S. control, where was the evidence of an Iraq–al-Qaeda connection? Where was the evidence for Bush's assertions that "al Qaeda has been wounded" and that "we have seen the turning of the tide" against terrorism?

3. Had the president earned the right to don a military uniform by dint of his own service record, which was, at best, spotty?[5]

4. What (aside from the obvious) was the purpose of having the president make his entrance via an S-3B Viking Jet? Reporters

---

[4]One researcher reports that a Google search on the terms *Bush* and *swagger* produced over 8,000 results (Bennett 2007, pp. 45–48).

[5]Bush avoided service in Vietnam with a questionable stint in the National Guard in which he apparently failed to show up for duty after being transferred from Texas to Alabama and was somehow discharged eight months early so that he could attend business school.

were told that this was necessary because the ship was hundreds of miles offshore, out of helicopter range, and the president didn't want to delay the sailors who were now so close to home after many months at sea. But, in fact, the ship was just 30 miles offshore, well within helicopter range, when Bush's plane landed, and the shore leave of the sailors was delayed another day "as the ship made lazy circles just over the horizon to avoid distracting shots of the San Diego shoreline in news images of the landing and the speech" (Bennett 2005, p. 50).

But, of course, such questions were not asked, because the media were not striving for balance or critical distance. Instead, George W. Bush was again awarded the status of an icon, a figure unchallengeable by anyone, much less by the press:

NBC's Keith Olbermann said, "This was victory day. I mean we're seeing the sign aboard the *Lincoln* right now that reads 'Mission Accomplished.'"

Chris Matthews added, "More than that, Keith, it's a statement. It's saying to the Democratic Party or anyone else who wants to challenge this man for a full eight-year presidency, 'Try to do this. Look at me. Do you really think you've got a guy in your casting studio, your casting director can come up with, who can match what I did today?' Imagine Joe Lieberman in this costume, or even John Kerry. Nobody looks right in the role Bush has set for the presidency—commander-in-chief, medium height, medium build, looks good in a jet pilot's costume—or uniform, rather—has a certain swagger, not too literary, certainly not too verbal, but a guy who speaks plainly and wins wars. I think that job definition is hard to match for the Dems" (5/2/03).

Again, this valorization of George W. Bush carried important consequences. As *Time* magazine explained, "Again and again in interviews . . . Americans told *Time* that their faith in Bush is what ultimately overcame their reservations about his policy in Iraq" (3/3/03). This was a faith the press had gone to great lengths to create, and now, with the "mission accomplished," to sustain.

❖ CONCLUSION

Operation Iraqi Freedom was a glorious affair, according to press reports. From the regimental fanfares used to herald their war coverage, to the breathless odes to the power and precision of America's fearsome military machines, to the stories of high-fiving GIs taking out black-clad "scum of the earth" Fedayeen, to the Kodak Moments of a daring rescue and an Iraqi celebration of their liberation, and finally to the magic of the "Mission Accomplished" moment, the war was a "stunning success." Not only was it "one of the most stunning military campaigns ever conducted," a "precision war with a minimum loss of casualties," but it was also a war to preempt the dreaded WMD, which were found, again and again. And it was a war of liberation, its victors greeted by throngs of grateful Iraqis "emerging into the daylight . . . to thank the arriving troops and the politicians who sent them," while the president proclaimed, "The tyrant has fallen, and Iraq is free" (Fox News 4/9/03).

The war had all these qualities, if one could ignore the other side of the story, which the press usually could. This other story, the dark side of the moon to most Americans, was one in which

- Embedded journalists reported the "marine grunt truth," which, said one reporter, "became my truth" and resulted in the favorable coverage revealed by content analysis. Unembedded reporters, meanwhile, were turned away from the border, imprisoned, beaten, bombed, shot, and killed by U.S. forces.

- Department of Defense "Combat Cameras" and the "Platform for Truth" brought us news in which "military successes are briefed before they happen, civilian casualties are never confirmed, questions are rationed, follow-ups are frowned upon, full answers are not forthcoming" (Kampfner 2003).

- Jessica Lynch's "rescue" and the toppling of Saddam's statue at Firdos Square were the artifacts of public relations professionals.

- Many of the U.S. bombs dropped were "surgical" only in the sense that Jack the Ripper was said to be surgical: These were the especially lethal cluster bombs that shredded the men, women, and children of al-Hilla and Shuala. An estimated 10,000 civilians were killed in this first phase of the war.

- The WMD and the al-Qaeda connection were never found and never would be.

- Large anti-American demonstrations were already bubbling to the surface. As Al Jazeera continued to roll footage of Iraqi children victimized by the bombing, blood-soaked and crying in pain, Egyptian President Hosni Mubarak predicted "Now, there will be 100 bin Ladens" (ABC 3/31/03). Yeats' "rough beast" was now afoot—and slouching toward Baghdad.

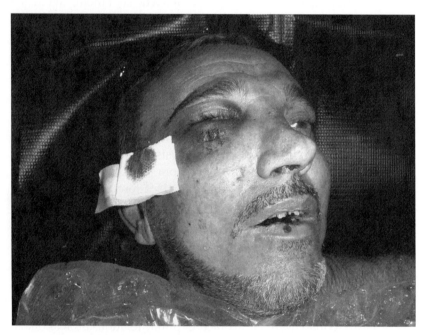

An injured Abu Ghraib detainee, packed in ice and plastic—one of the "interrogation techniques" approved for use by Donald Rumsfeld in 2003. Once such photos were revealed, would the press find the courage to follow the story wherever it led—even, if the facts warranted, to the doorstep of a still-popular wartime president?

5

Aftermath

What Rough Beast,
Its Hour Come Round at Last . . .

This chapter tells the story of how the press has covered the war in Iraq since the "Mission Accomplished" moment. We begin one year after that moment of triumph, with the war hip-deep in tragedy. By the spring of 2004, over 500 Americans and tens of thousands of Iraqis—many of them civilians—have been killed in the war.

And then the photos of Abu Ghraib appeared. When they did, a struggle began over who would write the caption for these pictures: Would it be the White House, for whom the caption was, "Disgraceful conduct by a few American troops, who disregarded our values"? Or would our independent press write its own story, based on a quickly emerging record of documents and testimony, a story that would connect the torture at Abu Ghraib to demands from the White House for "coercive interrogation" techniques?

Our next stop on the war's timeline is in the fall of 2004, when the first scientific effort to count Iraqi casualties appears—and itself becomes a casualty. The study's conclusion, that as many as 100,000 Iraqis had been killed in the first year and a half of war, was startling news. But it was also a direct challenge to the White House narrative, which held that our fight was with a ragtag band of Hussein loyalists, al-Qaedists, and "dead enders," not with the tens of thousands of women and children reported as killed by American bombs in this new study. But the White House need not have worried. The nation's news media obligingly either ignored the story or covered it with a smoke screen of misinformed skepticism.

Our tour of the war continues with stops at the following events:

- Bloody Fallujah: Once again, civilian casualties are dismissed as "unconfirmed reports."

- The Downing Street Memo: This smoking gun—saying plainly that the Bush administration intended to go to war when it said it did not, that the administration had no reliable intelligence about weapons of mass destruction (WMD) when it said it did, and so "fixed" the evidence to sell the war—is a big story in Britain, but is ignored and belittled by the U.S. press.

- Cindy Sheehan: The antiwar mother of a son killed in action is marginalized by the media.

- The CIA's Duelfer Report: This final report of weapons inspectors concludes that Saddam Hussein had no WMD at the time of the invasion and no plan for reviving such weapons. In a feat of amazing sleight of hand and cheek, press pundits actually use the report to justify the war.

- This pattern continues until the press finds its "final," vindicating story: "The surge is working!" This chapter will review that story, as well as the untold story of how the surge worked, by allowing ethnic cleansing to finish its bloody project.

We'll see that during this period, a strange disconnection occurs. While the press usually reports the constant barrage of horrifying news coming out of Iraq—the beheadings, hangings, mutilations, rapes, murders—White House and press spin doctors desperately try to minimize and rationalize those troubled reports into a story of hope and progress. It is as though the war is producing the pictures, but the White House and its compliant press are writing the captions. As the gap between the two widens, Americans come to believe the pictures, not the captions. And as the public turns against the war, so do many members of Congress.

During the Vietnam War, this turning of public opinion and some elites against the war had also been the press's "tipping point": "By 1968, the establishment itself and the nation as a whole were so divided that the media naturally took a far more skeptical stance toward administration policy than in the early years" (Hallin 1986, p. 162).

In Iraq, that didn't happen. Even as the public and one of the major parties turned against the war, the media remained steadfastly committed to an increasingly untenable cause. In the years between Vietnam and Iraq, something about our nation's media has changed, a matter we will revisit in Chapter 6.

❖ PICTURES FROM THE DARK SIDE

When President Bush declared, from the deck of the USS *Lincoln*, that "major combat operations in Iraq have ended," they had only just begun. By the time Bush gave his speech, 139 Americans had died in combat. In the following year, 416 more Americans would die on the battlefields of Iraq. A few months after that, the first scientific effort to measure Iraqi deaths due to the American invasion would put the number at 98,000.

And then, almost a year to the day after the landing on the *Lincoln*, CBS's *60 Minutes II* aired photos taken at the Abu Ghraib prison. At the request of the Pentagon, CBS had withheld the photos for two weeks. Then the network heard that the *New Yorker* was about to publish its own Abu Ghraib story, accompanied by the photos, and so they became public. Soon, there were thousands of photos showing horrific abuses of prisoners: photos of naked prisoners stacked up in pyramid formation; photos of naked prisoners on their hands and knees, leashed like dogs; and photos of prisoners forced to masturbate for the camera or posed in other humiliating simulated sex acts. There were photos of hooded prisoners attached to what looked like electrical wire, photos of naked prisoners cowering in the face of unmuzzled guard dogs, and photos of GIs posed, grinning, beside prisoners' corpses.

The Problem With Torture

The nation gasped, and approval of the war dropped—for the first time—below disapproval. A survey by the University of Maryland's Program on International Policy Attitudes showed large majorities of Americans declaring that "the United States is a moral leader" that "should not lower itself by engaging in torture or cruel or degrading treatment" (Program on International Policy Attitudes 2004).

In addition to this moral objection, there were other reasons to oppose a policy of torturing prisoners. One involved our obligations under the Constitution, under international law, and under treaties the United States had signed. Former General Counsel for the Navy Alberto Mora pointed out that a number of these laws and treaties, including the Constitution and the Geneva Convention on Torture, prohibit the U.S. government from inflicting cruelty on prisoners of war. Violating these treaties, Mora argued, would render U.S. troops vulnerable to the same treatment (Mayer 2006). Other reasons to be chary of torture, pointed out at the time in the alternative press, included the following:

1. The testimony of interrogation practitioners, who pointed out that coercive techniques are notorious for producing false intelligence. Army Colonel Stuart Harrington, for example, is a military intelligence specialist who has conducted interrogations in Vietnam, Panama, and Iraq during Desert Storm. Aside from being immoral and illegal, he says, coercion is "simply not a good way to get information. They'll just tell you anything to get you to stop." Air Force intelligence officer Colonel John Rothrock goes even further: "I don't know any professional intelligence officers who would think this [torture] is a good idea" (*Washington Post* 1/12/05);

2. The fact that many of the detainees at Abu Ghraib were innocent. As one of the military's own investigations pointed out, it was common practice for U.S. troops to "round up large quantities of Iraqis in the general vicinity" of an incident. This "cordon and capture" technique, the report said, put many Iraqis, "all too often including women and children," who were not insurgents and had "no intelligence value" into the Abu Ghraib prison (Schlesinger 2004). Reporter Thomas Ricks described the process as "indiscriminate cordon and sweep operations that involved grabbing whole villages and detaining thousands of Iraqis" (2006, p. 195). A separate Pentagon investigation also acknowledged that most of these detainees were

eventually released without ever having been charged with any wrongdoing (Fay 2004, p. 72). But not quickly. "Complicated and unresponsive release procedures," the report said, "ensured that these detainees stayed at Abu Ghraib" (Schlesinger 2004). The Red Cross estimated that, overall, from 70% to 90% of detainees at Abu Ghraib were arrested mistakenly, a figure confirmed by the Schlesinger report (*Washington Post* 5/20/04).

3. A third good reason to oppose torture was that it devastated the U.S. image in the world, and with it, the United States' "soft power"— its ability to lead, not by force of arms but by the force of the country's moral stature in the eyes of the world. World opinion of the United States fell like wet laundry after Abu Ghraib, in part because "to many foreign eyes, Abu Ghraib looked more like [a policy of] torture and less like the isolated abuse the administration claimed it was" (Bennett et al., 2007, p. 116).

Fixing Responsibility

Would the press find the courage to follow this story wherever it led, even, if the facts warranted, to the doorstep of a still-popular wartime president? Or would the media follow the lead of the president, who declared that the photos represented only "disgraceful conduct by a few American troops, who dishonored our country and disregarded our values."

Even at the outset, the press had good reasons, including a great deal of documentary evidence, to believe that the Abu Ghraib photos revealed a policy of torture, initiated at the highest levels of government. One of these documents was a list of interrogation techniques, approved for use at Guantanamo Bay, by Secretary of Defense Donald Rumsfeld. A number of these techniques bore an uncanny resemblance to actions depicted in the Abu Ghraib photos. Later, the Schlesinger committee blamed this memo for creating "confusion" among soldiers at Abu Ghraib (Schlesinger 2004).

Then there were the documents that laid out the Bush administration's legal position on coercive interrogation. The first was a memo by Jay Bybee of the Justice Department's Office of Legal Counsel. It asserted that, in the case of suspected terrorists, any coercive technique would be legal so long as it did not cause "death, organ failure or serious impairment of body functions" (*New York Times* 6/27/04). Another, by then-White House counsel Alberto Gonzales, advised the president that the War on Terror "renders obsolete [the Geneva Convention's] strict limitations on questioning of enemy prisoners and renders quaint some of its provisions" (*Washington Post* 5/18/04).

Indeed, long articles by the *New Yorker*'s investigative reporter Seymour Hersh came out soon after the photos emerged, hunting the torture policy down a trail of documents and informants to the top of the Pentagon, and from there to Guantanamo Bay, to Abu Ghraib, and to multiple U.S. detention facilities where the same coercive interrogation techniques were employed (2004a,b). Eventually, his conclusions would be confirmed by a bipartisan congressional committee report (Levin 2008).

How the Press Covered (Up) Abu Ghraib

In the summer of 2004, two very different stories would compete to become the caption attached to Abu Ghraib's implacable pictures. One was a story of policy, promulgated at the highest levels of government, directing interrogators to impose physical punishment on detainees in order to induce physical and psychological panic in them and thus extract intelligence information. The unvarnished word for such a policy is "torture." The other story was one of poor supervision and the unfortunate mistreatment of prisoners by a few low-level miscreants. Which story would prevail? Would the press tell "both sides," or would it make one of them the story and the other a nonstory?

To answer that question, a team of political scientists analyzed the coverage of Abu Ghraib in a sample of the nation's leading news sources, including the *New York Times*, the *Washington Post*, *USA Today*, the CBS Evening News, and eight other large, well-known newspapers. For one thing, the researchers asked what the press would name the scandal: Would Abu Ghraib's name be "torture," which "in both common usage and legal terminology" suggests an interrogation policy coming from the top of the chain of command? (Bennett et al. 2007, p. 90). Or would what happened be called "abuse," a word innocent of any connotation of a top-down policy, a word appropriate to describe the regrettable cruelty of a few low-level deviants?

The study found that in the *Washington Post*, which typified the coverage generally

> the most prominent characterization by far was abuse, with torture barely appearing in the news coverage, and only slightly more often in editorials. . . . The frame imbalance in the news coverage was

overwhelming, with just three percent of the stories offering torture as the primary definition of the photos. (Bennett et al. 2007, p. 92)

This was compared with 96% of stories using frames that tended to exculpate the White House (p. 92).

What's more, the few references to torture emerged for just a moment after the photos went public. After that, the familiar prowess of the White House spin machine took over. There followed a flurry of Rose Garden photo ops, televised interviews, appearances before Congress and even a surprise visit to Abu Ghraib by Donald Rumsfeld. At all of these events, the White House told—and the press reported—its story: that these abuses were the work of "a small number of troops who acted in an illegal, improper manner."

As this spin machine took over, references to torture all but disappeared. On CBS, for example, "eight of the ten uses of *torture* . . . appeared between April 29 and May 12." From May 12 until the story dwindled at the end of the summer, "torture was used only twice on the CBS Evening News to describe events at Abu Ghraib" (pp. 94–95).

Not long before the Abu Ghraib story broke, both the *New York Times* and the *Washington Post* had apologized to readers for relying too heavily on official sources, privileging their story of WMD above other stories, even when the other stories had compelling evidence on their side. Now, along with the rest of the mainstream press, they again relied heavily on official sources, privileging their story above the other story, which again had compelling evidence to support it.

If the press failed to tell both sides of the story of who was responsible, it failed again to tell the full story of the victims of Abu Ghraib. Here again, reporters, who were fully aware of the cordon and capture techniques used to round up so many innocent detainees, nonetheless dutifully quoted U.S. officials, who said, "They are deemed to be a security threat through multiple sources. It's that simple. If they were innocent, they wouldn't be at Abu Ghraib." "You know, they're not there for traffic violations, they're murderers, they're terrorists, they're insurgents" (*Washington Post* 5/12/04; 5/27/04). This "bad guy" frame outgunned the alternative, appearing three times as often in the *Post* as information about the mass arrests that had brought thousands of Iraqis to Abu Ghraib (Bennett et al. 2007, p. 114).

Throughout this period, the press often "game-framed" Abu Ghraib—rendering the debate a contest played by President Bush and his team for the PR trophy. In these stories, reporters became color commentators, describing the strategies and awarding style points to the White House for its performance (Bennett et al. 2007, p. 128).

In the end, the University of Maryland survey showed that most Americans were unaware that the secretary of defense had authorized use of the interrogation techniques pictured in some of the photos. They were unaware that many of the prison's detainees were arrested without evidence and that after being detained indefinitely, they were released without charge (Program on International Policy Attitudes 2004).

And so, as the story of a few grunts gone awry took hold, public approval for the war rebounded, to levels it had enjoyed in the days before America had ever heard of Abu Ghraib (Mueller 2006).

Finally, in 2009, a report of the Senate Armed Services Committee, signed by both the Republican and Democratic members, would produce an unheralded ending to this story. The report's unvarnished conclusion was that the horrors of Abu Ghraib were not, in fact, just the misguided actions of low-level soldiers:

- "Following the President's determination [that the Geneva Conventions did not apply to detainees in the War on Terror,] techniques such as waterboarding, nudity, and stress positions . . . used by enemies that refuse to follow the Geneva Conventions, were authorized for use in interrogations of detainees in U.S. custody."

- "Secretary of State Donald Rumsfeld's authorization of aggressive interrogation techniques . . . influenced and contributed to the use of abusive techniques, including military working dogs, forced nudity and stress positions in Afghanistan and Iraq." (Levin 2008)

Not one of the country's national newspapers considered this definitive and startling report a front-page story.

❖ A CASUALTY STORY BECOMES A CASUALTY

Just a few months after the Abu Ghraib photos went public, another bombshell of a story fell. But thanks to the media, which acted more like a bomb squad than a news disseminator, this explosive story never detonated.

In late October 2004, Britain's leading medical journal, the *Lancet*, published a study by researchers from Johns Hopkins and Columbia Universities. The study was the first attempt to scientifically measure the number of Iraqis who had died as a result of the war. The conscience-shocking number reported by the study was approximately 100,000—10 times more casualties than the previous, nonscientific estimates. What was worse, although many of the deaths were caused by insurgents (about 15%), or by the carjackers, kidnappers, and burglars running rampant in Iraq (33%), the plurality of the deaths (43%) were attributed to American bullets and bombs. "A style of engagement that relies heavily on air power has resulted in a lot—a lot—of civilian deaths," said lead researcher Les Roberts (Glass 2006).

In addition to this stunning finding, there was another reason for news editors to consider this an important story: It was credible. Lead author Les Roberts is "one of a handful of experts in the world who is a specialist in counting war dead." His estimates of war-related mortality in Burundi, Rwanda, Sierra Leone, Darfur, and the Congo were definitive—cited routinely and often by the world's press and its political leaders. The study itself employed the method Roberts had used in his previous studies, the standard epidemiological method for determining a country's mortality rate: a cluster sample survey of the country's households, randomly selected, so that "every household in Iraq had an equal chance that we'd visit them" (Glass 2006).

The report's conclusion was a conservative estimate. The researchers had risked their lives to include all 33 of the randomly selected clusters, including the crucible of violence known as Fallujah. But in the end, Fallujah's report of 53 deaths in just 30 surveyed households was too much of a statistical outlier to include in the calculations.

The Iraqi physicians who volunteered to do the house-to-house polling found their respondents willing to talk. Only 5 of 988 households refused the interview. And their respondents provided death certificates for deceased householders in 80% of the cases.

Surely this careful study, concluding that the Iraq War had wrought human tragedy on a scale previously unimagined, would command the media's attention. But instead, it didn't. Instead, ABC, CBS, and Fox News never mentioned the story. NBC gave it 21 seconds, CNN 14 seconds. Neither the *New York Times*, the *Washington Post*, nor any other major American newspaper deemed this a front-page story. The vast majority of the nation's newspapers never even mentioned the *Lancet* study.

Those few newspapers that did bother to look at the story tended to fix it with a curiously jaundiced eye. The *Washington Post*'s story set the mold for stories in other papers that leveled uninformed potshots at the study. After two brief paragraphs describing the study, the *Post* pounced: "Other experts immediately challenged the new estimate, saying the small number of documented deaths upon which it was based make the conclusions suspect. 'The methods that they used are certainly prone to inflation due to overcounting,' said Marc Garlasco, senior military analyst for Human Rights Watch. 'These numbers seem to be inflated. . . . I certainly think this is a reach'" (*Washington Post* 10/29/04). After that story appeared, Garlasco showed up as the designated hitter in a United Press International (UPI) story criticizing the study, and of course in the local papers that ran the story from the *Post* or UPI wire services.

But Marc Garlasco was an odd choice to serve as spokesman for a statistical critique of the study. "First, I'm not a statistician, I know absolutely nothing about it," Garlasco later admitted. "And when I talked to statisticians, they said, 'No, the method they're using is a really accurate one. This is a generally accepted model." Indeed, in this later interview, Garlasco allowed that a bomb is an undiscriminating weapon, and on this point, he truly was an expert. Before signing on with Human Rights Watch, Garlasco had worked for the Pentagon as a "targeting analyst," planning bombing missions and later visiting bomb sites to determine how accurate the attack had been. He recalls the bomb meant for "Chemical Ali," the man who had headed Saddam's bioweapons program in the 1980s. From a closed-circuit Pentagon television,

> We watched the Predator hit the building and see bodies fly out of it, legs kicking in the air like rag dolls. We erupted in cheers, we were ecstatic. "We got Chemical Ali! This is great!" Three weeks later I'm standing in that bomb's crater with a 70 year old man. He's got tears in his eyes, telling me how 17 members of his family, including his grandchildren, were killed. This was one of those strikes where we did everything right. We had the bad guy, the mission was weaponeered correctly, and yet it was the wrong place to hit at that time, and people died. (Glass 2006)

The bomb, it turned out, had hit the intended building but had also destroyed neighboring buildings. Chemical Ali was not, as it happened, in the vicinity when the bomb struck. "He was a legitimate target, but this goes to show how difficult the job really is," said Garlasco (Glass 2006).

As the *Post*, UPI, and AP stories expressed an untutored skepticism, other news editors considering whether and how to run the *Lancet* story were also contending with the furious campaign to discredit the report going on in the right-wing media. Here, basic facts were often deliberately distorted or ignored in the effort to poison the wells of the *Lancet* study. A recurring objection from the right was that the study was unreliable because the war had kept researchers from going to certain sites. But as we've seen, the opposite was true: The doctors doing the polling insisted that they visit all 33 sites, including perilous Fallujah, because the work was that important. Nonetheless, this right-wing flak took its toll. As one newspaper editor put it, "if the study is flawed, and we give it credence, we're hit with a 'liberal bias' complaint" (Glass 2006).

This is not to say that the study had no limitations. There were two important caveats, and both were acknowledged in the report itself. The first was that the researchers did not attempt to distinguish between civilian and insurgent deaths, on the reasonable assumption that respondents would be leery of declaring allegiances in the midst of a civil war. But the study nonetheless shed light on civilian casualties. Half the reported dead were women and children. Even if we make the extremely unlikely assumption that all the men who died were insurgents, we are still left with a huge number of civilian deaths.

But critics got the most traction from the study's second limitation—its sample size and confidence interval. Because the researchers' 2004 budget was smaller than they would have preferred, so was their sample size, which made the confidence interval large—between 8,000 and 194,000 deaths. Again, however, the right-wing press's treatment of this limitation badly distorted the truth, and the mainstream press bought into the distortion. "The range for deaths was wider than Rosie O'Donnell's rump, so the researchers merely split the difference," howled the right's *American Spectator* (8/21/07). And the mainstream online paper *Slate* added this much requoted thumbs-down: "This isn't an estimate, it's a dartboard" (10/29/04).

The problem with these objections is that they assume all numbers included in the confidence interval are equally likely to be the correct number, when, in fact, the probability curve for the confidence interval is bell shaped, with the estimate of 100,000 deaths at the top of the bell. Put another way, the confidence interval allowed only a 2% chance that the correct number was as low as 8,000 and a 90% chance that it was 44,000 or above.

Three months after the report was released, the *Chronicle of Higher Education* conducted a detailed investigation of the study and its reception, and concluded, "On its merits, the study should have received more prominent play." The public health professionals interviewed by the *Chronicle* had "uniformly praised the paper for its correct methods and notable results" (2/4/05).

Over the next two years, the war's appetite for human carnage was voracious. U.S. casualties were often in the hundreds per month. And so, in 2006, the *Lancet* team went back to Iraq and returned with an even more unthinkable number: 655,000 "excess deaths" due to war. This time, the study was better funded, and the confidence interval was much smaller. But once again, right-wing media went on the attack, this time proclaiming that their 2004 attacks had discredited all reports from this team and charging any mainstream media that would give the study credence with liberal bias. Amazingly, *Slate*'s pithy falsehood about the 2004 study was applied again and again to the 2006 study, as in this article from the *Washington Times*:

> Dr. Les Roberts burned the media in 2004 by irresponsibly hyping a supposed death toll of 100,000. . . . As *Slate*'s Fred Kaplan showed, the study proved no such figure. The authors' survey really determined that the death toll was somewhere between 8,000 and 194,000. As Mr. Kaplan put it, "This isn't an estimate, it's a dart board." (10/12/06)

Once again, the mainstream press surrounded the study with a smoke screen of misinformed skepticism. Repeatedly, the press gave "both sides" of the story by counterpoising scientists with administration officials, as if they were equally qualified to comment on epidemiological methodology. The Associated Press story, for example, was headlined, "Iraq Death Toll Study Has Mixed Reaction":

> The new study . . . was released Wednesday. . . . But just how good are its conclusions? "I don't consider it a credible report," President Bush said Wednesday. Neither does Gen. George Casey, the top American military commander in Iraq. "I've not seen a number higher than 50,000, and so I don't give it much credibility at all." However, several biostatisticians and survey experts were supportive of the work. (10/12/06)

Since the *Lancet* studies, two more scientific investigations of Iraq War casualties have been conducted. The first, conducted by Iraq's health ministry, estimated 400,000 war deaths as of late 2006. *The New England Journal of Medicine* published the results. In an accompanying editorial, the *Journal* noted "substantial limitations" of the study that may have caused it to undercount the war dead (1/31/08).

Finally, a study by Opinion Research Business, a respected London-based polling firm at work in Iraq since 2005, estimated in 2007 that Iraq War casualties numbered 1.2 million. In the United States, only one leading newspaper, the *Los Angeles Times,* and one radio service, NPR, chose to report this stunning news.

❖ THE BLOOD-DIMMED TIDE

In February 2006, Sunni fighters bombed the Askariyah Mosque in Samarra, one of Shiite Islam's holiest shrines. If the conflict had not been a full-blown civil war before, it was now. By the second half of 2006, Iraqi deaths had reached all-time highs. Over the course of that year, the number of civilian deaths—since the invasion in 2003—would double. Baghdad's central morgue had recorded 522 deaths in August 2003, 386 in August 2004, and 555 in November 2005. By July 2006, the number was 1,417 (IraqBodyCount.org).

And yet, according to war chronicler Thomas Ricks, the Bush administration was reluctant to acknowledge Iraq's downward spiral (*New York Times* 2/10/09). And why should it, when the White House's increasingly unbelievable story—that "staying the course" was the proper course—was still the dominant narrative in the mainstream press?

But a funny thing happened on the way to "victory." As the president and the press held fast to a discredited story, these opinion leaders lost their followers. Try as they might to spin cataclysmic events into something less terrible than they were, history was against them. Reality had ripped open the underbelly of the "Iraq mission," and all the guts were spilling out. For example:

April 2004: American forces begin a ferocious aerial bombardment of Fallujah, a hotbed of insurgent activity. But they are forced to suspend the attack when popular uprisings break out across Iraq, in protest against the civilian casualties caused by the bombing. The *New York Times* describes the situation this way: "The outrage, fed mostly by unconfirmed reports of large civilian casualties, forced the Americans to withdraw. American commanders regarded the reports as inflated, but it was impossible to determine independently how many civilians had been killed" (11/8/04). In two subsequent articles the *Times* again refers to "unconfirmed reports" of civilian casualties (11/9/04; 11/15/04). But, in fact, reliable agencies had investigated Fallujah casualties, and all confirmed that indeed hundreds of civilians had been killed in the April assault. The head of Fallujah's main hospital put the number at 800. Based on their extensive evaluation of numbers from local hospitals and health ministry officials, Iraq Body Count estimated 600. The Associated Press reported that "two football fields were turned into cemeteries with hundreds of freshly dug graves, some with names of women, some marked specifically as children" (4/30/04).

Military officials reported that 70% to 90% of the city's 300,000 people eventually fled the violence and became refugees (*Extra!* 11/16/04).

May 1, 2004: Three days after the photos of Abu Ghraib are made public, President Bush celebrates the one-year anniversary of "Mission Accomplished":

> One year later, life for the Iraqi people is a world away from the cruelty and corruption of Saddam's regime. At the most basic level of justice, people are no longer disappearing into political prisons, torture chambers and mass graves.

The press dutifully quotes the president, without noting the stark irony that his words represented against the backdrop of Abu Ghraib.

May 11, 2004: A video is released showing Nicholas Berg, an American contractor, being beheaded by Iraqi insurgents.

May 31, 2004: Four Blackwater contractors are shot and burned in their cars, before a cheering crowd dismembers the corpses and hangs two of them from a bridge.

October 7, 2004: The CIA's Duelfer Report, the final report of U.S. weapons inspectors searching for WMD, concludes that Saddam Hussein had no WMD at the time of the invasion, and "no formal, written strategy or plan for the revival of WMD." Undeterred, *U.S. News & World Report*'s Michael Barone found some thinly sourced speculation in the report about what Saddam might have done in the future, if UN sanctions were ever lifted. Unbelievably, he used these shards of speculation to conclude, "The report makes it plain that George W. Bush had good reason to go to war in Iraq and end the regime of Saddam Hussein" (10/8/04).

May 1, 2005: The Downing Street Memo is revealed. After meetings with CIA Director George Tenet and other high-level U.S. intelligence officials in the summer of 2002, the head of Britain's foreign intelligence service, Sir Richard Dearlove, reported back to Prime Minister Blair. His gobsmacking memo reveals these details:

- Eight months before the war begins, while the White House is saying that war is only a "last resort," American officials tell Dearlove that war is "inevitable."

- Tenet tells Dearlove that the war will be "justified by the conjunction of terrorism and WMD." But, says Tenet, "The case [for war] was thin. Saddam was not threatening his neighbors, and his weapons capability was less than that of Libya, North Korea or Iran." So,

- "The intelligence and facts are being fixed around the policy."

Here it was: the smoking gun in the hands of the White House; a memo from a very reliable source, saying clearly that the administration had made up its mind to go to war in 2002, while telling the American people the opposite, and had decided to sell the war with "fixed" intelligence. But the Downing Street Memo, which had "caused an enormous stir in Great Britain, went virtually unnoticed in the United States. Coverage in the American press was sparse and, when it appeared at all, was distinctly defensive. No newspaper saw fit to publish the document" (Danner 2006, p. xvi).

May 30, 2005: Vice President Cheney tells the nation that the insurgency is "in its last throes" (CNN, *Larry King Live* 5/30/05).

Summer 2005: Cindy Sheehan, mother of a son killed in Iraq, camps out near Bush's ranch in Crawford, Texas, in protest against the war. ABC's Dan Harris minimizes her efforts: "While Cindy Sheehan gets a lot of media attention, only 13 percent of Americans want an immediate withdrawal of U.S. troops" (8/25/05). This was highly misleading. While Americans were sensible enough not to opt for "immediate withdrawal," something no one advocated, an August 25 Harris poll found 61% of Americans wanted to bring home "most U.S. troops within the next year" (*Extra!* 9/1/05).

March 19, 2006: A November 2005 report that civilians in Haditha had been killed by a roadside bomb turns out to be false. Instead, according to eyewitnesses, U.S. marines "went on a rampage after the [IED] attack, killing 15 unarmed Iraqis in their homes, including seven women and three children" (*Time* 3/19/06).

May 1, 2006: On the third anniversary of "Mission Accomplished," President Bush says Iraq has reached "a turning point" on the way to "victory in this war on terror."

June 20, 2006: The mutilated bodies of two U.S. soldiers who had been kidnapped four days earlier are found. An Iraqi Defense Ministry official said the soldiers "were killed in a barbaric way" (*USA Today*).

July 2006: Five U.S. soldiers are charged with the rape and murder of a young Iraqi girl and with the murder of her family members to cover up their crime.

July 2006: The deadliest month of the war so far, 1,666 IEDs detonate, killing at least 3,438 Iraqi civilians (*New York Times* 8/15/06).

August 21, 2006: Bush acknowledges that Iraq had "nothing" to do with 9/11. For a president who had referred to 9/11 over a dozen times during the press conference announcing that war on Iraq had begun, and had never stopped connecting Hussein to al-Qaeda and to 9/11, this was a stunning admission. Only 3 of the nation's 12 largest newspapers make it a front-page story. Incidentally, 2 of those 12 newspapers do not cover the story at all.

September 11, 2006: Vice President Cheney says that when war critics urge withdrawal from Iraq, "Terrorists are encouraged" (*Meet the Press* 9/11/06).

September 24, 2006: A new National Intelligence Estimate finds that "the American invasion of Iraq has helped spawn a new generation of Islamic radicalism and that the overall terrorist threat has grown since 9/11" (*New York Times* 9/24/06).

October 8, 2006: The number of U.S. casualties reaches its highest levels "in the spiral of sectarian violence" (*Washington Post*).

October 19, 2006: "The number of Iraq and Afghanistan veterans who have been treated for post-traumatic stress disorder (PTSD) doubled—from nearly 4,500 to over 9,000—between October '05 and June '06" (McClatchy).

November 20, 2006: "Seven out of ten Iraqis say they want the U.S. to leave within a year" (World Public Opinion Poll).

November 23, 2006: "In the deadliest attack since the American invasion," 144 people die (*New York Times*).

January 2, 2007: More troops now disapprove of the president's handling of the war than approve of it (*Military Times*).

January 3, 2007: U.S. soldiers' death toll reaches 3,000.

January 10, 2007: President Bush announces a "surge" of 20,000 additional troops. "The new strategy that I announce tonight will help us succeed in the war on terror" (CNN 1/11/07).

Who's Captioning These Pictures?

Throughout this period, the media continued to provide a steady diet of pro-war pundits, who did what they could to soften the blows of bad news. Fairness and Accuracy in Reporting's (FAIR) annual survey of media sources showed that centrist, mostly pro-war think tanks received the most citations (45%). Conservative, very pro-war institutes were right behind, at 40%. Progressive, antiwar think tanks increased their media presence in 2006 by a significant 11%, but that still left them with only 16% of all press citations (Dolny 2007).

In a separate content analysis, Media Matters for America assessed "the balance of voices" on the influential Sunday morning television talk shows aired during 2005 and 2006. Their results showed that

> the right has a distinct advantage in . . . the debate on Sunday morning. . . . One sees instances again and again in which panels feature conservative voices, centrist or neutral voices and no progressive voices. . . . Republicans and conservatives had the advantage on every show, in every category mentioned.

Overall, Republican and conservative guests outnumbered Democrats and progressives by a margin of 44% to 27%. Counting only elected officials and administration spokesmen, the Republican advantage was 62% to 37%. Conservative journalists were nearly twice as likely as their progressive counterparts to appear on the Sunday shows, and there were nearly three times as many right-leaning panels as there were left-leaning ones. Even after Democrats took back the Congress in 2006, "the overall ideological contours of Sunday-morning television did not change: Republicans and conservatives still hold the advantage" (MediaMatters.org/reports/Sundayshowreport 2007).

And finally, a third major content analysis showed that the othering and demonizing of Islam continued unabated throughout this period. "Almost half of all statements about Islam have been negative in the American network news," during 2007 and 2008, reported Media Tenor (9/10/08). These included televangelist Pat Robertson's reference to Islam as a "bloody, brutal type of religion" (*The 700 Club* 4/28/06). And Glenn Beck's rant against

> all you Muslims who have sat on your frickin' hands and have not been marching in the streets saying, "We need to be the first ones in the recruitment office lining up to shoot the bad Muslims in the head." I'm telling you, with God as my witness . . . human beings are

not strong enough, unfortunately, to restrain themselves from putting up razor wire and putting you on one side of it. (8/10/06)

And Michael Savage's observation that, "When I see a woman walking around with a burqa, I see a hateful Nazi who would like to cut your throat and kill your children" (*Savage Nation* 7/2/07).

The Final Stretch

Ever since the "Mission Accomplished" moment, a strange disconnection had appeared in the press. On one hand, the news usually reported the incessant barrage of horrific events taking place in Iraq. On the other hand, White House and press spin doctors desperately tried to minimize and rationalize those horrific reports into stories of hope and progress, stories that would make "staying the course" a sensible strategy. It was as though Iraq had provided the pictures, but the U.S. press and politicians supplied the captions. And after watching this spectacle for a long time, Americans came to believe the pictures, not the captions. An ABC/*Washington Post* poll asked, "Do you think the United States should withdraw its military forces from Iraq in order to avoid further U.S. military casualties, even if that means civil order is not restored there?" In May 2004, 40% of Americans said "Yes." By July 2007, it was 59% (Hart 2007). In a December 2007 AP poll, 60% of respondents opted for a six-month timeline to withdraw all U.S. troops. At this point, only one major newspaper, the *Los Angeles Times*, had editorially endorsed withdrawal (Mitchell 2008, p. 140).

But most papers, instead of taking voters' opinions seriously, airily lectured and dismissed the American people. Shortly after the 2006 midterm elections, in which exit polls showed again that most Americans supported withdrawal, a *New York Times* headline scoffed, "Get Out of Iraq Now? Not So Fast, Experts Say" (11/15/06). And sure enough, the story assembled three reliably pro-war pundits to say it.

Exasperated NBC reporter Norah O'Donnell went one better, saying of a six-month withdrawal, "There is not one military or foreign policy expert who thinks you could actually, feasibly do that, and second, that it would be a good idea" (11/26/06). All the armchair experts O'Donnell had in mind apparently knew more about the situation than the Iraqi people, two thirds of whom said, "The presence of U.S. forces is making the security situation worse" (*USA Today* 3/20/07). And by implication, O'Donnell's list of people who were not "military or foreign policy experts" included former National Security Chief William Odom, former CIA Director John Deutsch, Boston University military historian Andrew Bacevich, former Senator George McGovern, former Under Secretary of State William Polk, along with the majority of congressional Democrats who had voted for withdrawal resolutions. All had advocated, some of them in books on the subject, the withdrawal that "not one expert" thought was a good idea.

All were met with the press's unshaken faith in the war it had bolstered, as in this scolding from ABC reporter Jake Tapper, bemoaning "once-cautious Democrats now trying to outflank one another on the antiwar left," while "many analysts caution against a withdrawal that is too sudden and say the bill Democrats voted for today could make matters worse" (5/07). Once again, the two pro-war pundits Tapper chose to quote did indeed warn against withdrawal.

"The Surge Is Working!"

With the press as its faithful megaphone, the Bush administration seemed oblivious to the spiraling violence and the dissident experts, oblivious to the beleaguered Iraqis and the weary U.S. public. In fact, says Thomas Ricks, the administration "might never have contemplated the major revisions in strategy and leadership that it would soon make" if not for the election of 2006. But when, in November, the Republican Party lost control of Congress, the White House changed course, turning to a new team of military experts "whose advice had been disregarded and even denounced during the run-up to the war" (Ricks, in *New York Times* 2/10/09).

Because withdrawal would never be an option for the Vulcans of the Bush White House, the once-spurned strategies of the new military team were the only port left in a very bad storm. These new strategies, generally credited to General David Petraeus and Lieutenant General Raymond Odierno, included bribing and arming the Sunni sheiks of Anbar province, who had once been hostile to U.S. forces, in exchange for their cooperation.

But the tactic that press pundits and pro-war politicians first plumped and then took credit for was "the surge"—a net addition of about 30,000 U.S. troops into Iraq. President Bush announced the surge on January 10, 2007. Immediately, violence levels leapt upward. Civilian deaths rose by 13% in March and another 29% in May, over and above the already record-high numbers of late 2006 to early 2007 (BBC 4/2/07; Reuters 6/3/07). Overall, 2007 would prove to be the deadliest for U.S. forces since the war had begun. By August, coalition deaths would toll 4,000. In the first 11 days of May, 234 men murdered by death squads were dumped in the streets of Baghdad (*Guardian* 5/13/07).

But during the second half of 2007, the violence had begun to subside—by 70% between June and October, said the Iraqi government (Reuters 10/22/07). The only inference media pundits could draw was that the surge they had urged was working—miraculously. The *New York Times'* David Brooks gloated, "Before long, the more honest among the surge opponents will concede that Bush, that supposed dolt, actually got one right" (6/24/08). NBC's Chris Matthews added, "The surge's success has been a point of honor for [Republican presidential candidate John] McCain" (7/6/08). CNN's Candy Crowley agreed, "Few would argue about the success of the surge in Iraq" (6/29/08). The surge "turned Iraq heading into a stable, democratic country," chimed in Fox's Fred Barnes (7/9/08). On NBC's *Today Show*, guest Michael O'Hanlon parsed the implications for the coming election: "I think Senator McCain has a lot to brag about for the last couple of years. He's been one of the original advocates of the surge strategy, which has worked well" (7/4/08).

The press also proclaimed that "cocksure surge opponents, drunk on their own vindication," would now have to explain themselves (*New York Times* 6/24/08). For example, Barack Obama.

- "Shouldn't he have to account for opposing the surge, which has enhanced the safety of Iraqis and American GIs?" (*Los Angeles Times* 6/26/08).

- "How do you [Obama] escape the logic that John McCain was right about the surge?" (ABC News' George Stephanopoulos 9/7/08).

- "Why can't Obama bring himself to acknowledge the surge worked better than he and other skeptics thought it would?" (*USA Today* editorial 7/20/08).

The Untold Story of the Surge

There were at least three things wrong with the press mantra, "The surge is working." The first problem was that, somehow, the surge was working in places where there was no surge. In Anbar province, for example, violence had declined months before the surge began, "nor were very many extra troops ever sent there." Indeed, says distinguished Middle East historian Juan Cole, the Anbar Awakening "depended on there not being much of a troop escalation. Had large numbers of troops been committed, they would have stirred up and reinforced the guerilla movement" (Cole 2008). In Anbar, it was bribing and arming insurgents, not surging against them that quelled the violence. Nonetheless, Anbar's relative calm was claimed as vindication by surge supporters: "Because of the surge, we were able to go out and protect [Anbar province]. And it began the Anbar Awakening," said John McCain, getting both his dates and his numbers wrong (quoted in *New York Times* 7/22/08).

Perhaps it is not surprising that pundits and politicians wanted to wrap Anbar's huge reduction in violence in the mantle of the surge. After all, who wants to claim credit for the fact that "Bribing and arming insurgents is working!"

A second problem, far more serious, was that the surge could be said to have "worked" in the same sense that the Holocaust "worked." That is to say, the surge worked by completing the process of ethnic cleansing in Baghdad. Juan Cole describes what happened:

> Escalation troops began by disarming the Sunni Arabs in Baghdad. Once these Sunnis were left helpless, the Shiite militias came in at night and ethnically cleansed them. Shaab district near Adhamiya had been a mixed neighborhood. It ended up with almost no Sunnis. Baghdad in the course of 2007 went from 65 percent Shiite to at least 75 percent Shiite. My thesis would be that the United States inadvertently allowed the chasing of hundreds of thousands of Sunni Arabs out of Baghdad (and many of them had to go all the way to Syria for refuge). Rates of violence declined once the ethnic cleansing was far advanced, just because there were fewer mixed neighborhoods. (Cole 2008)

Off the air, CNN correspondent Michael Ware, stationed in Baghdad during the surge, reaffirmed Cole's point:

> The sectarian cleansing of Baghdad has been—albeit tragic—one of the key elements to the drop in sectarian violence in the capital. The days of mixed neighborhoods are gone. If anyone is telling you that the cleansing of Baghdad has not contributed to the fall in violence, then they either simply do not understand Baghdad or they are lying to you. (in Cole 2008)

By September 2007, with the Sunnis driven from Shiite Baghdad, the Mahdi Army of Muqtada al-Sadr concluded a cease-fire with U.S. and Iraqi troops. Cole explains, "Since the United States had inadvertently enabled the transformation of Baghdad into a largely Shiite city, a prime aim of the Mahdi Army, they could afford to stand down." Because al-Sadr's army had been responsible for so much bloodshed, this cease-fire, made possible by ethnic cleansing, was by itself an important contributor to the reduction in violence (Cole 2008).

The final problem with the "surge is working" stories was that they rarely acknowledged the other side of the coin: that two years after the surge began, despite the reductions in violence, Iraq remains one of the most dangerous places on Earth. Juan Cole offers an eye-opening comparison: "Thirty years of Northern Ireland troubles left about 3,000 dead, a toll still racked up in Iraq every five months" (2008).

Even more disturbing than the fact *that* violence persists is the reason *why* violence persists. Iraq Body Count's recent annual report states that "Most of these reductions have been attributed to declining inter-community violence. The most notable reduction in violence is in Baghdad." Of course, this finding dovetails with Cole's argument that Baghdad quieted once ethnic cleansing was complete. "On the other hand, areas outside the capital have seen far less dramatic reductions in violence, and dozens of civilians are still being killed in conflict-related violence throughout Iraq on a relentless, daily basis."

Why? While interethnic violence has declined, violence between "coalition military and those who oppose them" has not declined. In other words, the U.S.-insurgent battle, already the number one known killer of civilians, now accounts for an ever-increasing share of the ongoing violence in Iraq (IraqBodyCount.org 12/08).

❖ OBAMA AND BEYOND

In the 2008 presidential election, voters pulled the levers they hoped would bring change, just as they had in 2006. An astounding 75% of them said "the country is headed seriously off on the wrong track," and 63% of all voters "disapproved" of the Iraq War (ABC 11/4/08). Barack Obama, the candidate who had opposed the war, opposed the surge, and promised to bring combat troops home within 16 months of taking office, won election with 53% of the votes cast to his opponent's 46%—a landslide by recent American standards.

The nation's news media reacted by lecturing Obama on the folly of his Iraq pledge. This, as we've already seen, began during the campaign. "Now that the surge is nearly complete, with reduced violence to show for it, will Obama moderate his views on pulling troops out? And when? So far, he hasn't" (MSNBC 7/1/08). Then Obama said, during a press conference, that he would "continue to refine" his Iraq policy and that "I've always said that the pace of our withdrawal would be dictated by the safety and security of our troops and the need to maintain stability" (7/3/08). The press reacted as though Obama's promise to withdraw was now, thankfully, a thing of the past—despite the fact that the candidate held a second press conference later that same day to assert that his position on Iraq had not changed. On ABC's *This Week*, Ted Koppel explained

> Obama's advisers have conveyed to him what I'm sure he has known all along. And that is, U.S. troops are in a part of the world that produces a huge amount of oil and natural gas. We will have U.S. troops in that region for years to come, whether we want to or not. And I think Senator Obama has come to that realization. He's come to realize you cannot pull all the troops out of Iraq, unless you want to put them somewhere else. This is not a time to be saying, yes, we're going to pull all the U.S. troops out of there come what may. (7/6/08)

The *Washington Post* exulted that Obama's "strident and rigid posture" in favor of a phased withdrawal was now giving way to a "worthy, necessary attempt to create the room for maneuver he will need to capably manage the war. He has taken a small but important step toward adjusting his outdated position on Iraq to the military and strategic realities of the war he may inherit" (7/8/08).

On *Fox News Sunday*, Mara Liasson declared that backing away from his pledge was "what the American people want a commander in chief to do" (7/6/08). This came as polls showed over 60% of Americans agreeing that "the U.S. should set a timetable for withdrawal by announcing that it will remove all its troops from Iraq by a certain date" (CNN 7/29/08).

If Obama becomes president, scolded the *New York Times*' Thomas Friedman, "The Iraqis will tell him on day one that we can't leave Iraq because it will explode" (7/23/08). As Friedman wrote this, Iraqi Prime Minister Nouri al-Maliki had just called for a U.S. withdrawal (*Der Spiegel* 7/19/08). This followed the lead of the Iraqi Parliament, which had, "without note in the U.S. media," called for a withdrawal timetable in May 2007 (alternet.org 5/9/07). These actions, in turn, followed the lead of the Iraqi people, who have consistently favored U.S. withdrawal since 2004 (*Extra!* 11/12/07). By the time Friedman schooled Obama on what "the Iraqis will tell him on day one," 70% of Iraqis were demanding a U.S. withdrawal (Channel 4 3/5/08).

2009: Change?

After the election, the mainstream press continued to root for signs that Obama would break his campaign promise and ignore both U.S. and

Iraqi public opinion by keeping combat troops in Iraq indefinitely. When the president-elect picked incumbent defense secretary and surge supporter Robert Gates to continue in that role, and then picked Hillary Clinton, who had unapologetically voted to authorize force in Iraq, as secretary of state, the press rejoiced. Under a headline proudly trumpeting its biases, "Campaign Promises on Ending the War in Iraq Now Muted by Reality," the *New York Times* praised Obama for what the paper hoped would be a breaking of his campaign promise: "The impression is of a political leader converting to governance from electioneering" (12/2/08).

In an editorial typical of many in the nation's op-ed pages, the *San Francisco Chronicle* agreed:

> Obama's decision to keep Defense Secretary Robert Gates has angered the anti-war left, as it signals that Obama is prepared to drop his pledge to withdraw U.S. combat troops from Iraq within 16 months. Now the question is: When did Obama know he would not honor his pledge—during the primary . . . or over time? . . . Either way, Obama is where he should be on the issue. (12/3/08)

The "liberal" panelist on *Fox News Sunday*, Mara Liasson, added, "I think choosing [Gates] makes a lot of sense. I think if there was any concern during the campaign that Obama would kind of reflexively and literally stick to this sixteen month timetable, that's gone" (11/30/08).

Imagine the media's confusion and chagrin when, after all their confident predictions and patient tutoring, President Obama nonetheless said, about a month into his term: "Let me say this as plainly as I can. By August 31, 2010, our combat mission in Iraq will end" (*Los Angeles Times* 2/28/09).

Afghanistan Again

As we saw in Chapter 2, the American media hailed the war in Afghanistan as a great military victory, which would lead, as President Bush had promised, "to an Afghanistan that is prosperous, democratic, self-governing."

But even as the press's roving eye moved on, eager to follow the Bush White House to the next war, Afghanistan remained—remained in the grip of its brutal warlords, at the mercy of a resurgent Taliban, hooked on a heroin trade that kills more Americans than terror ever will, drowning in poverty, starvation, and violence.

Since then, only half the reconstruction aid promised by the United States ever arrived and was funneled through corporate contractors that gave a lot (to politicians) and took a lot (of profits) but left little improvement in Afghanistan. For example, DynCorp received $1.6 billion in no-bid contracts to train Afghan police but left them "incapable of carrying out routine law-enforcement work," according to government inspectors (Jones 2009).

In the fighting that has continued in Afghanistan, long after the press declared victory, 600 U.S. soldiers have died—155 in 2008 alone. The United States continues to spend about $2 billion each month on military operations in Afghanistan, a figure that may double as a troop surge begins this year (Heller 2009). The civilian death toll jumped a staggering 40% from 2007 to 2008, thanks in part to stepped-up U.S. bombing runs. Ironically, on the day the American electorate voted for change, an Air Force strike in Afghanistan killed about 40 members of a wedding party. This was at least the sixth wedding smashed by U.S. bombs in Afghanistan and Iraq since December 2002 (Tomdispatch.com 11/13/08). Afghan President Hamid Karzai used his congratulatory phone call to Barack Obama to plead for an end to the attacks.

The media's considered reaction to Afghanistan's plight was perhaps predictable: Only another troop surge, they declared, would solve the problem. On the front page of the *New York Times*, Michael Gordon led with a fearless and false declaration: "Military experts agree that more troops are required to carry out an effective counter-insurgency campaign [in Afghanistan]" (12/1/08).

But, in fact, many military experts did not agree. Rory Stewart, author of an award-winning book on Afghanistan, argued that "a sudden surge of foreign troops will be unhelpful and unsustainable. . . . Well-focused, long-term assistance in which we appear a genuine partner, not a frustrated colonial master, could help Afghans achieve [stability]" (alternet.org 12/8/08). Military historian Andrew Bacevich suggests an Anbar Awakening instead of a surge:

> The chief effect of military operations in Afghanistan so far has been to push radical Islamists across the Pakistani border. As a result, efforts to stabilize Afghanistan are contributing to the destabilization of Pakistan, with potentially devastating consequences. . . . The war in Afghanistan won't be won militarily. It can be settled—if imperfectly—only through politics. The real influence in Afghanistan has traditionally rested with tribal leaders. The basis of U.S. strategy in Afghanistan should therefore become decentralization and outsourcing, offering cash and other emoluments to local leaders who will collaborate with us in keeping terrorists out of their territory. (*Newsweek* 12/8/08)

Despite these concerns about a military solution, when President Obama announced that 17,000 additional troops would go to Afghanistan while the administration conducted a full-scale review of U.S. strategy in that region, the nation's press applauded. The *Baltimore Sun* seemed disappointed only because the troop increase was not larger, calling it

> a relatively modest increase that falls short of the 30,000 reinforcements discussed by military planners earlier this year, as concerns have grown about the increasingly violent struggle there with Taliban forces and al Qaeda terrorists. . . . Retired Marine General James Jones, now President Obama's national security advisor, headed up two recent studies of Afghanistan. His conclusion: "We cannot afford to lose." (2/18/09)

The *Washington Post*'s report was based entirely on the thinking of the U.S. commander of forces in Afghanistan, General David McKiernan, who told us that "the U.S. will have to have about 60,000 troops in Afghanistan for at least the next 3 or 4 years to combat an increasingly violent insurgency" (12/19/09). A few days later, in a follow-up story, the *Post* added: "Pretty much everyone agrees that if you want to deny al Qaeda a haven, you have to defeat or defuse the Taliban" (2/22/09). The *Philadelphia Inquirer* agreed: "Yes, we need to be in Afghanistan. We can't afford to let Afghanistan become another Taliban-run sanctuary for al Qaeda, which could lead to another 9/11" (2/24/09).

As is often true of conventional wisdoms, this one was more conventional than wise. Afghanistan-based *Christian Science Monitor* reporter Anand Gopal has recently pointed out that the Taliban is "far from monolithic," a coalition of convenience made up of "nationalists, Islamists and bandits." For most of them

> foreign fighters, especially al Qaeda, have little ideological influence . . . al Qaeda's vision of global jihad doesn't resonate in the rugged highlands and windswept deserts of Afghanistan. Instead, in a world of endless war, roving bandits and Hellfire missiles, support goes to those who can bring security. (Gopal 2008)

The inference is clear: With a Taliban that may be willing, for the right price, to sever its ties with al-Qaeda, and an Afghan people who long only for peace, war should not be our only option.

The Contested Terrain of the Future

At this writing, it is too early to say with any assurance what the "Obama Doctrine" of American foreign policy may look like. What can be said is that the prevailing winds in which this president's course will be steered tend to push the ship of state to the starboard. Those rightward-blowing winds include the forces, described in Chapter 1, that have impelled America toward empire. Above all, these forces include the primordial power of corporate capitalism, now grown into a military-industrial complex that feeds millions of Americans and funds our federal officeholders. That power has recently been on display again, as a series of megabanks and Wall Street investment firms followed greed to the brink of failure. But the concentration of wealth and power vested in these institutions is now such that their failure would shock and awe the world's economic system, and so, one after another, the hapless taxpayer was forced to bail them out.

That power will push the new administration to stay in Iraq. Barack Obama has already made concessions to that power. Tellingly, the new administration's first budget proposes an *increase* in military spending over the last Bush budget: There will be no "peace dividend" even after the election of the antiwar candidate (alternet.org 4/9/09). Obama has also said all along that a "residual force" of perhaps 30,000 to 50,000 troops will remain in Iraq after "combat forces" have left. The forces of empire have already seen to it that the world's largest and most expensive U.S. embassy has been firmly planted in Baghdad. This $592 million, 104-acre compound will house 1,200 employees from 14 federal agencies, and, of course, will need protection, a solid pretext on which to maintain a large military force in Iraq indefinitely. This is to say nothing of the 14 "enduring" U.S. military bases dotted around Iraq, many of them large enough to have bus routes, car dealerships, shopping malls, fast food restaurants, and traffic jams. They were built, deliberately, to last, and to make it hard to walk away from such an enormous "investment."

President Obama has pledged that he will honor a provision that the Iraqi government fought for in its Status of Forces Agreement with the United States—a provision that says all U.S. troops, including "residual forces," are to leave Iraq by the end of 2011. But Obama will be under enormous pressure from the military-industrial establishment to renegotiate that agreement and to remain in Iraq. Already, military planners are confident of the outcome.

> Military commanders, despite this Status of Forces Agreement . . . are already making plans for a significant number of American troops to remain in Iraq beyond that 2011 deadline, assuming that . . . agreement would be renegotiated. One senior military commander told us that he expects large numbers of American troops to be in Iraq for the next 15 to 20 years. (NBC 2/27/09)

On the other hand, a progressive, antiwar movement has mushroomed in response to the Bush presidency and is now centered in the presidency of Barack Obama. Early inklings suggest that the new president and his "base" may yet prove to be a force in their own right. Todd Lindberg, a conservative political scientist who studies voting behavior, admits with some regret that "we are now two elections ('06 and '08) into something big. This . . . is just the latest sign that the country's political center of gravity is shifting from center-right to center-left" (*Washington Post* 11/16/08).

As public opinion shifts, we would expect that, for commercial reasons, the mass media might adjust its message to stay in tune with its audience. Again, there are auguries of such a shift. MSNBC, which just a few years ago fired its only "tired old liberal," Phil Donahue, has now given its prime-time lineup over to the genuinely progressive voices of Rachel Maddow and Keith Olbermann.

On the other hand, it is a bit much to expect corporate media to now offer a sustained critique of corporate power. Conservative Joe Scarborough remains the face of MSNBC's morning show, for example. For reasons to be outlined in the next chapter, when our mass media move "left," they end up in the center, a place that remains perfectly congenial to corporate capitalism. Any attempt by Obama to move beyond that congenial center is likely to be met by furious resistance from the corporate establishment, including its mass media. It seems that we have fallen under the spell of the ancient Chinese curse that says to its victims, "May you live in interesting times."

❖ CONCLUSION

When its watchdog fails, society is robbed. Of course, the media is not the only institution bearing responsibility for the catastrophe of Iraq, and indeed, as journalists themselves have often insisted, the war might have proceeded even if the press had been more vigilant. We'll never know. We do know, however, what didn't work: the press's failure to check and balance elite power and to offer the public a full spectrum marketplace of ideas was not the way to prevent disaster.

Let us consider, for a moment, some of the costs of this systemic failure:

- At this writing, 5,181 American soldiers have fallen in the wars of the 21st century. Estimates are that perhaps 20% of the 1.5 million

Americans who have been deployed in Iraq—about 300,000 people—have returned with PTSD; 320,000 have sustained brain injuries. U.S. veterans are committing suicide at a rate of 6,256 per year, 120 each week, 17 a day. This reflects a suicide rate increase of 500% between 2002 and 2007 (alternet.org 9/11/08).

- Nobel Prize winning economist Joseph Stiglitz estimates that the total cost of the Iraq War will be between $4 trillion and $5 trillion. "And remember," he cautions, "that's just the cost for America" (alternet.org 5/19/09).

- Director of MIT's Center for International Studies John Tirnan estimates that about 1 million Iraqis have been killed in this war, that there are perhaps 1 to 2 million war widows and 5 million orphans in Iraq (*Nation* 2/2/09).

- The United Nations estimates that there are about 4.5 million displaced Iraqis—more than half of them refugees—or about one in six citizens. Only 5% of displaced Iraqis have returned to their homes in the past year (*Nation* 2/2/09).

- As the war in Afghanistan is reheated, the International Committee of the Red Cross has sent out this plea:

  We cannot sufficiently stress the unbearable levels of individual and collective suffering that Afghan men, women, and children have had to endure over three decades, and that they continue to endure at levels that defy belief. For the past three years The Red Cross has repeatedly drawn attention to the increasingly severe impact of the conflict on the civilian population. Never, however, has our concern been quite as acute as it is now. The conflict is intensifying and affecting wider parts of Afghanistan. Civilian casualties are significantly higher than a year ago. (alternet.org 3/16/09)

When Vice President Cheney warned, in 2002, that war would require us to "visit the dark side," he wasn't kidding. On the other hand, Hegel reminds us, "The owl of Minerva flies at dusk" (1967). Wisdom, he means, can emerge from darkness, from disaster. With that in mind, let us proceed to a final question.

A globe in the lobby of the *Los Angeles Times* building, November 7, 2006. On the day this photo was taken, *Los Angeles Times* editor Dean Baquet resigned over continuing budget cuts by the *Times'* parent company. Such cuts have been especially hard on two important beats: investigative journalism and international news, represented, ironically, by this globe. Altogether, the already-depleted number of foreign-based reporters dropped another 25% in just four years after 2002.

6

Why?

This chapter will take up the question that by now seems urgent: Why? Why has the press failed, in its coverage of 21st-century wars, to watchdog elites and to stock a full shelf of alternative perspectives? We will focus on three powerful forces that contributed markedly to this tragic failure.

The first is the defining characteristic of American media. The fact that they are mostly owned by a few, very large, very profit-centric corporations means that, for U.S. news, the bottom line is the bottom line: The commercial imperative—maximize profit—is the industry's first commandment.

Add to this picture the fact that several media sectors are now experiencing the corporate equivalent of oxygen deprivation—declining profits—and we have a commercial imperative in crisis, driving the news business into more and more desperate business strategies. The first of these have been massive staff cuts, especially in two areas that are crucial in reporting war and foreign policy. One is investigative reporting—the kind that allowed the Knight Ridder team of Landay and Strobel to get the weapons of mass destruction (WMD) story right—as we saw in Chapter 3.

A second victim of staff cuts has been foreign-based reporters. And might the lack of them, we'll ask in this chapter, have something to do with Americans' failure to understand "Why do they hate us"?

In the media business, as we'll see, a direct corollary of the commercial imperative is the need for a large and affluent audience, which, in turn, has its own corollaries. We'll see how its twin commandments, do not bore and do not offend your audience, produce precisely the trivial, uncritical news described in earlier chapters.

We'll also ask whether advertisers, who, after all, pay the piper, also call the tune. And we'll see that more and more, information comes to Americans in the form of "soft news," where dumbing down content and ginning up emotions have gone to extremes.

The second basic force defining today's news is the power of establishment elites to define, and confine, the issues. Here we'll ask, Why would the press so privilege the very power elites whom the Founders thought the press should check and balance? Here, we'll meet the press's Achilles heel—its need to fill large volumes of air or page with increasingly small staffs. Elites, in turn, have found just the right Paris's arrow for this Achilles heel: the public relations industry, with its irresistible photo ops, pseudoevents, video news releases (VNRs), and myriad other forms of attractively prepackaged news. We'll also look at the quiver of sticks and carrots elites can use to coax and punish the press. And finally, we'll see that corporate commercial news has now created its own star system, one that allows top reporters to become part of the Washington power elite—if they have adopted that elite's assumptions and values, the unquestioned conventional wisdom about a beneficent United States and its right to invade, which has caused so much suffering in the 21st century.

Finally, we look at a powerful new voice in the American conversation, representing another face of corporate power. In our time, corporate money has created an expressly right-wing surround sound system—a multitude of mass media platforms working to envelop their audience in a constant din of conservative stories. This right-wing media empire is, as we'll see, now fully integrated with our mainstream mass media.

Unfortunately, this right-wing media empire often seems devoted not to telling the truth, but to winning the battle by any means necessary—including the use of half-truth and untruth, in a politics of intemperate resentment, where opponents are seen not as fellow citizens, but as an evil enemy that must be defeated, and let the ends justify the tactics. This voice has been one of the forces furiously pushing the nation toward war.

At the end, our chapter on "Why?" will lead us only to another question, which we'll address in the conclusion of this chapter: How? How can we do better? How can we move toward a media system that serves democracy better than the current system of corporate ownership—a system less interested in selling the people and more interested in telling the people?

❖ THE COMMERCIAL IMPERATIVE

"Politics is business," Lincoln Steffens said, and "that's what's wrong with it." In fact, he went on to say, "That's the matter with everything," and he included journalism on his list (1957, p. 4). In our time, much—perhaps most—of the bankruptcy in the marketplace of ideas can be traced to a generally thriving business in the other marketplace.

The commercial imperative of that other marketplace is, of course, profit. This chapter will argue that the profit motive is perhaps the basic source of the biases reviewed in this book. Of the forces converging on a news that is *against* thinking and *for* the way things are, the profit motive is the granddaddy of them all.

Industry to Business: The New Ownership of the News

In fact, Lincoln Steffens, writing in 1904, hadn't seen nothin' yet. The corporate game of "engulf and devour" that began in the 1970s did not overlook the profitable news business. Today, *Time* magazine and CNN are both the property of the Time Warner corporation, along with 290 other companies, including HBO and many other cable channels; Warner Brothers Studios; Little, Brown and Company publishing group; Road Runner; and a host of Internet sites. Fox News and the *Wall Street Journal* are owned by the News Corporation, which also owns a myriad of television stations, movie and TV studios, cable channels, newspapers, magazines, satellite TV systems, book publishers, sports teams, and Internet sites.[1] To paraphrase Thorstein Veblen, the news "industry" has become a "business." To paraphrase Vince Lombardi, these days, "Profit isn't everything; it's the only thing."

---

[1]Continually updated information about the ever-changing kaleidoscope of media ownership can be found in these Web sites: *Columbia Journalism Review* (click on "Who Owns What" at www.cjr.org); the media reform group Free Press (www.freepress .net/content/ownership); and the *Online Journalism Review* (www.ojr.org).

Gone is the crusading owner–editor who purchased a press because, for better or worse, he had something to say. Gone is Hodding Carter, whose valiant little Greenville, Mississippi, *Delta Democrat Times* fought racism in the heart of the South, at the height of its power. Owners today have other goals in mind.

> Today, corporations do not purchase . . . media properties for sentimental reasons. . . . They buy them as investments that will yield a maximum return as quickly as possible. . . . This is not what media executives talk about in public. But in private they and their acquisition agents are unequivocal. Christopher Shaw, the merger expert . . . speaking at a session of potential media investors, said, "No one will buy a 15 percent margin [media] property without a plan to create a 25 percent to 40 percent margin." (Bagdikian 1987, p. 7)

Who are these new owners? The multinational media corporations (MMCs) are governed by boards of directors "very similar" to those of large nonmedia corporations. About two thirds of those directors are corporate executives, bankers, or corporate attorneys (Herman and Chomsky 2002, pp. 10–11). This is not a group given to sentimentalizing about their companies' responsibilities or the common good. Indeed, when GE took over NBC and installed one of its corporate lawyers as its president, he firmly declared that the network's overriding responsibility was to "shareholders." At that point, a member of the news division asked whether the network had another responsibility—whether the news was "a public trust." "It isn't a public trust," replied the boss. "I can't understand that concept" (Auletta 1991, p. 475).

Other media giants, for example, the *New York Times* and *Washington Post* companies, are still controlled by the families whose progenitors built them. And isn't this where the flame is kept? To a greater extent, perhaps it is. But even here, owners must put a premium on the bottom line. Failure to do so will displease the commercial banks they rely on for loans, as well as the Wall Street analysts who determine the value of the companies' publicly traded stocks. When they are unhappy, the stock price goes down. So does the family fortune. Back in 1969, John Knight, CEO of family-owned Knight newspapers, could defiantly proclaim to an audience of Wall Street analysts, "Gentlemen, I will not become your prisoner." But by 2004, Knight's successor would sheepishly admit, "Since I have been CEO, the number of meetings [with Wall Street investors and analysts] has increased dramatically, and institutional investors expect you to call on them" (Meyer 2004, p. 175).

Thanks to this new ownership circuitry and its inherent need to maximize the bottom line, the transition from "industry" to "business"—from passion for product to passion for profit—is rushing to completion. As Douglas Henwood says in his definitive study of the new corporate logic, we live in a time "When MBA's Rule the Newsroom."

"Crisis" in the Newsroom

As we shall see, profit maximization and good journalism are often a two-lane highway—each heading in opposite directions. And the MMCs that tell most of our society's news and other stories have a strong preference for the lane that leads to rich stockholders and poor news. And how much stronger will that preference be when profit itself is perceived to be in peril? In the 21st century, as the MMCs bemoan a "crisis" of profitability, we are in the midst of finding out.

The Decline of Newspapers

The problem is most acute in the newspaper business, with three swords of Damocles hanging over its head.

The First Is a Decline in Advertising Revenue

Under competition from the Internet, one of newspapers' main cash cows—classified advertising—has already wandered off the ranch and on to cheap and sometimes free sites such as Craigslist. Can other ads be far behind? ("State of the News Media 2008" 2008, p. 16). Newspapers' share of advertising had already declined from 35% to 20% in the half century before 2000, as television arrived to compete for those dollars (Meyer 2004, p. 210). In 2007, newspaper earnings fell another 8% "for the first time in a non-recessionary year" ("State of the News Media 2008" 2008, p. 16).

Then, in 2008, the U.S. economy melted down, and as its advertising disappeared, so did some of the newspaper business. The Tribune Company, owner of the *Los Angeles Times*, the *Chicago Tribune*, the *Baltimore Sun* and other dailies, has filed for bankruptcy, as have the *Philadelphia Inquirer* and the *Minneapolis Star Tribune*. The *Detroit News* and the *Detroit Free Press* will limit home delivery to three days a week. The *Seattle Post-Intelligencer* and *Christian Science Monitor* have scuttled their print editions all together, and will exist only online; along with this change, the *Post-Intelligencer* will reduce its news staff by about 90%. Denver's *Rocky Mountain News* has closed, and the *San Francisco Chronicle* is near death.

Next Is Audience Decline

To some extent, reducing the size of their audience has been a deliberate strategy on newspapers' part. Known as "trimming the fringe," the strategy reduces the number of low-income readers who are not sought after by the advertisers who provide, on average, 82% of newspaper revenue (Meyer 2004, p. 37). A recent *Columbia Journalism Review* survey of fringe trimming at 90 of the nation's largest papers found this typical response: "The inner city, from an advertiser's standpoint, is undesirable, and for that reason, we put the least amount of effort into it" (Cranberg 1997, p. 54). "It's a rational business decision," says a Wall Street analyst, "focusing on quality circulation rather than quantity, shedding the subscribers who cost more and generate less revenue" (Pena 2007, p. C1).

Former *Chicago Tribune* editor James Squires calls this culling "the dirty little secret of newspapering . . . an economic formula that is ethically bankrupt . . . for a business that has always claimed to rest on a public trust" (Cranberg 1997, p. 54).

But of course, these planned and "rational" readership reductions are not the losses big media fears. The fearsome losses are the unplanned and unwanted migration of newspaper readers to the competition—to television, now digital, with its hundreds of new channels, and to the Internet, with its millions of sites. Since 2000, the larger U.S. papers have said good-bye to about 10% of their readers (Pena 2007, p. C1).

Perhaps worst of all, a disproportionate share of the lost readers are young people—the future of the business and a very attractive cohort to advertisers, because they are more "malleable" (Mindich 2005, p. 53). In the early 1970s, 49% of 18- to 29-year-olds were reading a newspaper daily. By the late 1990s, only 21% were doing so (Putnam 2001, p. 252).

Wall Street Casts a Cold Eye on the Newspaper Business

Wall Street, which demands ever-increasing profits, has been predictably hard on newspapers' decline: The price of newspaper stock has fallen by over 30% in the last two years. The *Minneapolis Star Tribune* was sold to investors for half of what McClatchy had paid for it eight years earlier. Recently, the New York Times Company wrote down the value of its *Boston Globe* by 40% ("State of the News Media 2008" 2008, pp. 15–17).

The Upside of the Newspaper Business

None of the above gloom is to say that the newspaper business can no longer be profitable. Prior to the economic meltdown of 2008 to 2009, most newspapers were returning handsome profits. The problem is that an industry used to stratospheric profits is facing a future of merely atmospheric profits, and that is an adjustment the MMCs are unwilling to accept.

Journalism professor Philip Meyer sees two strategies open to newspapers:

Nurture: Accept that profits will decline, from the 20% to 40% the industry has enjoyed, to a more normal level for retail products of 6% to 8%. Build a creative Internet presence that complements and enhances the paper. And above all, invest in "product improvement" to lock in the golden goose—the distinctive attribute that will cause readers and advertisers to continue to support newspapers: news quality. Meyer argues persuasively that "readers' perceptions of value are substantially related to the quality of news," and that "trusted newspapers are able to ask more from advertisers" (Meyer 2004, pp. 54–55, 46).

Harvest: Refuse to accept declining profits, even in declining circumstances. Adapt by raising prices and slashing costs. Squeeze the golden goose until it turns green. Because the MMCs and Wall Street share a strong preference for maximum profits and short-term returns, this "harvesting" strategy has been the industry's standard operating procedure.

Changing Times for Television

By certain measures, television news also seems to be treading troubled waters. Despite new anchors and millions spent on promotion, network evening news lost another million viewers in the last year, "roughly the same number it has lost in each of the last 25 years" ("State of the News Media 2008" 2008, p. 15). In just the last 10 years, the percentage of people who regularly watch network TV news dropped from 60% to 34%. As recently as 1978, the "Big Three" networks commanded about 90% of the prime-time audience; today, their share is half that number. And again, the dropouts have been disproportionately young. Today, the average age of a network news viewer is 60 (Mindich 2005, pp. 72ff.).

But as we look more closely, TV's financial picture becomes more nuanced—and brighter. Television has compensated for its fragmenting audience by simply devoting more airtime to advertising. In 1981, 23 minutes and 20 seconds of the nightly news half hour was devoted to news. By 2000, 18 minutes and 20 seconds went to news, and the rest to advertising (Mindich 2005, p. 99). And because it is a "trusted" medium for news, TV continues to charge advertisers premium prices for airtime ("State of the News Media 2008" 2008, p. 2). All of the three largest networks have recently seen hefty revenue growth for both morning and evening news, in some cases by double digits ("State of the News Media 2008" 2008).

In cable news, too, business is good. Fox has seen its profits grow by a third, recently overtaking CNN in that department. CNN's profits also continue to grow, by 13% in a recent year, and even MSNBC is beginning to see "meaningful profits" for the first time ("State of the News Media 2008" 2008).

For local TV stations, news has been an increasingly important source of revenue. Unlike the network feed, whose ad revenue has to be shared between the network and the local station, local news is a cheap form of locally produced programming, carrying ads whose payments go entirely to the local station ("State of the News Media 2008" 2008).

Despite these sunny indicators, it is the gathering clouds that preoccupy the MMCs and their Wall Street analysts.

The Commercial Imperative in Warp Drive

Here, then, is the news media in the early morning of the 21st century: Most of it is owned by ever-fewer corporations, which are single-mindedly focused on profit, at a time when they perceive a crisis of profitability. How will this economic "base" influence the "superstructure" of news gathering and news content? Have we gone from a time of a commercial to a "hypercommercial" imperative?

Death by a Thousand Cuts

The process began with the media merger mania of the 1980s, resulting in "massive staff cutbacks," leaving the networks "shadows of their former selves" (Pintak 2006, p. 54). This process of acquire and cut continued, even through the go-go 1990s, when media profits soared. When the Gannett Corporation took over New Jersey's *Asbury Park Press*, for example, the new owner announced that within a year, the paper's award-winning news staff would be cut by a fourth, and the news hole would be significantly smaller (Layton 2002b, p. 143).

Such draconian cutbacks have been typical, and they have only increased in the profit-imperiled 2000s. Between 2000 and 2005, newsroom staffing at daily papers had dropped by 3,000 people, or about 5%. And then, as the profit crunch became more acute, staffing dropped by another 1,000 in 2006 alone ("State of the News Media 2008" 2008, p. 18). Disproportionately, these cuts have been inflicted by the corporate-owned news media. After cutbacks totaling 14% of *Time* magazine's newsroom staff in 2005 and 2006, *Time* announced cuts of nearly 300 more news people, and will close its bureaus in Los Angeles, Chicago, and Atlanta ("State of the News Media 2008" 2008, p. 19).

Then came the epic recession of the late 2000s, and it was raining pink slips: Job cuts during the first months of 2009 totaled 300 at the *Los Angeles Times*, 205 at the *Miami Herald*, 156 at the *Atlanta Journal-Constitution*, and so on.

Network news, too, was rendered lean and mean by the process of acquire and cut. The NBC news staff, for example, was slashed by 28% in just the first round of cutbacks by GE (Auletta 1991, p. 562). In the present "crisis," news staffs are declining again, by about 10% between 2002 and 2006. Since 2006, NBC has announced another 300 staff cuts, another 5% of its remaining news staff ("State of the News Media 2008" 2008, p. 19).

Perhaps worst of all, these cutbacks fell hardest on two particularly important types of journalist: the investigative and the foreign-based reporter.

Farewell, Muckrakers

Investigative reporters are those whose particular portfolio is the watchdog function: "to afflict the comfortable and comfort the afflicted," without the usual limitations of time and budget. This is the type of reporter who might have investigated the administration's case for war in Iraq. Indeed, this was the mantle donned by the Knight Ridder reporters who did question the White House claims. Mandated by their editor to get the story behind the story, and given time and resources to do so, they did this sort of reporting, after Vice President Cheney declared that the Iraqis had "reconstituted their nuclear program and may have a nuclear weapon soon."

From what I was able to learn just educating myself about the kind of infrastructure required to build a weapon and knowing [after a month of reading UN inspectors' reports] that the UN had destroyed what the Iraqis had had, this just seemed to be really weird and wrong. So I started making phone calls. I talked to somebody who follows this issue, not a senior official, but a working stiff and this person's words to me were, "The vice president is lying" (in Borjesson 2005, p. 366).

Unfortunately, this kind of "enterprise" reporting is expensive, and in the present climate, "if it can't be justified financially [i.e., can't be shown to generate more revenue than it costs] it can't be justified" ("State of the News Media 2008" 2008, p. 17). And so a five-year study of investigative journalism on TV news found that this watchdog of the people had "all but disappeared from the nation's commercial airwaves." What remains of investigation, about 1% of TV news, is often such fluff as "women illegally injecting silicone at parties" or lapdog stories consisting of "spoon-fed leaks from government sources" (McChesney 2004, p. 81).

In print, the heroic journalism that blew the lid off of My Lai and Watergate gave rise to "investigative units . . . that are now mostly gone in the wake of budget cuts and profit pressures" (Bennett and Serrin 2005, pp. 177–178).

Goodbye, World

In the 1950s, half of the Americans surveyed said "foreign policy" was the most important news subject. Today, 8% think so (Baum 2003, p. 22). And no wonder, since the press has so marginalized international news. Today, a foreign story that can't deliver war or a natural or financial disaster "has little chance of entering the American consciousness" (Arnett 2002, p. 66).

That's because "broadcast television has essentially left the field" of international news (Arnett 2002, p. 8). Even the 24-hour news specialist, CNN, had only 35 correspondents outside the United States— half the staff the BBC maintains (Rampton and Stauber 2003c, p. 174).

Time devoted to foreign coverage on the three largest broadcast networks fell from 4,032 minutes in 1989 to 1,382 in 2000. Even after 9/11, foreign coverage came back only halfway, to 2,103 minutes in 2002. And once the Taliban and Saddam Hussein had been toppled, attention to the world again declined rapidly (Rampton and Stauber 2003c, p. 175). In the heyday of Walter Cronkite, 40% of TV news was international. Now, such coverage is in the single digits (Arnett 2002, p. 67).

At newspapers, the money crunch has made expensive foreign bureaus a major casualty. "Washington bureaus for such chains as Gannett, Hearst and Scripps eliminated or greatly pared" world coverage (Arnett 2002, p. 67). But that was just the beginning. The number of foreign-based newspaper reporters dropped a further 25% between 2002 and 2006 ("State of the News Media 2008" 2008).

Overall, the United States, the world's only military and media superpower, has fewer correspondents stationed in foreign capitals than any other major Western nation (Bagdikian 2004, p. 94). No wonder, then, that an overwhelming majority of Americans say they "lack the background" to understand overseas news, offering "powerful evidence" that the public's "broad interest in international news is most inhibited by the public's lack of background information in this area"

(Kohut 2002, p. 87). Middle East–based reporter Lawrence Pintak points out that CBS, typical of most of the major MMCs, has had no full-time bureau stationed anywhere in the Arab world since 1985. Lacking any knowledge of the Arab language or culture, reporters there fall back on stereotype and government press releases to tell the story of the Middle East. "Might that have something to do with America's failure to understand," he asks, "why 'they' hated 'us'?" (2006, p. 97)

Perhaps not surprisingly, this death by a thousand cuts has led to a rash of resignations by editors, quitting in protest over the dismantling of the capacity to responsibly report the news. After another memo from corporate headquarters told him to slash his staff and "reconsider" the substantial space devoted to foreign news, Editor Jay Harris of the *San Jose Mercury News* had had enough. In a postresignation speech, he asked, "When the interests of readers and shareholders are at odds, which takes priority? When the interest of the nation and an informed citizenry and the demands of the shareholders for ever-increasing profits are at odds, which takes priority?" (Laventhol 2001, p. 18).

Maximizing Audience: The Commercial Imperative in Wartime

As we've seen, the first resort of the MMCs in a time of imperiled profit is to cut staff, leaving the news ever more vulnerable to the public relations machinery of elites. But costs are only one side of the ledger. How does the news pursue the revenue side?

The MMCs' job has been defined as "delivering eyeballs to advertisers." For these companies, revenue is a function of the size and demographic profile of the audience—those readers or viewers who attract advertisers. And how might the MMCs corral this increasingly maverick audience? Their drastic staff cutbacks indicate that "improving quality" is not the strategy of choice. Instead, from the Mt. Sinai of audience maintenance come these twin commandments: Thou Shalt Not Bore Thine Audience; Neither Shalt Thou Offend Them. Either sin tempts the cancelled subscription, the changed channel, the wrath of the profit margin (Exoo 1994, p. 90ff.).

Do Not Offend

The "Rally 'Round the Flag" effect means that presidential approval ratings will spike upward when war is looming. And when the public approves of the president, "do not offend your audience" means not criticizing but applauding the commander in chief and his pro-war agenda. This press applause, of course, reinforces the rally effect: Indeed, "research has shown that the magnitude and duration of rallies depends in significant measure on the nature and extent of media coverage" (Baum 2003, pp. 212–213). After 9/11, the press applauded the president so much and criticized him so little that his approval ratings rally, from 51% to 86%, was the largest ever recorded.

The network that understood this logic best was Fox News. One analysis of the network's war coverage described it as complete trust in the Bush administration's decisions, use of jingoistic rhetoric, and contempt for all alternative narratives (Iskandar 2005, p. 166). "Fox," said the *New York Times*, "has pushed television news where it has never gone before: to unabashed and vehement support for a war effort, carried in tough-guy declarations often expressing thirst for revenge" (12/3/01).

Commercially, this strategy was stunningly successful. The operating profit at Fox nearly tripled in just one year after 9/11 (*Economist* 12/7/02). This did not go unnoticed at the other MMCs; many of them tried to "outfox Fox" (Iskandar 2005, p. 168). This was the time, for example, of dumping Donahue and piling on Armey, Savage, and Scarborough at MSNBC.

Then, as the rationale for war proved false and the fighting dragged on for years, public support began to dissipate and elites began to debate. In this, more normal moment, how would the law, Do Not Offend, be enforced? In general, the press proceeds by choosing sources, stories, facts, and themes that do not threaten established cultural values. These include the "hegemonic story" of America's place in the world, with its twin articles of faith:

1. That the United States is a "benevolent force in the world," making it "more just and democratic"

2. "That the United States, and the United States alone, has a 007-like right to invade any country it wishes" (Nichols and McChesney 2005)

Despite the ripest opportunity in a generation for doing so, the press did not question those assumptions or raise the subject of American economic imperialism. As we saw in Chapter 5, the issue for the media was not why we fight, but how. And the "how" was often praised by the press ("the surge is working!") even though the "why" had proven to be a ruse, and "working" meant only reducing the violence caused by the American invasion. "Most journalists who get plum foreign assignments already accept the assumptions of empire," says foreign correspondent Reese Erlich. "I didn't meet a single reporter in Iraq who disagreed with the notion that the U.S. has the right to overthrow the Iraqi government by force" (Solomon and Erlich 2003, p. 12). "Do we question the system?" mused a *Chicago Tribune* editor. "Of course not. If we did, we wouldn't be representative—or read" (Exoo 1994, pp. 90–91). There, in one basket, are the chicken and the egg. But which is which? Are the dearth and narrowness of debate in the news the effect—or the cause—of the American consensus? Isn't "being representative" a Catch-22? The popular mind will decide which ideas make the news, but the popular mind knows nothing of a wide range of alternative views, because they haven't made the news.

Do Not Bore: A Trivial Pursuit

Once it became clear that the news *could* make money, its new corporate owners moved to ensure that it *would*, by "making it look more like entertainment." This trend was exacerbated as television news's competition grew from three VHF channels to the hundreds available on digital cable and the hundreds of thousands on the Web. To combat this, Time Warner completely revamped its CNN HLN to look like a web page crammed with information. The channel hired an actress who struggled to read the news as its star anchor and began using catchy graphics that "appeared to be written by over-caffeinated junior high-school students" (Mindich 2005, pp. 49–50).

In this push toward an entertaining news, "the networks were able to draw upon a proven model of the successful blending of news with entertainment": local TV news. One writer calls it "the far side of infotainment" (Bennett 2007, p. 244). As an index of that, Rocky Mountain Media Watch compiled a "mayhem index" that measured the number of crime, accident, fire, natural disaster, and other scary stories on local TV news. As the mayhem index rose—to 60% of coverage, in one station's case—Media Watch concluded that local TV news had become "toxic": "severely unbalanced" in its emphasis on carnage and trivia, creating a "public health issue" that "goes beyond bad journalism" (Grossman 1998, p. 33).

The results of the new emphasis on infotainment are not hard to spot. Between 1968 and 1998, the "news quality" score for *60 Minutes* fell by over half. Today, 60% of segments on the show feature "soft news" topics—celebrity profiles, "lifestyle," crime, and human interest stories. Only 13% of stories deal with the "hard news" of politics. And that is as good as it gets: The news quality score for *60 Minutes* is much higher than that of its competitors, such as *Dateline* and *20/20*. Together, the five leading prime time newsmagazines devote just over 5% of their time to stories about government, the military/national security, foreign affairs, education, or the economy (Baum 2003, p. 38).

Meanwhile, on the nightly network news, murder stories were increasing by 600% between 1990 and 2000 (Mindich 2005, p. 78). The "Top 15 Single Week Stories," those given the most time by the network news, included the Don Imus firing, wildfires, the Senator Larry Craig gay sex scandal, and a spree killing. The sacking of shock jock Don Imus alone consumed more than one fourth of all networks' news time for a full week.

As we've already noted, this increased attention to the trivial and the terrible has come at the expense of our own subject, international relations. In the most recent year with available data, for example, "each of the following foreign stories accounted for one half of one percent or less of all [network news] coverage": the Israeli-Palestinian conflict, negotiations with North Korea, the violence in Darfur, and deteriorating U.S. relations with Russia ("State of the News Media 2008" 2008, p. 8). Lamenting the loss of international news, former president of NBC News Reuven Frank concludes, "Like all American companies . . . broadcasting had moved from supplying customers to maximizing stock prices and their managers' bonuses" (Arnett 2002, p. 74).

McPaper

Just as local news had modeled infotainment for the networks, so *USA Today* became the template for newspapers. The Gannett Corporation's baby, based on the most thorough market research ever done by a newspaper, quickly grabbed the nation's second largest circulation with its mix of brightly colored graphics, skimpy articles and expanded sports, weather, and gossip sections (Layton 2002b, p. 123).

The industry could hardly wait to follow, adding sections on fitness, food, pop music, computers, the local nightclub scene, making money, buying houses, cars, hobbies, pets, shopping malls, and on and on (Blankenburg 1992, p. 116). The transition from newspaper to "McPaper"—the news equivalent of tasty, nonnutritious fast food—had begun.

Once again, old news beats were shrunk to make room for the new. A recent State of the American Newspaper survey asks how the broadsheets' content has changed since the 1960s. Prior to 9/11, foreign news had declined from 20% to 5% of front-page stories (Stepp 2002, p. 93). "Broadcast television," said one analyst of the survey, "has essentially left the field [of international news]. . . . Magazines followed suit; foreign covers . . . are the newsstand kiss of death. . . . [Newspapers] that once rightly bragged on their foreign-affairs coverage . . . virtually gave it up" (Arnett 2002, p. 67).

One might have thought that 9/11 would change this attitude toward foreign news, but one would be wrong. A post-9/11 follow-up survey of the same newspapers found that "there's still not much foreign copy beyond the big [war] stories, and there is little to illuminate the values and cultures of different countries—the very kind of stories that might explain the anger seething in the Muslim world" (Arnett 2002, p. 87).

Game On

When important stories do manage to barge into the news, they are often trivialized, transformed from "substance" to "game." Indeed, argues James Fallows, "The habits that are most annoying and destructive in today's press coverage all make sense if we assume that we have eliminated the differences between news and sports" (1997, p. 160ff.).

When, for example, Senator Ted Kennedy gave a speech roundly condemning the war with Iraq, the press did not ask, Is it true? but Who will win? The case for Kennedy's serious charge, that the White House had exploited 9/11 and fudged the evidence to justify a war that was proving to be a tragedy, went unexamined. Instead, the press gave us the "Wham!" and "Pow!" of a political prizefight. News accounts excitedly reported Kennedy's punches: "Worst blunder in more than two centuries of American foreign policy." And his opponents' counterpunches: "Kennedy's hateful attack against the Commander in Chief would be disgusting if it were not so sad." This was followed by color commentary, speculating about who would "win." Would Kennedy's speech gain traction and KO Bush's war, or would the Champ win again? "The larger issue about selling the war based on false advertising was lost" (Bennett et al. 2007, pp. 17–18).

In fact, as we saw in Chapters 4 and 5, the game has framed much of the 21st-century's war and foreign policy coverage. Debates over warrantless wiretaps and Abu Ghraib became a matchup of White House versus Democrats: The Punch-up on the Potomac. The war itself was framed as a matter of tactics and ballistics—war as football, war as Wii. Wartime elections became horse race and handicapping.

No doubt, this game frame was entertaining. After all, people jump and down and shout at horse races. But was it enlightening? Was it really all right to make such vital matters as war or constitutional rights into a football game or a prizefight? As the issues gave way to the game, were Americans left with any real news, defined by Walter Lippman as "information on which citizens can act"?

News as Fleeting Shadows, Signifying Nothing

In addition to game-framing its stories, the news also trivializes social problems by fragmenting them. "Ours is a world of broken time and broken attention," Lewis Mumford said, and the media have done their share of that breaking (Postman 1985, p. 69). Press coverage severs events from their connection with other political events, with theory, and with history. They are signalized, not signified. As a result, they seem to come at us as discrete, random occurrences. Insofar as events are attributed to any causes at all, they are personalized—left on the doorstep of individuals, not institutions. Attention is turned from deep to surface explanations.

Political scientist Shanto Iyengar has measured this fragmentation, which he calls "episodic framing": "This frame depicts issues in terms of individual instances or specific events—the carnage resulting from a particular terrorist bombing, for example. Episodic coverage typically features dramatic visual footage and pictures."

Iyengar contrasts this frame with what he calls "thematic framing," which "places a public issue in a general context and usually takes the form of an in-depth, background report. . . . Thematic reports tend to be more sedate [than episodic stories] consisting primarily of 'talking heads.'"

And his findings? "In the United States, episodic framing is by far the predominant mode in news stories, largely as a result of market pressures" (Iyengar and McGrady 2007, p. 220). A similar study found that 69% of news stories were framed as "uncontexted" episodes (Baum 2003, p. 76).

In Chapters 2 and 3, our "reverse content analysis" showed that a good deal of arguably important information about Afghanistan and Iraq was forgotten—for example, the sordid history of U.S. collusion with Afghan warlords and with the "Butcher of Baghdad." Often enough, these facts were precisely the sort of historical context that is normally deemed "boring" to audiences and, therefore, "not news."

Soft News in Wartime

As the "hard news" about the world wanes, the "soft news" waxes. "Hard news" appears in places we usually think of as news outlets— the *CBS Evening News* or *Newsweek* magazine, for example. "Soft news" appears, for example, on cable's celebrity and crime-obsessed news-magazine shows, and on daytime and late-night talk shows. Current examples include *Extra, Access Hollywood, Nancy Grace, The Oprah Winfrey Show,* and *Late Night With David Letterman.* The soft news shows and networks are often owned by the same companies that bring us the hard news. Thus, they too abide by the commercial imperatives: Do not bore and do not offend. Indeed, because they are designed not to be "info," but rather just "'tainment," these shows take the commercial strategies apparent in hard news to extremes. The "news" on these shows offers "sensationalized presentation, human interest themes, and an emphasis on dramatic subject matter, like crime and disaster" (Baum 2003, p. 6). Conspicuously absent from the soft news is any mention of public policy or its causes and alternatives. In short, there is rarely any "information on which citizens can act" in the soft news.

Unfortunately, as Americans turn away from hard news sources for their knowledge of the world, they are turning toward the mental chewing gum that is soft news. Today, more Americans than ever cite television as their main and most trusted source of news (Baum 2003, p. 58). And of those TV watchers, more tune to *Entertainment Tonight* or to *Oprah* than to *Nightline* or the *NewsHour* (Baum 2003, p. 62).

While soft news shows generally avoid political subjects, they do pay a surprising amount of attention to international conflict. But perhaps this is not so surprising. After all, when covered "softly," this arena is full of stories that won't bore or offend their audience. The opposite of boring is "water cooler effect"—what people are buzzing about at the office during a break—and war has it: spectacular pictures, heroes and villains, dramatic rescues, life and death stakes. "Like celebrity trials and sex scandals, foreign crises can be packaged as compelling human drama" (Baum 2003, p. 7). What's more, the general consensus among elites and the media about U.S. wars means that these stories "transcend" the partisan politics that viewers often find off-putting about hard news.

This movement of Americans toward an increasingly soft news is worrisome. The producer of Fox's tabloid TV show *Extra* defines soft news this way: "Simplicity transcends everything. Simplicity with great pictures will always win out" (Baum 2003, p. 45). Little wonder, then, that studies show an inverse relationship between soft news consumption and accurate political information, or that soft news viewers are "mainstreamed" more often than others into agreeing with a popular policy, even though it may be misconceived (Baum 2003, p. 290). Little wonder that soft news contributed to the unusually strong and fateful "rally 'round the president" effect that gave George Bush the tailwind to go, repeatedly, to war (Baum 2003, p. 223).

Advertisers: Paying the Piper, Calling the Tune?

Dallas Smythe famously observed that the business of mass media is "delivering eyeballs to advertisers." Of course it is. After all, our hyper-commercial mass media rely on advertisers to pay the bills and turn the profits. The vast majority of television and magazine revenue comes from advertisers, as does over 80% of newspaper revenue (Meyer 2004, p. 37).

So it is advertisers who pay the media piper. Do they also call the tune? Indeed they do, say journalists. A Pew Research Center survey of 300 journalists found that nearly half of them acknowledged con-sciously engaging in occasional self-censorship to serve the commercial interests of their employer or advertisers; only one quarter said that this never happened to their knowledge ("Self Censorship" 2000). In a separate survey, investigative TV reporters admitted that advertisers had "tried to influence the content" of news stories (73% said "yes"), that they had "tried to kill" news stories (60% said "yes"), and "suc-ceeded in influencing a news report" (40%). They also reported that there had been pressure from within their TV stations to "not produce stories that advertisers might find objectionable" (59.2%) and to "pro-duce news stories to please advertisers" (55.8%) (*Extra!* 7/8/97).

Journalists used to take pride in the "wall of separation between church and state" in the news business. The "church" was the news-room, where the public trust was honored, where journalists could challenge the powers that be. The "state" was the business side of the paper, where the news was sold to audiences and advertisers. The point was that state did not dictate to church. The church's marching orders should come from its mission, its vital role as people's watchdog and marketplace of ideas. The church's orders should not come from the commercial interests of advertisers.

But today, the news business looks like Jericho, as its walls come tumbling down. For example, the nation's fourth-largest advertiser, the Chrysler Corporation, has sent a letter to 50 of the nation's leading magazines, saying in part,

> It is required that Chrysler Corporation be alerted in advance of any and all editorial content that encompasses sexual, political or social issues . . . that might be construed as provocative or offensive. . . . These [alerts] are to be forwarded . . . prior to closing to give Chrysler ample time to review. . . . As acknowledgment of this letter, we ask that you sign below and return to us no later than February 15. (*Columbia Journalism Review* 9–10/97, p. 30)

The president of the American Society of Magazine Editors protested that "this is a road we can't go down." And yet, Chrysler's manager of media relations was able to report that of the 50 letters sent to major magazines, demanding acceptance of Chrysler's terms, "every single one" was signed and returned. Shortly afterward, Chrysler threatened to withdraw its ads from *Esquire* magazine unless a politically controversial story was killed. *Esquire* obliged and killed the piece, causing a senior editor to resign in protest, saying, "That act signals a terrible narrowing of the field available to strong, risk-taking work. . . . Events of the last few weeks signal that, in effect, we're taking marching orders from advertisers" (*Columbia Journalism Review* 9–10/1997, p. 32).

Given the passion that its life and death stakes arouse, war coverage, in particular, is a minefield of potential offenses to advertisers that must be traversed very carefully. As Richard Dale of Deutsch Advertising explains, "After a segment about a chemical attack that includes a shot of a disfigured face, it might not be the best time to talk about Oil of Olay skin care" (Bettig and Hall 2003, p. 96). So it was that in the Gulf War, networks courted advertisers with assurances that their commercials would be inserted into news shows replete with "upbeat images or messages about the war, like patriotic views from the home front" (Bettig and Hall 2003, p. 96).

Any editors thinking of criticizing the 21st-century wars in Iraq or Afghanistan would need to consider the fate of the *New Yorker* during the Vietnam War. In 1966, the *New Yorker* "attained the largest number of ad pages sold in a year by any magazine of general circulation in the history of advertising." Then, in 1967, the magazine took a stand, in issue after issue, against the war. It did so at a time when most major media continued to support the war. As it did so, "a strange disease struck." The magazine's circulation held steady, but the number of ad pages "dropped disastrously."

The magazine's editor at the time, the legendary Wallace Shawn, explained his position: "To be silent when something is going on that shouldn't be going on would be cowardly. We published information we believed the public should have and we said what we believed." But would today's mass media corporations support an editor like Shawn? "Are you kidding?" answered a magazine executive. "One bad year like the one The *New Yorker* had in 1967 and either the editorial formula would change or the editor would be out on his ear. It happens regularly" (Bagdikian 2004, pp. 218–227).

❖ ESTABLISHMENT SOURCES

Throughout this book, we've seen that many of the shelves in the press's marketplace of ideas are bare. Indeed, at crucial moments, it seemed that the only ideas available were the limited fare of the top shelf. In other words, the "debate" about war was dominated by high-echelon elites and officials. In fact, news sources were "indexed" according to their proximity to power (Bennett et al. 2007, p. 36). And so the watchdog of the people became something like the opposite—the megaphone of the powerful. This meant that the crucially important debate about war or peace in Iraq was thoroughly dominated by the Bush administration's house of cards case against Saddam Hussein.

This was not for want of credible experts willing to challenge the case for war, as we have seen throughout the book. They were there. But the indexing rule meant that a Mohammed al Baradei, head of the UN's International Atomic Energy Agency (IAEA) and awarded a Nobel Prize for his work, but lacking "decider power" or "spin capacity," would be ignored and belittled for challenging White House assertions. Meanwhile, Ahmed Chalabi, convicted of a felony and written off by the CIA as a con man, but bearing the White House stamp of approval—would see his minions' fantasies quoted like the gospel in a yearlong deluge of news stories.

Why? Why would the press so privilege the very power brokers the Founders thought the press should check and balance?

Why Elites Dominate the News

The cornerstone of journalistic values is the norm of objectivity. Present in rough form as early as the earliest modern news, the norm was refined in the early decades of the 20th century into a bulwark for an emerging "profession" besieged by charges of crassness and bias. The job of the newsperson, it says, is to depict the world's important events accurately and disinterestedly.

The problem is how to choose unbiased facts when there are no such things. Given the infinitude of interesting facts, stories, leads, angles, and sources, and given that liberals, conservatives, and radicals of the right or left will always disagree over which of these facts are important and newsworthy, the question becomes, How can bias be avoided when bias is inevitable? Journalists have responded to this paradox with a set of "rituals"—elaborate contortions designed to soothe the insistent demand for objectivity "almost the way a Mediterranean peasant might wear a clove of garlic to ward off evil spirits" (Tuchman 1972, p. 662). This response to one paradox has created another: The norm of objectivity, in the professed service of freeing the people, has, in fact, helped shackle us to a cave-wall shadow show.

The first rule of the objectivity ritual is the ritualized telling of "both sides" of a story, using "authoritative" sources (Tuchman 1972, pp. 665–670). Telling "both sides" as delivered by credible sources sounds like a laudable goal. But let's consider it. The phrase itself, "both sides of the story," reveals the feet-of-clay assumption underpinning this practice: It presumes that there are only two sides to a story, when, in fact, there are many. And defining "credible sources" as those with "decider" or "spin" capacity limits the two sides to elites who tend to agree on the basic goals of American foreign policy. This is a particularly troubling practice in international affairs, where the number of "deciders" is so small (Bennett et al., 2007, p. 132).

And so, as we saw in Chapters 2 through 5, a "third side," offering a fundamental critique of our 21st-century wars, questioning their goals, and indeed, the goals of American foreign policy generally, was "not news." Repeated content analyses found that "alternative perspectives" from progressive advocacy groups were almost entirely absent from the news. During this period, foreign journalists expressed dismay about the exclusion of American left-wing intellectuals from the American press, because these are respected and often-quoted figures abroad (McChesney 2004, p. 103).

We also saw that from 2001 to 2003, when most elites agreed on the "need" for war, the definition of "credible sources" meant that "both sides of the story" were not told. Reflecting on this coverage, many journalists have since made clear that they are satisfied they did their jobs properly, despite the one-sided coverage. And why not? After all, the journalists had performed their rain dance for objectivity: How could they be to blame if the truth did not emerge?

"I think the questions were asked. It was just a drumbeat of support from the administration. It is not our job to debate them," said ABC's Charles Gibson. (Alterman 2008)

"My job isn't to assess the government's information and be an independent analyst myself. My job is to tell readers of the *New York Times* what the government thought about Iraq's arsenal." (Judith Miller, in Massing 2004, p. 62)

"When people talk about oil having been the reason for the war, I think they are correct. . . . But I certainly have to give proper deference. . . . If the president says I am going to war for reasons x, y and z, I can't very well stand there and say, 'The president is not telling you the truth.' I as a reporter at least have to say, 'Here's what the President . . . the Secretary of Defense . . . the Director of the CIA . . . what the members of Congress are saying.' . . . And when everyone . . . with one voice are more or less agreeing, are you suggesting that the American press corps then say, 'Well, horse manure'?" (Ted Koppel, in Borjesson 2005, p. 31)

This pious refusal on the part of the press to do its job as people's watchdog has been satirized recently by the nation's Aristophanes, *The Daily Show*. Here host Jon Stewart quizzes "reporter" Rob Cordrey on the puzzling coverage of the Swift Boat controversy:

Stewart: Here's what puzzles me most, Rob. John Kerry's record in Vietnam is pretty much right there in the official records of the U.S. military, and hasn't been disputed for 35 years.

Cordrey: That's right, Jon. And that's certainly the spin you'll be hearing from the Kerry campaign over the next few days.

Stewart: That's not a spin thing, that's a fact. That's established.

Cordrey: Exactly, Jon, and that established, incontrovertible fact is one side of the story.

Stewart: But isn't that the end of the story? I mean, you've seen the records, haven't you? What's your opinion?

Cordrey: I'm sorry, "my opinion"? I don't have opinions. I'm a reporter, Jon, and my job is to spend half the time repeating what one side says, and half the time repeating the other. Little thing called "objectivity"—might want to look it up someday.

Stewart: Doesn't objectivity mean objectively weighing the evidence and calling out what's credible and what isn't?

Cordrey: Whoa-ho! Listen, buddy: Not my job to stand between the people talking to me and the people listening to me.

For the mass media, trying to attract a mass audience, "the safest place to be is in the 'non-ideological' space found in an understanding of news as whatever the most powerful officials say it is. The press does this as if official sources were somehow free of biased intent" (Bennett et al. 2007, p. 132). So it was that in 2005 and 2006, even as public support for the war was plummeting, the definition of "credible sources" meant that the press remained "slavishly committed to telling an increasingly unbelievable story" (Bennett et al. 2007, p. 174).

The Public Relations Arrow and the Press's Achilles Heel

As we have already seen, the term *news business* is not a metaphor. Between the lines of every day's news is a profit–loss ledger. This means that every editor's life is a struggle against the commercial elements: space, time, and cost. Daily, the newsperson must

1. Fill a "news hole" large enough to carry a heavy load of advertising lineage.

2. Do this with a staff that will not weigh too much on the debit side of the ledger. Thanks to several rounds of cost cutting, this staff is lighter than ever.

3. Do it under deadline—and in the age of the Internet and the 24-hour news cycle, that deadline is "right now."

The problem with these press constraints is this: Where the fourth estate lacks time and staff to get the story, the other estates—those "covered" by the press—have been happy to fill the breach. In fact, government and corporations have responded to the press's need for an agenda and for information by creating a full-blown industry—the public relations business.

By the 1920s, it was estimated that more than half the stories appearing in the *New York Times* originated in the work of press agents. Today, the public relations army is more formidable than ever. Estimates are that from 30% to 50% of the now-huge White House staff is involved with media relations. Over the past five years, Pentagon spending on advertising and public relations has grown by 63%, to at least $4.7 billion in 2009 (alternet.org 2/7/09). Its press agents now outnumber Pentagon reporters by about four to one. One estimate put the number of full-time PR staffers in just the air force at over 1,300. Is it any wonder that over 60% of front-page stories in the *Washington Post* and the *New York Times* are "inspired" by establishment press releases, press conferences, TV appearances, and "non-spontaneous events" (Exoo 1994, p. 107).

This last category remains one of the most ingenious products of the public relations machine—the pseudoevent. This is a happening staged by elites, to attract the media spotlight and bathe themselves in the warm glow of favorable publicity. It is designed to fit like a glove on the media's need for predictable, quickly coverable, dramatic events.

For the press, a diet of these handouts from elites' PR machines is cheap and filling: The stories are inexpensive to report and they quickly fill the voracious news hole. But they leave the press in the position of the inebriated man looking for his car keys under a street light. "Did you lose them here?" asks a police officer. "No," the man replies, "but the light's better here" (Fallows 1997, p. 144). When journalists follow the spotlight shone by PR handouts, are they looking where the light is, and missing the real story?

Staging the visually compelling destruction of Saddam's statue across the street from most journalists' headquarters was, as we have seen, a particularly ingenious and effective pseudoevent. But did it cause the press to miss the truth?

Together, these PR techniques are the "levers" Bennett et al. mean when they conclude that

> what carries a story is not necessarily its truth or importance, but whether it is driven by dominant officials . . . with the greatest capacity to use the levers of office to advance their news narratives . . . and the best communications operations to spin their preferred narratives. (Bennett et al. 2007, p. 29)

These levers are the "flywheel," says New York Times editor Philip Taubman, which allows those who control the levers to keep their story churning through the news, while an opposing story may appear once and then fade like May flowers (Bennett et al. 2007, p. 38). In order to move this flywheel, the Bush administration spent $1.8 billion in a two-and-a-half-year period on PR contracts, a figure that dwarfs similar spending by previous administrations (Nichols and McChesney 2005, p. 65). That spending, in turn, bought these sorts of tactics:

1. VNRs: Dressed up to look and sound like a news report, these PR concoctions told the administration's side of the story. But they are distributed free of charge to TV stations across the country and are often used by local television as a cheap and easy way to fill the news hole. The Pentagon's own "Hometown News Service" alone produced 750,000 news releases to the "14,000 newspapers, TV and radio stations subscribing to Hometown's free service." The service's "good news" stories have touched 41 million Americans via local news outlets (Bennett et al. 2007, p. 144).

2. A somewhat mysterious PR firm known as the Lincoln Group created pro-U.S. news and bribed Iraqi news editors to run it as their own copy (Mozzetti and Daragahi 2005).

3. A number of news columnists and broadcast pundits were paid as much as $240,000 to support administration policy in their commentary (Mueller 2006, p. 65).

4. Retired generals and admirals were so omnipresent in the coverage of the Iraq war that one writer said ours "looked like Chilean TV after a coup." They have also been part of the White House PR campaign. This program, undisclosed until recently, refers to these analysts as "surrogates" for the administration. The retired brass were "wooed in hundreds of private briefings with senior military leaders," including officials with significant influence over contracting. Such contracts are highly prized among lobbyists for military contractors, such as the "surrogates." Together, they represent more than 150 arms makers, "as lobbyists, senior executives, board members or consultants" (*New York Times* 1/21/08). In return, the surrogates carried White House talking points on the air and in print, sometimes even when "they suspected the information was false or inflated. Several analysts acknowledged they suppressed doubts because they feared jeopardizing their access. It was them saying, 'We need to stick our hands up your back and move your mouth for you,'" said one former Green Beret and Fox analyst (*New York Times* 4/21/08).

Sticks

Irresistible photo ops, free VNRs, payoffs to pundits and access to high-level officials—these are the carrots a White House can offer the MMCs. But when those fall short, the government also has sticks with which to poke and prod the media into line. These include the following sticks:

1. *Censorship.* As we saw in Chapter 4, the war coverage of embedded reporters was completely subject to the censorship of unit commanders. Meanwhile, unembedded reporters were actively discouraged and sometimes physically barred from reporting the war. The Pentagon has also barred the press from covering the arrival of caskets at Dover Air Force Base. An October 2001 memo from Attorney General John Ashcroft suggested that agencies should refuse Freedom of Information Act requests whenever they could find a reason to do so.

2. *Information control.* The Bush White House has been notoriously good at "Message Discipline," that is, "develop a message that you want the press to get and don't let reporters distract you," leading one reporter to describe the presidency as "weirdly impenetrable" by the press. For the White House staff, absolute loyalty to the message is a job requirement. Those who wander off message "are in some professional danger," according to a *Washington Post* White House reporter (Mueller 2006, pp. 33, 52–59).

3. *Sanctions.* The Bush White House routinely withdrew cooperation from reporters whose copy was displeasing. Recall, for example,
the Knight Ridder team who had the temerity to challenge the WMD
story in the fall of 2002. They were barred from joining the other journalists on the defense secretary's plane "for at least three years" (*Editor
and Publisher* 5/23/07). The administration also tried to have
unfriendly reporters removed from their beats, and complained incessantly to editors about negative coverage (Alterman 2003, p. 215). In
December 2003, for example, Lawrence Di Rita, spokesman for the
Department of Defense, sent a letter to the *Washington Post* complaining about the coverage of reporter Thomas Ricks, and then met with
Ricks' editors to press the case. The complaint against Ricks suggested
that he was "soliciting comments from too many people and giving too
little weight to official statements" (Fritz et al. 2004, p. 50). Jefferson
would have called this, "Doing his job."

Journalists' Incentives: "Everybody Wants to Be at Versailles"

Distinguished journalist James Fallows has tried to explain how and
"why the values of journalists have changed," and how their current
practices "undermine democracy" (1997, p. 6).

In the new media environment, Fallows sees a "mixture of financial, social and professional incentives" that have produced a "star system" among journalists, giving them the potential to

> command power, riches and prestige that few of their predecessors
> could have hoped for. Yet this new personal success involves a terrible
> bargain. The more prominent today's star journalists become, the
> more they are forced to give up the essence of real journalism. (1997,
> pp. 6–7)

Here is what happened. In the 1950s and 1960s, the networks' news
divisions were not moneymakers. They existed because the network
founders, the Paleys and Sarnoffs, felt some obligation to inform the public, and because, back then, the FCC required that the networks devote
some time to public affairs programming. As a result, network news was,
in those days, poor but free: As unprofitable enterprises, they were not
lavishly funded, but they were free to define the news as they saw fit.

Then, in the early 1970s, "*Sixty Minutes* changed journalism for one
simple reason: It made money." This opened the networks' eyes to the
possibility that news could add to, not subtract from, the bottom line.
Suddenly, news divisions were flush with cash—annual budgets went

from $3 million to $4 million to half a billion between the 1960s and the 1990s (Fallows 1997, p. 55). But as his mentor tells Barton Fink in the Coen brothers' film of the same name, "You have come to the attention of the studio head. Fink, you do not want to come to the attention of the studio head." With increased budgets came increased interference by the network in news decisions, leading to more "game" and less "substance." Today, says Fallows, "the entire press has become the sports page" (p. 151).

A profitable TV news also created a star system. With their good ratings and relatively low production costs, TV newsmagazines and political talk shows proliferated. Then, one after another, the all-news channels popped up. With all of this airtime to fill, TV turned to reporters, including the best-known print reporters, as analysts, panelists, and commentators. Suddenly, lots of journalists were receiving more exposure than journalists had ever dreamed of.

And that fame quickly led to fortune, when corporations and other interest groups offered five-figure fees to these new celebrities as featured speakers at their conferences. Thus, television became a reporter's ticket to the gravy train of the lecture circuit. But TV was not open to just any reporter. Its golden tickets are reserved for "prominent" reporters—the ones who do the big stories—the stories that score interviews with the highest-level officials.

In Chapter 3, we met *New York Times* reporter Judith Miller, who had Cheney and Rumsfeld on her Rolodex, and was often on television. We also met Jon Landay and Warren Strobel, who did not and were not. Asked if they had ever been invited to be on television, the Knight Ridder reporters admitted that they had not, "Unless you count C-Span" (Moyers 2007).

The elite journalists with ready access to elite newsmakers "are not typical of all American reporters, most of whom work in small markets and are still underpaid." But "Bigfoot" reporters, says Fallows, are "representative" of American journalism, "since they are the standard others envy and aspire to, and since they dominate the face that journalism presents to the public" (p. 78)

Unfortunately, the Bigfeet's newfound status is altering their perspective. "It is a major problem that journalists have come to identify with the rich or upper middle class, rather than with the poor," says Charles Peters, editor of the *Washington Monthly*. And why not? Today, the median salary for a journalist of the 40 largest circulation newspapers in the country was nearly double the median income for all U.S. workers (*Los Angeles Times* 12/8/02). Accordingly, recent surveys have shown that members of the Washington press corps are more pro-business and conservative than most Americans on the economy, militarism, and regulation of business (McChesney 2004, p. 104).

Borrowing a leaf from *Power Elite* theorist C. Wright Mills, Bennett et al., suggest that this worldview is only to be expected in

> a media system where the same people—journalists and politicians— attend the same social functions, send their children to the same private schools . . . and attend the same parties. They also tend to live in the same communities—Bethesda, Chevy Chase . . . old town Alexandria, or a Washington address followed by NW. (2007, p. 199)

In all these settings, views and attitudes are shared. "We have to recognize that the press is part of this establishment, a prominent part of this establishment," says prominent establishment member and State Department spokesman Robert Callahan. "And the whole political spectrum, when we are talking about Washington, is very narrow" (Bennett et al. 2007, p. 134).

This establishment consensus, as we have seen, supports U.S. wars. For journalists, said one reporter, this meant that

> if you were against the [Iraq] war, you were marked as some kind of left-wing throwback, or an isolationist, someone who didn't get it. . . . [On the other hand] pro-war writers were being read—they were having an impact on the debate. . . . Pro-war writers and pundits were getting TV time, which could (and did) lead to other career intangibles like book deals, greater brand recognition, magazine awards, and what not. . . . And what were the consequences for getting it wrong? Zip. In fact, most of the . . . pro-war writers have risen to greater heights within the . . . media world. (Hastings 2009)

Violating the consensus, on Iraq for example, that emerges from this establishment, says *Harper*'s publisher John MacArthur,

> puts you out of step with 95 percent of your colleagues. . . . You feel left out. . . . You stop getting invited to parties, and people say you're a crank and a weirdo. You're not part of the team anymore. . . . Nobody likes to be isolated socially. Everybody wants to be at Versailles. Washington is Versailles. They want to be close to *le roi soleil*, they want to be part of the power structure, and if taking the official leak from the official source, getting close to Cheney, to Rumsfeld—if that brings you credit and invitations and promotions, it's a great way to live. If you go contrary to that, you wind up back in Cleveland. (Borjesson 2005, pp. 98–99)

❖ MAINSTREAMING THE RIGHT

There is a new voice in the American conversation, and it is a powerful one. The conservative movement has created a media empire of its own—and has fully integrated it into our mainstream mass media. In the 21st century, this voice has been one of the implacable forces pushing the nation to war.

The story of the right-wing media begins in the 1970s. By this time, as we saw in Chapter 1, the economies of Europe and Asia had recovered from their pummeling at the hands of World War II, and these new foreign competitors, now on the U.S. doorstep with their cars, consumer electronics, and so on, had created a "crisis of profitability" for American corporations.

To restore its profit position, American business saw that it would have to take a bigger piece of what was now a smaller pie. Workers, consumers, and government would have to settle for less. A 1974 *BusinessWeek* editorial saw the magnitude of the task:

> It will be a hard pill for many Americans to swallow—the idea of doing with less so that business can have more. Nothing that this nation or any other nation has done in modern economic history compares in difficulty with the selling job that now must be done to make people accept this new reality. (in Dreier 1987, p. 65)

How could such a "selling job" be accomplished? William Simon, a millionaire, junk bond venture capitalist, and former Reagan treasury secretary, had the answer. His manifesto called for "nothing less than a massive and unprecedented mobilization" with funds "rushing by the multi-millions" from corporate donors to a network of pro-business pundits, think tanks, journals, book publishers—and media outlets to showcase all of the above (Simon 1978).

The corporate community heard the call. In particular, foundations established by the Coors (beer), Olin (munitions and chemicals), Scaife (banking), Bradley (auto parts), Koch (oil and natural gas), and Smith Richardson (pharmaceuticals) fortunes provided the crucial seed money—with the last four of these dubbed the "four sisters" of the conservative movement. These funds were then matched by even larger corporate foundations—Amoco, Alcoa, Rockwell, Ford, and so on ("Buying a Movement" 1996).

By 1980, this funding network had already established 70 right-wing think tanks that would provide a steady stream of conservative pundits and ideas to the media. This was just one prong of the right's multimedia onslaught, but even at that, by 2000, contributors had lavished over $1 billion on just their 20 largest institutes, out of the more than 500 conservative think tanks that corporate seed money had established by then (D. Brock 2005, p. 49).

And that was just the beginning. By the 21st century, corporate money had created a right-wing surround sound system—a multitude of mass media platforms working together to envelop its audience in a constant din of conservative stories. And while the right spoke through this magnificent megaphone, the left's unfunded message was often inaudible, amplified, as one writer said, by a tin kazoo. "It doesn't take a rocket scientist," said the head of the National Committee for Responsive Philanthropy, "to figure out that the millions spent by [conservatives] have enabled them to virtually dictate the issues and terms of national debates" (D. Brock 2005, p. 49).

Unfortunately, imbalance wasn't the only problem with the conservative media. Often, critics charged, these media seemed devoted, not to telling the truth, but to winning the battle by any means necessary, including the use of half-truth and untruth (Jamieson and Cappella 2008, p. 245). What's more, says *Columbia Journalism Review* editor Michael Massing, this same win at all costs philosophy has led to a "politics of personal destruction, promoting a mindset in which opponents are seen not as fellow citizens to be debated and persuaded but as members of a subhuman species who must be isolated and stamped out" (2009, p. 16).

The formidable weapons of this conservative media arsenal include:

The Idea Factories: Think Tanks, Journals, Book Publishing

Business's blitzkrieg began by laying a foundation of "scholarly opinion." By endowing a host of think tanks, book publishers, and journals, big business provided the money, time, research resources, collegial setting, and publications in which conservative thinkers and their ideas could flourish.

Up sprang the Heritage Foundation, the Cato Institute, the American Enterprise Institute, the Hoover Institute, the National Bureau of Economic Research, and more than 500 Mini-Me's of these conservative think tanks.

Then, rather than try to publish their findings in established, peer-reviewed periodicals, the right simply founded its own journals: the *Weekly Standard,* the *Public Interest,* the *American Spectator,* the *New Criterion,* and so on. All of them were designed to influence opinion, ladeling out free copies and press releases to opinion leaders, policy makers, and mainstream news outlets ("Buying a Movement" 1996).

Likewise, why endure the rigorous process of blind peer review of books, when the right could simply publish its own books—and buy enough copies to make its books "best sellers"—ready for their close-up in prime-time news. And so Rupert Murdoch would acquire HarperCollins and publish books by Sean Hannity, Peggy Noonan, and Dick Morris. And Alfred Regnery, a Reagan administration antipornography crusader who resigned after police found a large stash of hard-core porn in his home, took over the family publishing business and began publishing political porn. Regnery's salacious list includes *The Myth of Heterosexual AIDS; Year of the Rat: How Bill Clinton Compromised U.S. Security for Chinese Cash; Shut Up & Sing: How Elites from Hollywood, Politics, and the UN Are Subverting America; Leftism Revisited: From de Sade and Marx to Hitler and Pol Pot;* as well as *Unfit for Command,* the scurrilous book that swift-boated John Kerry's presidential campaign, and a series of fearmongering tracts arguing that Islam preaches jihad against nonbelievers, in order to subject them to its "oppressive and supremacist" yoke (Spencer 2005; 2006).

After publication, these books are heavily promoted by the conservative movement. Corporate funders buy these books in bulk and distribute them free to right-wing book clubs, or as premiums for subscriptions to conservative journals. Because just a few thousand sales in a given week can push a book onto a best-seller list, these bulk sales often make the crucial difference. The *New York Times* Best-Seller list marks books bought in such bulk sales with an inconspicuous dagger. But otherwise, the mainstream media treats these books as bona fide best sellers, and their best-selling authors are ready for their mainstream media appearances. "It's not uncommon for a Regnery author to be interviewed on 200–300 radio shows," said Alfred Regnery (D. Brock 2005, p. 357).

With this, the first outpost had been taken. The field of public policy was "awash with academic studies" that came to the "right" conclusions, explained Edwin Feulner of the Heritage Foundation. From there, said Dr. Feulner, "Sell it and resell it every day by keeping the product fresh in the consumer's mind," disseminating these conclusions to "thousands of newspapers" (Exoo 1994, p. 110). Today, Heritage alone spends over $8 million per year on public relations. That money buys a 365/24/7 media hotline, disseminates a "hot sheet" to thousands of news agencies weekly, runs its own TV and radio studios in its Capitol Hill offices, blast-faxes its "mentions" in major news outlets to thousands of smaller ones, runs "training camps" for reporters, and scores about 40 mentions in major media every week. Given that spin capacity, it is no wonder that, as we have seen in repeated content analyses, this decade's war coverage has showcased many more conservative think tanks than liberal ones.

Any Means Necessary

Unfortunately, the quantity of this right-wing "scholarship" far exceeds its quality. *Columbia Journalism Review* editor Trudy Lieberman has devoted an entire book to documenting the false claims, shaky statistics, fixed polling, and other "clever gimmicks" that Heritage, Cato, and other conservative think tanks have deployed. For example, the Cato Institute issued a major report discrediting Head Start, just as the Clinton administration was seeking increased funding for the program. The study became a story in newspapers across the country, which quoted Cato's author as the "expert" in the field, saying that "heredity so strongly determines behavior that early intervention is a waste of time." But as Lieberman learned, the study's author, John Hood, "Research Director" of the John Locke Foundation, a corporate-funded Cato wannabe, was neither a scholar nor an expert on childhood development, and had done no original research. The report, said Lieberman, did little more than string together other critics' often clearly erroneous criticisms of Head Start (Lieberman 2000).

Meanwhile, lurid, tabloid-like rumors about the Clintons' personal lives became the standard fare at the *Weekly Standard,* a journal founded by the dean of the neoconservative movement, Irving Kristol, and paid for by Rupert Murdoch. One such tale, endlessly retold in right-wing media, was that of Gary Aldrich, a "best-selling" Regnery author whose supposedly eyewitness descriptions of Bill Clinton's shenanigans were, he later admitted, "hypothetical" (D. Brock 2005, p. 357).

One of the stars to emerge from this conservative farm system is Ann Coulter. She is a graduate of the right's National Journalism Center, funded by William Simon and the Four Sisters to teach journalists the "right" way to report the news. Its graduates have gone on to careers at the *New York Times,* NPR, CNN, and so on. Coulter's first book was published by Regnery and her next by Murdoch's HarperCollins. Her books are heavily promoted through the Conservative Book Club and through conservative journals and Web sites, which offer free copies of her books, bought in bulk, by conservative foundations.

Ms. Coulter lives her principle, which is that "journalism is war by other means." Here is a sample of her thinking: On John Walker, an American who fought with the Taliban, she said, "We need to execute people like John Walker to physically intimidate liberals, by making them realize that they can be killed too." On the race-motivated truck-dragging death of African American James Byrd, she said, "There is a constitutional right to hate!" On a group of 9/11 widows who had endorsed John Kerry for president, she said, "I've never seen people enjoying their husbands' deaths so much." To an antiwar, disabled Vietnam vet, she said, "People like you caused us to lose that war!"

One of Coulter's most recent books is *Treason: Liberal Treachery From the Cold War to the War on Terrorism*. Here, she reveals that her hero is Joe McCarthy, the man whose name is, literally, synonymous with demagoguery, with leveling the charges of treason against liberals and leftists that wrecked so many innocent lives in the 1950s. But in Coulter's book, "His targets were Soviet sympathizers and Soviet spies. . . . Liberals denounced McCarthy because they were afraid of getting caught." In fact, his colleagues in the Senate censured him, Republicans and Democrats alike, and no one named by McCarthy was ever convicted or even charged with plotting against the United States. Her book then goes on to emulate her hero's work, using made-up or distorted facts and out-of-context quotations to demonstrate that Harry Truman, John F. Kennedy, Lyndon Johnson, Hubert Humphrey, and Tom Daschle were all traitors.

In the mainstream media, this lunatic screed is celebrated and rewarded. During the Iraq War, Coulter was a frequent guest on all the major news networks, was lovingly profiled in *Newsday*, the *New York Observer*, the *New York Times*, and a *Time* magazine cover story. Her syndicated newspaper column is carried by over 100 newspapers across the country. And so, as some prominent public figures began to speak out against the war, Ann Coulter warned them, using both right-wing and mainstream media bullhorns:

> As George Bush said, "You are with the terrorists or you are with America." Now we're getting a pretty clear picture of who is with the terrorists. As Patton said, "I like when the enemy shoots at me; then I know where the bastards are and can kill them." (AnnCoulter.com)

Right-Wing Idea Factories and the War in Iraq

One of the less-noticed, but more-influential, writers to emerge from the conservative idea complex was Laurie Mylroie, who wrote on the Middle East and was affiliated with the American Enterprise Institute. Her first book, *The War Against America: Saddam Hussein and the World Trade Center Attacks: A Study of Revenge*, argued that Iraq was somehow implicated in the 1993 bombing of the World Trade Center.

Writing in the *Washington Monthly*, Johns Hopkins professor and bin Laden expert Peter Bergen called Mylroie "the neo-cons favorite conspiracy theorist," and argued persuasively that "virtually all evidence and expert opinion" contradicted Mylroie's thesis (12/03).

After 9/11, Mylroie argued that the mastermind behind that attack was, again, an Iraqi intelligence agent. When no evidence could be found for that theory, she wrote *Bush vs. the Beltway: How the CIA and the State Department Tried to Stop the War on Terror.* In this book, she imagined a conspiracy among U.S. officials to hide the truth about Saddam's role in 9/11. "She is, in short, a crackpot, which would not be significant if she were merely advising, say, [crackpot serial candidate for president] Lyndon LaRouche," said Bergen (*Washington Monthly* 12/03). He meant that, instead, Mylroie and her ideas were "informing" the U.S. government. Her work became a central pillar in the administration's case for war and was cited often by Dick Cheney, Paul Wolfowitz, and other White House hawks.

And finally, one more notable achievement of the conservative ideas complex. With grants from the Bradley Foundation and from Rupert Murdoch, Irving Kristol's son William founded the grandly titled and grandly ambitious Project for the New American Century (PNAC). Under its auspices, neoconservatives devised the idea of preemptive war, with or without international support, against Iraq—a war we could win, oil reserves we wanted, against a dictator already despised by the American people. Before it became the Bush Doctrine, it was PNAC's.

On 9/11, the day of al-Qaeda's assault on America, Kristol said, "I think Iraq is, actually, the big unspoken elephant in the room today." On September 20, PNAC published an open letter to President Bush in the *Washington Times,* calling for Saddam's overthrow. In July 2002, Kristol's Murdoch-funded journal, the *Weekly Standard,* published "The Coming War with Saddam," which provided the script for the ubiquitous TV appearances made by PNAC members during the campaign for war. Kristol had begun PNAC as a way of trying to marry the themes of conservatism and "national greatness." Once the war began, his dream had come true: Patriotism, the war, and the Republican Party were now a plural marriage; "national greatness conservatism" and the New American Century were alive and well.

The Right-Wing Bullhorn: Newspapers, Television, Radio

As William Simon's memo had prescribed, the "wholesale" production of conservative ideas in think tanks, journals, and books would need "retail" outlets: television, radio, and newspapers that would deliver these ideas to the masses and make them what Gramsci called "the common sense."

Newspapers in Media Power Centers

One of the wealthy entrepreneurs who answered the call for right-wing media was the Reverend Sun Myung Moon. The Moon-founded Unification Church is somewhat unorthodox. Moon has declared that he is the "new Messiah" and that he seeks to lead an "automatic theocracy to rule the world" (*Extra!* 8/9/87).

But his politics are very orthodox indeed—orthodox conservative and Republican. In 1982, Moon founded the *Washington Times* "to fulfill God's desperate desire to save this world," by spreading a conservative message. Apparently, the paper's management imposed that message too heavily on the *Times'* founding editor, editorial page editor, and several members of their staff. All of them resigned, charging that Moon's managers continually interfered with the paper's editorial independence. Later, the rewriting of headlines and stories to reflect GOP spin became so common that reporters had a name for it: "Prudenizing," after the managing editor who did this work (Confessore 2002).

Being one of just two newspapers in the hometown of the national press gives the *Washington Times* considerable bullhorn power for its dubious version of the truth. For example, two months after 9/11, Bill Clinton gave a speech at Georgetown University. In it, he said that the United States is still "paying the price" for slavery. His comment was completely unrelated to the 9/11 attack, which he also discussed, later in the speech. But the *Washington Times'* headline read, "Clinton Calls Terror a US Debt to Past, Cites Slavery in Georgetown speech."

That same day, the story of Clinton's "infamy" became a highlight of the Internet's Drudge Report and of right-wing talk radio. That night, Fox News took the baton: "He's implying a moral equivalence between us and Osama bin Laden and his terrorists," said Fred Barnes (11/8/01). On *The O'Reilly Factor*, *Washington Times* editor Jeffrey Kuhn, in a righteous indignation worthy of Elmer Gantry, denounced Clinton as "morally reprehensible" (11/8/01).

Rupert Murdoch has added two more reliably conservative newspapers to the fold. His tabloid paper, the *New York Post*, has been described by the *Washington Journalism Review* as "s-curves of sex, scandal and screw the facts." Or as the *Columbia Journalism Review* put it, "The *New York Post* is no longer a journalistic problem. It is a social problem—a force for evil" (Shawcross 1997, p. 188).

The *Post* not only supported the war, but it helped to lead the right-wing media's fight to boycott antiwar performers, calling them "appeasers": "DO NOT AID THESE SADDAM LOVERS!" commanded a typical *Post* headline.

The paper is not well thought of in journalistic circles, but it is located in the media capital of the world, and that, again, gives it bullhorn power. When the *Post* reported that Hillary Clinton had called an aide "a fucking Jew bastard" during her close Senate race in 2000, the story instantly popped up on every news network and in indignant editorials in the *Washington Times,* the *Wall Street Journal,* and the *National Review.* The story, it turned out, was written by a former *National Enquirer* reporter. The "victim" was a campaign aide who had lost his law license for taking a bribe. He had told this story to numerous reporters without ever mentioning the "Jew bastard" part, was not Jewish, and later apologized in writing to Clinton for spreading false rumors about her (D. Brock 2005, p. 176).

Religious Right TV

One of the ingenious prongs of the right's offensive involved evangelical Christians. It is surprising to recall that this recently staunchly Republican voting bloc was, as recently as the 1970s, largely apolitical. In 1976, this group had voted for Jimmy Carter, not because of his politics, but because the moderate Democrat had described himself as an evangelical Christian. A Coors-funded operative named Paul Weyrich thought of a way to change that: wed evangelical Christianity to conservative politics by creating right-wing TV preachers, sponsored by corporate dollars, on newly available cable channels. And lo, after millions of dollars in corporate seed money, there were the ministries of the right Reverends Jerry Falwell and Pat Robertson, telling their listeners, "It's going to be a spiritual battle. There will be Satanic forces. We are not going to be coming up just against human beings" (D. Brock 2005, p. 189).

By the 1980s, the audience for Christian right TV was estimated to be at least 30 million per week. Robertson, Falwell, and Focus on the Family's James Dobson are also frequent guests on the mainstream TV news and talk shows. There, they are treated with the respect due a thoughtful commentator, despite the fact that all three men have openly expressed profoundly intolerant and undemocratic views. Robertson's 1991 book *The New World Order,* for example, claimed that an international conspiracy of Jewish bankers controlled the world's financial system. He also opined that "the feminist agenda . . . encourages women to leave their husbands, kill their children, practice witchcraft and become lesbians." Dobson, whose own audience is 29 million, describes feminists as women who "never married, didn't like children, and deeply resented men" (D. Brock 2005, pp. 191–195).

Naturally, all of these televangelists have been ardent supporters of our 21st-century wars. On his show, *The 700 Club*, Robertson interviewed a Regnery author whose book, *Dangerous Diplomacy*, had attacked the U.S. Department of State for having reservations about going to war in Iraq. "I read your book," fumed Robertson. "When you get through you say, 'If I could just get a nuclear device inside Foggy Bottom, I think that's the answer. We've got to blow that thing up!" (D. Brock 2005, p. 194).

Ready for Prime Time: Fox News

Ensuring that the media's message was pro-corporate would be much easier, conservatives understood, if corporations were in charge of the media. And so their policy goal became "media deregulation"—the repeal of any laws or regulations that restricted corporations' power to own and control the mass media.

For example, the "Fairness Doctrine," issued by the FCC in 1949, required that when a controversial issue is discussed on TV or radio, the airing station must present contrasting viewpoints. By the 1980s, the corporate media movement was in full swing, contributing substantially to the 1980 election of Ronald Reagan, the most conservative president since Herbert Hoover. By 1987, the Reagan FCC had repealed the Fairness Doctrine, and in so doing opened the door for Rush Limbaugh and Fox News. Now, more than ever, to paraphrase Will Rogers, freedom of the press belonged to the fella who owned a TV or radio network.

The first fella to use this new right to own a TV network and use it to promote his own views, unrebutted, 24 hours a day, was Rupert Murdoch. By 1996, the year Fox went on the air, the right had already spent decades and billions "working the ref"—slamming the mainstream media with the charge of "liberal bias." Indeed, major right-wing institutes such as Accuracy in Media and the Media Research Center were established with the sole purpose of bird-dogging the mainstream media, making the charge of "liberal bias" the equivalent of the Hollywood blacklist, and thus browbeating the mainstream press into a more conservative posture. There was no reliable evidence that this liberal bias actually existed.[2] As the dean of the Annenberg

---

[2]For good reviews of the evidence concerning the "liberal bias" charge, see McChesney 2004, chap. 3; Alterman 2003.

School of Communication at the University of Pennsylvania, Kathleen Hall Jamieson says, "Content analysis has failed to demonstrate a systematic liberal bias in press reports on politics." Indeed, she adds, "In three different studies, it was the [mostly conservative] ideological disposition of editors and publishers that predicted bias." As one indication of that overall bias, newspapers endorsed George W. Bush over his opponents by a ratio of about two to one (Jamieson 2000, p. 187).

But repeating the charge of "liberal bias" incessantly, and citing as evidence any statement by mainstream media that is critical of a conservative politician or idea, ultimately had its chilling effect. By the time of Fox's debut, the Big Lie had taken hold: Not only did three fourths of Republicans believe in the chimera of liberal bias, so did half of all Democrats (D. Brock 2005, p. 109).

And so, in a stroke of audacious and ingenious rhetorical chicanery, Fox News presented itself as the alternative to the "liberally biased" mainstream media. In the words of its slogans, Fox was "fair and balanced," objective, fact-based, and neutral: "We report, you decide."

But in choosing his "fair and balanced" news team, Murdoch drew mostly from the right-wing media system. As head of Fox, Murdoch chose Roger Ailes, who had run the notorious race-baiting presidential campaign of the senior George Bush in 1988. Asked whether it was ethical to tie Bush's opponent to African American murderer–rapist Willie Horton, Ailes said, "The only question is whether we depict Willie Horton with a knife or without one." Ailes' partner in the campaign, Lee Atwater, said that Ailes "had two settings: attack and destroy" (D. Brock 2005, p. 231).

The senior correspondents at Fox also tended to be groomed by the right's media machine. Brit Hume, formerly of ABC News, moonlighted as a writer for the *Weekly Standard* and the *American Spectator.* Tony Snow had been an editor at the *Washington Times,* and later became George W. Bush's press secretary.

At Fox, the process of giving the news a conservative slant is not subtle or complicated. It is simple and straightforward. Former Fox producer Charles Reina describes it:

> Not once in the 20+ years I had worked in broadcast journalism prior to Fox—including lengthy stays at The Associated Press, CBS Radio and ABC/*Good Morning America*—did I feel any pressure to toe the management line. . . . But the roots of FNC's [Fox News Channel's] day-to-day on-air bias are actual and direct. They come in the form of an executive memo distributed electronically each morning, addressing what stories will be covered and, often, suggesting how they should be covered. The Memo . . . has ensured that the [Bush]

administration's point of view consistently comes across. . . . The war in Iraq became a constant subject of The Memo. . . . For instance . . . one day . . . The Memo warned us that anti-war protestors would be "whining" about U.S. bombs killing Iraqi civilians, and suggested they could tell that to the families of American soldiers dying there. Editing copy that morning, I was not surprised when an eager young producer killed a correspondent's report on the day's fighting—simply because it included a brief shot of children in an Iraqi hospital. (Poynter.org)

We Distort; You Decide

Once again, however, imbalance—promoting a particular point of view—is not the most serious charge Fox faces. Rather, it is the way in which that point of view is advanced: If no holds are barred, if facts and truth are trampled to get to the "right" conclusions, then news is a tool of hegemony, not democracy. For example, the jewel in Fox's prime-time crown is *The O'Reilly Factor*, often the highest-rated program on the all-news channels. Media watchdog Fairness and Accuracy in Reporting (FAIR) has devoted an entire book, *The Oh Really Factor*, to a chronicle of O'Reilly's willingness to prevaricate. A typical moment occurred in 2004, when law professor David Cole appeared on the show to discuss the bipartisan 9/11 Commission Report. Cole reports that as the show was being taped, O'Reilly instructed his producers to edit out a snippet of Commission Chairman Tom Keane saying that no evidence existed of a link between Saddam Hussein and al-Qaeda. O'Reilly then claimed, for the cameras, that Keane had, in fact, confirmed such a link. When Cole challenged O'Reilly's assertion, his host went "berserk," called Cole "an SOB," and shouted that he "would never, ever, be invited back on the show again." When the segment aired, Cole's challenge to O'Reilly and the host's outburst had been edited out (MediaMatters.org 6/30/04).

As a former Fox editor, Matt Gross describes the prevailing attitude at the station:

> The facts of a story just didn't matter at all. An executive editor was sent down from the channel to bring us in line. His first directive to us: Seek out stories that cater to angry, middle aged white men who listen to talk radio and yell at their televisions. The idea was to get those viewers out of their seats, screaming at the TV, the liberals, by running a provocative story. (Poynter.org)

Such "reporting" helps us understand why Fox viewers, in particular, seemed ignorant of the most basic facts about the Iraq War. A survey conducted by the University of Maryland's Program on International Policy Attitudes found that viewers who relied on Fox for information about the war were substantially more likely than viewers of any other network to be misinformed. Respondents were asked if the evidence linked Hussein and al-Qaeda, if WMD had been found in Iraq, and if world opinion approved of the Iraq War. Results showed that Fox News viewers were the worst informed, while the PBS–NPR audience was the best informed—a laurel for public media, a subject we will return to in the conclusion of this chapter. While 67% of Fox viewers mistakenly thought that evidence had linked Saddam Hussein to al-Qaeda, only 16% of the PBS–NPR audience was under this delusion. Fox watchers were three times more likely than the nearest network to hold all three misperceptions. Among the PBS–NPR audience, however, an overwhelming majority did not harbor any of these mistaken beliefs. This finding held across partisan and ideological lines. In other words, even among pro-war, Bush-supporting conservative Republicans, those who watched PBS were much better informed than those who relied on Fox; Democrats who watched Fox were much more misinformed than those who turned to PBS or NPR (Kull, Ramsay, and Lewis 2003).

But misinformed viewers were not the only damage done by Fox's war coverage. The network acted as chief of the patriotism police, hurling the charge of disloyalty at war critics angrily and often. Its enemies list included journalists. CNN correspondent Christiane Amanpour, referred to by Fox as a "spokeswoman for al Qaeda," said

> I think the press was muzzled, and I think the press self muzzled. I'm sorry to say, but certainly television and my station was intimidated by the administration and its foot soldiers at Fox News. It did, in fact, put a climate of fear and self-censorship, in terms of the kind of work we did. (*USA Today* 9/14/03)

At a seminar to discuss the recent failures of news coverage, Dan Rather expanded on Amanpour's point, to include the chilling effects on mainstream journalists of the entire right-wing echo chamber. Speaking of the Four Sisters–funded Media Research Center, Rather said

> They are all over your telephones, all over your e-mail, all over your mail, and it creates an undertow in which you say to yourself, "You know, I think we're right on this story, but we better pick another day." Next thing you know, your boss will say, "If we run this story we're asking for trouble with a capital T. Why do it, why not just pass on by?" That happens; I'm sorry to report that happens.

Tom Brokaw, seated next to Rather on the stage that day, referred to the head of the Media Research Center, Brent Bozell's "pressing of a button" as "a kind of tsunami. He's well organized, he's got a constituency, he's got a newsletter, he can hit a button and we'll hear from him" (*Nation* 11/1/04).

Right-Wing Radio

The Reagan administration repeal of the Fairness Doctrine also created the possibility of right-wing radio. Creating the reality was Rush Limbaugh. In 1988, Limbaugh decided to take his New York–based talk show national, and the time was right. AM radio station owners, losing listeners to the clearer signals of their FM competitors, were looking for a savior, and Limbaugh was it: His show reliably delivered his audience of disaffected male conservatives, and he did it for free!

Limbaugh has always provided his show, paid for by his lucrative WABC contract, on "barter deal" terms to small local stations. That is, they do not pay cash for the show. They merely allow Limbaugh's syndication company to sell some of the show's ad time. It was an offer AM radio couldn't refuse. Within two years, Limbaugh was on 244 stations, and within seven years, 660 stations. Today, Limbaugh has an audience of 12 million people each day (Mann 2009).

The formula was so successful that soon Limbaugh imitators were everywhere. By the mid-2000s, conservative organizer Paul Weyrich estimated the number of right-wing radio talk show hosts at 1,700.

By 1994, conservative leaders would credit Limbaugh for that year's Republican congressional landslide victory. Newt Gingrich called it, "The first talk radio election." Added Republican Congressman Vin Weber, "Talk radio, with you in the lead, is what turned the tide" (D. Brock 2005, p. 290).

Soon, the newly elected Republican Congress would return the favor, changing telecommunications law to lock in conservative control of radio. For decades, federal law had encouraged local and diverse ownership of radio, by limiting ownership to 24 stations nationwide, and no more than 2 stations in any one local market. The Telecommunications Act of 1996 erased these limitations, creating a government-sanctioned oligopoly, and all but ending diversity of views on radio. Today, three companies own half the radio stations in the United States.

The largest of these, and the chief beneficiary of the new law, is Clear Channel Communications. Its top executives are proud Republicans and were major financial contributors to George W. Bush (buzzflash.com 4/18/03). Clear Channel is also the syndicator of Rush Limbaugh, Matt Drudge, and other right-wing radio shows.

During the war, Clear Channel banned a long list of "peace" songs, as we saw in Chapter 2, and also sponsored pro-war rallies and then covered them as news. At the same time, Cumulus Broadcasting, the second largest radio conglomerate, banned the Dixie Chicks from its airwaves for making an antiwar statement. The third radio behemoth, Citadel Communications, boasts more than 200 stations; it is owned by a right-wing financier and former board member of the *American Spectator.*

In talk radio, even more so than in other media, the right's disregard for facts and pit bull debating style are *de rigueur.* We have already met the wit and wisdom of the aptly named Michael Savage (8 million listeners). But Limbaugh's thoughts are no less punchy: When the photographs of Abu Ghraib emerged, Limbaugh pooh-poohed,

> This is no different from the Skull and Bones Initiation, and we're going to ruin people's lives over it? We are going to really hammer them because they had a good time. You ever heard of emotional release? You ever heard of the need to blow off some steam?

When a prominent environmentalist died of breast cancer, Limbaugh played the sound of a chainsaw and said, "She's finally been cut down to size! She'll never be able to bark up the wrong tree again!" He calls the National Organization for Women "a terrorist organization" and feminism "a way of bringing unattractive women into the mainstream of society" (just as, Stephen Colbert asks, talk radio has done for unattractive men?). On the man Limbaugh calls "Osama Obama": a man with a "perverted mind," a "revolutionary socialist," a "liar" who "wants to destroy America and the middle class," a "front man for terrorists" who wants to "turn the country into Castro's Cuba or Mugabe's Zimbabwe."

Once again, entire treatises, including books by FAIR and the Environmental Defense Fund, have been written on Limbaugh's embrace of falsities that serve his point. In his book on right-wing radio, political scientist David Barker found a significant correlation between listening to Limbaugh or four other conservative radio stars and being less informed and more misinformed about basic political facts than nonlisteners (Barker 2002, p. 24).

For example, during the 2008 presidential campaign, syndicated right-wing radio and Fox News host Sean Hannity used his programs to portray Barack Obama as a "treacherous enemy of the people." The centerpiece of his campaign was an hour-long episode of *Hannity's America* called "Obama and Friends: A History of Radicalism," which featured the "insights" of one Andy Martin. Martin had run for Congress in 1996, listing his goal as "to exterminate Jew power in America." In Hannity's special, Martin asserted, without evidence, that Obama is "secretly a Muslim," that he was recruited to his job as a community organizer in Chicago by former radical William Ayers, who engineered Obama's political career to bring about a "socialist revolution" in America. Whenever he is asked for evidence of these charges, Mr. Martin says, "That is my opinion—expert opinion, if you will," and "I don't pretend to be an exclusively fact-based reporter" (Salon.com 10/8/08).

While the conservative movement generally is, after two devastating election defeats, currently in some disarray, its media machine is not. In fact, remarkably, the often angry, intemperate, intimidating, mendacious, misleading voice of the right-wing surround sound system is now one of the "two sides" designated by the mainstream media to carry our national debate. It was enough to make even a mainstream columnist for the mainstream media wonder,

> When Rush Limbaugh sneezes or Newt Gingrich tweets, their views ricochet from the Internet to cable television and into the traditional media. It is remarkable how successful they are in setting what passes for the news agenda. . . . While the right wing's rants get wall to wall airtime, you almost never hear from [progressives who worry about] how close Obama's advisers are to Wall Street, or how long our troops will have to stay in Afghanistan, or how much he will be willing to compromise to secure health care reform. . . . Why are their voices muffled when they raise legitimate concerns, while Limbaugh's rants get amplified? For all the talk of a media love affair with Obama, there is a deep and largely unconscious conservative bias in the media's discussion of policy. The range of acceptable opinion runs from the moderate left to the far right and cuts off more vigorous progressive perspectives. By dragging the media to the right, Rush and Newt are winning. (E. J. Dionne, *Washington Post* 6/4/09)

❖ CONCLUSION

We have come full circle, and we conclude where we began: asking how important a free press is to democracy. In Chapter 1, we saw that, for Jefferson and Madison, the answer was simple. Without a free press, Ms. Sherwin, Jane Q. Public, is blind and deaf to the world she is supposed to be governing: no free press, no free country—no democracy.

We also asked what Ms. Sherwin needs from the press in order for her to "be [her] own governor," and to make democracy work. The answer was that democracy needs the press to perform two vital functions. The first is that of watchdog of the people, guarding against the tendency, as the Founders saw it, of those in power to pursue their own interests instead of the people's. This is especially true in war, Madison argued, which is "the true nurse of executive aggrandizement," the occasion when elites most like to help themselves to wealth and power.

For democracy's sake, the press must also perform the role of "marketplace of ideas"—a rich bazaar of competing ideas from which to choose. As Justice Hugo Black put it, "The First Amendment rests upon the assumption that the widest possible dissemination of information from diverse and antagonistic sources is essential to the welfare of the public."

Throughout this volume, we have seen the press act not as the watchdog of the people, but as the lapdog of the powerful. Repeatedly, the news media failed to challenge the White House's mendacious stories about war. From the deceit over WMD, to the duplicity about Abu Ghraib, and the half-truth of the "surge is working"—all of these administration tall tales and many more were given a free pass, endorsed and retold by the press.

We have also seen that there are shelves missing from the news media's marketplace of ideas—stories, thoughts, and thinkers that aren't there. In particular, the untold story of American foreign policy, the story of American empire, together with its smaller stories— chapters and verses—has been left out of the press's account of our 21st-century wars. And so, as our reverse content analysis has shown, the story of U.S. corporate power and its uneasy truce with democracy is not there: the story of oil, the history of the U.S. fist in the Middle East's face, the story of dissidents and why they dissented, stories of weapons inspectors and what they didn't find, stories of cluster bombs and civilian casualties, stories of military budgets the size of aircraft carriers, sailing on in war and in peace—all these important stories have been curiously, conspicuously absent from our news.

These failures of the press as watchdog and ideas emporium have helped lead to a long, dark night for American politics. Not only has the news failed to tell the full story of war, but it also missed the domestic story of the century—the looming economic meltdown— again, by deferring to corporate power, leaving us in the worst recession in 60 years (Lieberman 2008).

But as Hegel reminds us, night is when Minerva's owl of wisdom takes flight. Political scientists tell us that Americans may be at a moment of epiphany, based on the bitter politics of this decade, able to say that perhaps, after all, "Greed isn't good," and "War is not the answer;" and "Allowing a few very large, profit-obsessed corporations with political agendas of their own to control our society's stories is not the best way to deliver democracy's oxygen—information and ideas" (Edsall 2009; Holland 2009).

If the idea of a citizen uprising to demand better media seems utopian, let us remind ourselves that it has already happened. In 2003, a determinedly pro-business FCC had decided to push through a next round of deregulation that would give the MMCs ownership of even more media. But a chorus of American voices arose as one to say, "No." Public hearings on the issue became "standing room only affairs with 400–1,000 attendees," and said an FCC commissioner, "Not one of them stood up to say, 'I want even more concentration in our media ownership.' Not one" (McChesney 2004, p. 275). Then citizen action groups entered the fray, a united left and right—the NRA and MoveOn, acting together—along with journalists' professional organizations, the Newspaper Guild, and the International Federation of Journalists, who argued that concentrated ownership was bad for journalism. Together, in what one commissioner described as "a miracle," they stopped the FCC in its tracks.

Today, this openness to a new media model is crucial, because, in the newspaper business, the old model is dying. The broadsheets had hoped that declining ad revenue in their print editions would ultimately be offset by increasing ad revenue from their online versions. After all, Internet advertising was increasing rapidly and reliably. Then, in the fourth quarter of 2008, Internet ad value declined for the first time—ever—and with it, the hopes of the newspaper business for recovery (Isaacson 2009).

This is a perilous situation. Our newspaper industry still employs about 50,000 reporters—the vast majority of those practicing journalism in this country.

> As journalists are laid off and newspapers cut back or shut down, whole sectors of our civic life go dark. . . . Much of local and state government, whole federal departments and agencies, American activities around the world, the world itself—vast areas of great public concern—are neglected. Politicians will work increasingly without independent scrutiny and without public accountability. (McChesney and Nichols 2009, p. 2)

What is to be done? As the business model that has not served us well dies, we have a once in an aeon opportunity to ask, What model can replace it, and serve us better? The way to save American journalism, and to improve it, is to understand, as Jefferson and Madison did, that the news is a "public good": It provides a vital social function, arming a "people who mean to be their own governors with the power that knowledge gives" (Madison 1822). In this way, a free press serves the general public, not just the individuals who consume the news. Therefore, like roads or schools, this vital social function is not best provided by private business, but by the people, acting collectively, to see that their crucial need for information is met. We have witnessed the heavy cost when that need was not met by the commercial media in their 21st-century war coverage. As Madison said, so accurately describing our plight, "A popular government without popular information is but a prologue to a farce or a tragedy, or perhaps both."

Several scholars have suggested ways of moving from commercial to public media, from selling the people to telling the people (McChesney and Nichols 2009). The simplest would involve government subsidies to newspapers, paid automatically, according to a formula, so that governments could not threaten or bribe newspapers into toeing a party line. Sweden's support of newspapers in that country has prevented ownership concentration and fostered a lively debate among a wide range of ideas and interests (Gustafson and Hulten 1997). Others have suggested that newspapers be endowed, as universities are, and be run as public trusts, possibly in connection with journalism schools (Cole 2009). This is the model that supports Britain's *Guardian,* an award-winning newspaper, widely praised for its Iraq coverage (Bennion 2008).

For the United States, this is uncharted territory. Capitalist hegemony is more complete here than in other democracies. So it is not surprising that our public spending on mass media is only a fraction of what other democracies spend: Canada spends 16 times more per capita than the United States; Germany 20 times more; Japan 43 times more; Britain 60 times more; and Finland and Denmark 75 times more. And there is evidence that these public media polities may be doing something right. For example, the United States leads most of these countries in the percentage of college educated citizens but trails most of them in daily newspaper and TV news viewing (Mindich 2005, p. 100).

But as Thoreau warns us, "The light that puts out our eyes is darkness to us." Historically, he means, the brightest new thinking has been labeled folly. Just ask Galileo or Mandela. This will make a media revolution more difficult.

But "only that day dawns to which we are awake," Thoreau continues, and "there is more day to dawn." He means simply that there is room for improvement. And who, having reviewed this wretched record of recent war coverage, could disagree? It is enough to put us in mind of Matthew Arnold's bleak forecast for modernity: "And we are here, as on a darkling plain, swept with confused alarms of struggle and of flight, where ignorant armies clash by night."

Let us then imagine a different future and a free press: one that is free, not just from government censorship, but also, by virtue of being publicly subsidized, free from the commercial constraints described in this chapter. A press that is not indentured to owners, to advertisers, to Wall Street, to ratings, or circulation figures—one that is truly free to report "without fear or favor," and to include a wide bright spectrum of ideas.

Yes, we have been armies of the night. And yes, "The light that puts out our eyes is darkness to us." But "only that day dawns to which we are awake," and "there is more day to dawn." "The sun," Thoreau concludes, "is but a morning star."

References

Abercrombie, Nicholas, Brian S. Turner, and Stephen Hill. 1980. *The Dominant Ideology Thesis.* Sydney, Australia: Allen and Unwin.

Ackerman, Seth. 2001. "Networks of Insiders." *Extra!* November–December, p. 11.

Ackerman, Seth. 2002. "Afghan Famine On and Off the Screen." *Extra!* May–June, pp. 7–8.

Ackerman, Seth. 2003. "The Great WMD Hunt." *Extra!* July–August, p. 10.

Advertiser. 2005. "Warlords, Women Are Election Winners." October 8, p. 60.

Afary, Janet, and Kevin Anderson. 2007. "The Iranian Impasse." *The Nation.* July 16/23, pp. 35–40.

Ahmed, Akbar. 1992. *Postmodernism and Islam.* London: Routledge.

Alter, Jonathan. 2001. "Blame America at Your Peril." *Newsweek.* October, pp. 15, 41.

Alterman, Eric. 2003. *What Liberal Media?* New York: Basic Books.

Alterman, Eric. 2008. "Silence of the (MSM) Lambs." *The Nation.* June 30.

Alterman, Eric, and Mark Green. 2004. *The Book on Bush.* New York: Penguin.

Ambrose, Stephen. 1980. *Rise to Globalism: America's Foreign Policy, 1938–1980.* 2nd ed. New York: Penguin.

Amnesty International. 2003. "Iraq: Civilians Under Fire." March 8. http://www.amnesty.org/

Anderson, Robin. 2003. "That's Militainment!" *Extra!* May–June, pp. 6, 9.

Ansen, David. 2001. "Hollywood Goes to War." *Newsweek.* December 3.

Apple, R. W. 2001. "Awaiting the Aftershock." *New York Times.* September 12, p. A24.

Arnett, Peter. 2002. "Goodbye, World." In *Breach of Faith,* ed. Gene Roberts. Fayetteville: University of Arkansas Press, pp. 8, 66, 67, 74.

Asimov, Nanette. 2001. "Why Suicide Terrorists Embrace the Unthinkable." *San Francisco Chronicle.* September 23.

Associated Press. 2003. "Bush: Iraq Success Is Spurring Attacks." October 28.

Astor, Dave, and Chris Nammour. 2002. "Ready for Iraq, But Are They Ready for the War at Home?" *Editor & Publisher.* November 4.

Auletta, Ken. 1991. *Three Blind Mice.* New York: Random House.

Bagdikian, Ben. 1987. *The Media Monopoly.* Boston: Beacon Press.

Bagdikian, Ben. 2004. *The New Media Monopoly.* Boston: Beacon Press.

Baker, Russ. 2003. "The Big Lie." *The Nation.* April 27.

Baldauf, Scott, and Ashraf Khan. 2005. "New Guns, New Drive for Taliban." *Christian Science Monitor.* September 26, p. 1.

Barker, David C. 2002. *Rushed to Judgment.* New York: Columbia University Press.

Barry, John. 2001. "A New Breed of Soldier." *Newsweek.* December 10.

Barthel, Diane. 1988. *Putting on Appearances.* Philadelphia: Temple University Press.

Baum, Matthew. 2003. *Soft News Goes to War.* Princeton: Princeton University Press.

Bennett, W. Lance. 2005. *News: The Politics of Illusion.* 6th ed. New York: Longman.

Bennett, W. Lance. 2007. *News: The Politics of Illusion.* 7th ed. New York: Longman.

Bennett, W. Lance, and William Serrin. 2005. "The Watchdog Role." In *The Press,* eds. Geneva Overholser and Kathleen Hall Jamieson. New York: Oxford University Press.

Bennett, W. Lance, Regina Lawrence, and Steven Livingstone. 2007. *When the Press Fails.* Chicago: University of Chicago Press.

Bennion, Jackie. 2008. "The Guardian, 'Unlimited.'" PBS. http://www.pbs.org/

Bernstein, Richard. 2001. "Counterpoint to Unity: Dissent." *New York Times.* October 6, p. A13.

Bettig, Ronald, and Jeanne Lynn Hall. 2003. *Big Media, Big Money.* Lanham, MD: Rowman & Littlefield.

Blankenburg, William. 1992. "Unbundling the Modern Newspaper." In *The Future of News,* eds. John Look et al. Baltimore: Johns Hopkins University Press, p. 116.

Blum, William. 1995. *Killing Hope.* Monroe, ME: Common Courage Press.

Blum, William. 2000. *Rogue State.* Monroe, ME: Common Courage Press.

Borjesson, Kristina, ed. 2005. *Feet to the Fire.* New York: Prometheus.

Breed, Warren, 1958. "Mass Communication and Socio-cultural Integration." *Social Forces* 37:109–116.

Bremer, Paul. 2000. "Countering the Changing Threat of International Terrorism." Washington, DC: National Commission on Terrorism.

Brock, David. 2005. *The Republican Noise Machine.* New York: Three Rivers Press.

Brock, James. 2005. "Merger Mania and Its Discontents." *Multinational Monitor.* July–August.

Bumiller, Elizabeth. 2002. "Traces of Terror: The Strategy." *New York Times.* September 7.

Burnett, John. 2003. "Embedded/Unembedded II." *Columbia Journalism Review.* May–June, p. 43.

Bush, George W. 2002a. "Address at West Point." www.dartmouth.edu/~govdocs/

Bush, George W. 2002b. "The National Security Strategy of the United States." www.informationclearinghouse.info/article2320.htm

Bush, George W. 2002c. "Securing the Homeland, Strengthening the Nation." February 1. www.whitehouse.gov/

Bushell, Andrew, and Brent Cunningham. 2003. "Being There." *Columbia Journalism Review.* March–April, pp. 18, 20.

"Buying a Movement: A Report by the People for the American Way Foundation, 1996." People for the American Way. www.pfaw.org/

Callahan, David. 1994. *Between Two Worlds: Realism, Idealism and American Foreign Policy After the Cold War.* New York: HarperCollins.

Carter, Jimmy. 1980. "State of the Union Address [Carter Doctrine]." www.jim mycarterlibrary.org/

Chivers, C. J. 2003. "Islamists in Iraq Offer a Tour of 'Poison Factory' Cited by Powell." *New York Times.* February 9, p. 17.

Chomsky, Noam. 1992. *Deterring Democracy.* New York: Hill and Wang.

Clarke, Richard. 2004. *Against All Enemies.* New York: Free Press.

Coen, Rachel. 2002a. "Another Day, Another Mass Arrest." *Extra!* November–December, pp. 12–13.

Coen, Rachel. 2002b. "See No Evil." *Extra!* January–February, pp. 6–8.

Coen, Rachel, and Peter Hart. 2003. "Brushing Aside the Pentagon's 'Accidents.'" *Extra!* May–June, p. 18.

Cole, Juan. 2008. "A Social History of the Surge." *Informed Comment.* http://www.juancole.com

Cole, Juan. 2009. "The End of Newspapers?" March 1. http://www.juancole.com

Collins, Chuck. 2008. "Talking Points: Economic Meltdown." Institute for Policy Studies. October 27. www.ips-dc.org/

Conetta, Carl. 2002. "Strange Victory: A Critical Appraisal of Operation Enduring Freedom and the Afghanistan War." Commonwealth Institute Project on Defense Alternatives Research Monograph 6. January 30. http://www.comw.org/

Confessore, Nicholas. 2002. "Bad News." *American Prospect.* October 7.

Cooper, Gloria. 2004. "The Censors." *Columbia Journalism Review.* July–August, p. 58.

Corn, David. 2003. *The Lies of George W. Bush.* New York: Crown.

Cowell, Alan. 1991. "Kurds Fall Back From Iraq Forces." *New York Times.* March 27, p. 1.

Cox, Liz. 2002. "Sunday Morning." *Columbia Journalism Review.* September–October.

Cranberg, Gilbert. 1997. "Trimming the Fringe." *Columbia Journalism Review.* March–April.

Cranberg, Gilbert. 2003. "Bring Back the Skeptical Press." *Washington Post.* June 29, p. 54.

Crossette, Barbara. 2001a. "Feverish Protests Against the West Trace to Grievances Ancient and Modern." *New York Times.* October 22, p. B4.

Crossette, Barbara. 2001b. "Taliban's Ban on Poppy a Success, U.S. Aides Say." *New York Times.* May 20, p. A7.

Danner, Mark. 2006. "The Secret Way to War." *New York Review of Books.* December 13, pp. xvi, 15.

Dillow, Gordon. 2003. "Grunts and Pogues: The Embedded Life." *Columbia Journalism Review.* May–June, p. 33.

Dolny, Michael. 2002. "Think Tanks in a Time of Crisis." *Extra!* March–April, p. 28.

Dolny, Michael. 2003. "Spectrum Narrows Further in 2002." *Extra!* July–August.

Dolny, Michael. 2007. "Think Tank Sources Fall, But Left Gains Slightly." *Extra!* March–April.

Dreier, Peter. 1987. "The Corporate Complaint Against the Media." In *American Media and Mass Culture,* ed. Donald Lazere. Berkeley: University of California Press, p. 65.

Easterbrook, Gregg. 2000. "Apocryphal Now." *New Republic.* September 11.

Economist. 2005. "Multi-Multi-Party Democracy." October 22.

Edsall, Thomas. 2009. "Democrats Make Massive Gains." http://www.huffingtonpost.com.

Eisenhower, Dwight. 1961. "Farewell Address." http://www.milestonedocuments.com/

El Baradei, Mohammed. 2003. "Status of the Agency's Verification Activities in Iraq as of January 8, 2003. www.iaea.org/NewsCenter/Statements/2003/

Elliott et al., Michael. 2001. "We're at War." *Time.* September 24, p. 5.

Engstrom, Nicholas. 2003. "The Soundtrack for War." *Columbia Journalism Review.* May–June, p. 45.

Exoo, Calvin F. 1994. *The Politics of the Mass Media.* New York: West.

Extra! Update. 2001. "Suppressed Voices, History Alive on the Internet." December, pp. 1–3.

Fallows, James. 1997. *Breaking the News.* New York: Vintage.

Fay, Major General George. 2004. "Investigation of the Intelligence Activities at Abu Ghraib." www.army.mil/

Featherstone, Liza. 2003. "Parallel Universe at the Times." *Columbia Journalism Review.* July–August, p. 60.

Fisk, Robert. 2002. "Did Saddam's Army Test Poison Gas on Missing 5,000?" *Independent.*

Flanders, Laura. 2002. "It's Not Just the Veil." *Extra!* January–February, pp. 10–12.

Foer, Franklin. 2002. "Flacks Americana." *The New Republic.* May 20, pp. 5, 24.

Freeman, Richard. 2007. *America Works.* New York: Russell Sage Foundation.

Friel, Howard, and Richard Falk. 2004. *The Record of the Paper: How the New York Times Misreports U.S. Foreign Policy.* New York: Verso.

Fritz, Ben, Bryan Keefer, and Brendan Nyhan. 2004. *All the President's Spin.* New York: Touchstone.

Gaddis, John L. 1972. *The United States and the Origins of the Cold War, 1941–1947.* New York: Columbia University Press.

Gans, Herbert. 1979. *Deciding What's News.* New York: Pantheon.

Garten, Jeffrey. 1997. "The Root of the Problem." *Newsweek.* March 31, p. 16.

Gates, David. 2001. "The Voices of Dissent." *Newsweek.* November 13, p. 2.

Gellman, Barton, and Thomas E. Ricks. 2002. "U.S. Concludes Bin Laden Escaped at the Bora Fight." *Washington Post.* April 17, p. A1.

Gellman, Barton, and Walter Pincus. 2003. "Depiction of Threat Outgrew Supporting Evidence." *Washington Post*. August 10.

Gibbs, David. 2002. "Forgotten Coverage of Afghan 'Freedom Fighters.'" *Extra!* January–February, pp. 13–16.

Gitlin, Todd. 1987. "Television's Screens: Hegemony in Transition." *American Media and Mass Culture*, ed. Donald Lazere. Berkeley: University of California Press.

Glass, Ira. 2006. "What's in a Number?" *This American Life*. November 3. Chicago: Chicago Public Radio.

Goodwin, Jan. 2002. "An Uneasy Place." *The Nation*. April 29, p. 20.

Gopal, Anand. 2008. "Who Are the Taliban?" *The Nation*. December 22, pp. 17–20.

Gordon, Joy. 2002. "Cool War." *Harper's*. November, pp. 43–49.

Gramsci, Antonio. 1971. *The Prison Notebooks*, eds. and trans. Quinton Hoare and Geoffrey Smith. New York: International Publishers.

Green, Miranda. 2002. "Islamic World Strongly Opposed to U.S. Foreign Policy, Survey Shows." *Financial Times* (London). February 27.

Greenspan, Alan. 2007. The Age of Turbulence. New York: Penguin.

Greenwald, Robert (Director). 2004. *Uncovered: The Whole Truth About the Iraq War* [DVD]. Culver City, CA: Brave New Films. http://bravenewfilms.org/

Grossman, Lawrence. 1998. "Does Local TV News Need a Nanny?" *Columbia Journalism Review*. May–June, p. 33.

Gustafson, Karl, and Olof Hulten. 1997. "Sweden." In *The Media in Western Europe*, ed. Bernt Stubbe Ostergaard. London: Sage.

Hacker, Andrew, ed. 1964. *The Federalist Papers*. New York: Washington Square Press.

Hallin, Daniel. 1986. *The Uncensored War*. New York: Oxford University Press.

Hanson, Christopher. 2003. "American Idol." *Columbia Journalism Review*. August–September, pp. 58–59.

Harbrecht, Douglas. 2003. "Toting the Casualties of War." *Business Week Online*. February 6.

Harrison, Bennett, and Barry Bluestone. 1988. *The Great U-Turn*. New York: Basic Books.

Hart, Peter. 2001. "Covering the 'Fifth Column.'" *Extra!* November–December, p. 18.

Hart, Peter. 2003. "Crazy Like a Fox." *Extra!* May–June.

Hart, Peter. 2007. "No Way Out." *Extra!* November–December.

Hart, Peter, and Seth Ackerman. 2001. "Patriotism and Censorship." *Extra!* November–December, p. 6.

Hart Peter, and Jim Naureckas. 2002. "Fox at the Front." *Extra!* January–February, p. 9.

Hastings, Michael. 2009. "Backing the Iraq War Was the Smart Career Move." June 17. http://mediachannel.org/

Hegel, G. W. F. 1967. *Hegel's Philosophy of Right*. New York: Oxford University Press.

Heller, Z. P. 2009. "Let's Rethink Escalation in Afghanistan Before It's Too Late." January 26. http://www.alternet.org/

Hellman, Christopher. 2006. "The Runaway Military Budget: An Analysis." *Friends Committee on National Legislation Newsletter.* March.

Herman, Edward, and Noam Chomsky. 1988. *Manufacturing Consent.* New York: Pantheon.

Herman, Edward, and Noam Chomsky. 2002. *Manufacturing Consent.* New York: Pantheon.

Hersh, Seymour. 2003. "Selective Intelligence." *The New Yorker.* May 12, p. 44.

Hersh, Seymour. 2004a. "Torture at Abu Ghraib." *The New Yorker.* May 10, p. 45.

Hersh, Seymour. 2004b. "The Gray Zone: How a Secret Pentagon Program Came to Abu Ghraib." *The New Yorker.* May 24.

Hickey, Neil. 2002. "Access Denied." *Columbia Journalism Review.* January–February.

Hirsh, Michael, and John Barry. 2001. "How to Strike Back." *Newsweek.* September 24.

Holland, Joshua. 2009. "The Results Are In: Americans Now Aligned More Closely with Progressive Ideas." May 30. http://www.alternet.org/

Howard, Sir Michael. 2001. "Mistake to Declare This a War." *The RUSI Journal* 146, no. 6.

Human Events. 2001. "Public or Media Approval?" December 17. International Affairs.

Ireland, Doug. 2001. "This Isn't the End of It." *In These Times.* December 24.

Isaacson, Walter. 2009. "How to Save Your Newspaper." *Time.* February 16.

Isikoff, Michael, and Evan Thomas. 2003. "Follow the Yellow-Cake Road." *Newsweek.* July 28, p. 22.

Iskandar, Adel. 2005. "The Great American Bubble." In *Bring 'Em On,* eds. Lee Artz and Yahya Kamilipour. Lanham, MD: Rowman & Littlefield.

Iyengar, Shanto, and Jennifer McGrady. 2007. *Media Politics: A Citizen's Guide.* New York: Norton.

Jackson, Derrick. 2006. "Income Gap Mentality." *Boston Globe.* April 23.

Jackson, Janine. 2004. "War's Iconic Image a Psy-Ops Creation." *Extra!* August, p. 3.

Jamieson, Kathleen Hall. 2000. *Everything You Think You Know About Politics . . . And Why You're Wrong.* New York: Basic Books.

Jamieson, Kathleen Hall, and Joseph N. Cappella. 2008. *Echo Chamber.* New York: Oxford University Press.

Jefferson, Thomas. 1816. "Letter to Charles Yancey." In *Thomas Jefferson on Politics and Government.* http://etext.virginia.edu/jefferson/quotations.

Jhally, Sut (Director). 1994. *The Killing Screens: Media and the Culture of Violence* [DVD]. Northampton, MA: Media Education Foundation.

Jhally, Sut (Director) 1997. *The Electronic Storyteller: TV and the Cultivation of Values* [DVD]. Northampton, MA: Media Education Foundation.

Johnson, Chalmers. 2004. *The Sorrows of Empire.* New York: Metropolitan.

Johnson, Peter. 2003. "War Protest Coverage Now in the Forefront; Some Find the Media's Attention Too Little, Too Late." *USA Today.* February 25.

Jones, Ann. 2009. "The Afghan Scam." January 12. http://alternet.org/
Jones, Seth. 2005. "The Danger Next Door." *New York Times.* September 23, p. A19.
Journalism.org. 2005. "The State of the News Media." http://www.stateofthe media.org/
Judis, John, and Spencer Ackerman. 2003. "The First Casualty." *The New Republic.* June 30.
Kampfner, John (Director). 2003. *War Spin* [Documentary]. BBC. May 18.
Katznelson, Ira, Mark Kesselman, and Alan Draper. 2002. *The Politics of Power.* USA: Wadsworth.
"Key Judgments [From October 2002 NIE]." 2002. U.S. Central Intelligence Agency. http://www.fas.org/irp/cia/product/iraq-wmd.html
Kingsolver, Barbara. 2002. "Misquoted Critic: There Are Many Ways to Love America." *San Francisco Chronicle.* January 17.
Kirk, Michael. 2009. *Frontline: Inside the Meltdown.* PBS. http://www.pbs.org/
Kohut, Andrew. 2002. "Public News Habits Little Changed by September 11." *Survey Reports.* Washington, DC: Pew Research Center for the People and the Press.
Kull, Steven, Clay Ramsay, and Evan Lewis. 2003. "Misperceptions, the Media, and the Iraq War." *Political Science Quarterly.* Winter 2003.
Kuttner, Robert. 2002. "Script the Pundits Well!" *The Daily Howler.* August 27. http://www.dailyhowler.com/
Landay, Jonathan, and Warren Strobel. 2002. "A Report Reveals Analysts Split Over Extent of Iraqi Nuclear Threat." Knight Ridder. October 4.
Landay, Jonathan, Warren Strobel, and John Walcott. 2002. "Some in Bush Administration Have Misgivings About Iraq Policy." Knight Ridder. October 8.
Laventhol, David. 2001. "Profit Pressures: A Question of Margins." *Columbia Journalism Review.* May–June, p. 18.
Layton, Charles. 2002a. "The Information Squeeze." *American Journalism Review.* September, p. 29.
Layton, Charles. 2002b. "What Do Readers Really Want?" In *Breach of Faith,* ed. Gene Roberts. Fayetteville: University of Arkansas Press.
Lemann, Nicholas. 2002. "The War on What?" *The New Yorker.* September 16.
Levin, Senator Carl. 2008. "Statement of Senator Carl Levin on Senate Armed Services Committee Report of Its Inquiry into the Treatment of Detainees in U.S. Custody." December 11. http://levin.senate.gov/newsroom/release .cfm?id=305734
Lieberman, Trudy. 2000. *Slanting the Story.* New York: The New Press.
Lieberman, Trudy. 2008."How Our Gutless Media Helped Trigger the Credit Crisis." *Columbia Journalism Review.* November 20.
Lincoln, Bruce. 2003. *Holy Terrors: Thinking About Religion After September 11.* Chicago: University of Chicago Press.
Lindblom, Charles. 1977. *Politics and Markets.* New York: Basic Books.
Lindblom, Charles. 1982. "The Market as Prison." *Journal of Politics* 44:327.
Lippmann, Walter. 1922. *Public Opinion.* New York: Free Press.
Lorch, Donatella. 2002. "The Green Berets Up Close." *Newsweek.* January 14.

Lustick, Ian. 2006. *Trapped in the War on Terror.* Philadelphia: University of Pennsylvania Press.

Madison, James. 1793. "James Madison on War." http://tiger.berkeley.edu/sohrab/politics/madison.html

Madison, James. 1822. "Letter to W. T. Barry." In *The Founders Constitution,* Ch. 18. Document 35. Chicago: University of Chicago Press.

Magdoff, Harry. 1969. *The Age of Imperialism: The Economics of U.S. Foreign Policy.* New York: Monthly Review Press.

Mann, Bill. 2009. "Limbaugh's Dirty Little Secret of Radio 'Success.'" http://www.huffingtonpost.com/

Mann, James. 2004. *The Rise of the Vulcans.* New York: Penguin.

Marcuse, Herbert. 1964. *One Dimensional Man.* Boston: Beacon Press.

Marx, Karl. 1988. *The Communist Manifesto.* New York: Norton.

Marx, Karl, and Frederich Engels. 1964. *The German Ideology.* Moscow: Progress.

Massing, Michael. 2003. "The High Price of an Unforgiving War." *Columbia Journalism Review.* May–June, pp. 34, 35.

Massing, Michael. 2004. "Now They Tell Us." *New York Review of Books.* February 26, pp. 3, 19, 21, 26, 36–40, 41, 43–45, 47, 51, 53–54, 55, 59, 60, 62.

Massing, Michael. 2009. "Un American." *Columbia Journalism Review.* January–February, p. 16.

Mayer, Jane. 2006. "The Memo." *The New Yorker.* February 27, p. 32.

McChesney, Robert. 1999. *Rich Media, Poor Democracy.* Urbana: University of Illinois Press.

McChesney, Robert. 2004. *The Problem of the Media.* New York: Monthly Review Press.

McChesney, Robert, and John Nichols. 2009. "Save America's Newspapers." March 23. http://mediachannel.org/

McCollam, Douglas. 2004. "The List: How Chalabi Played the Press." *Columbia Journalism Review.* July–August, p. 32.

McManus, Doyle. 2003. "Pentagon Reform Is His Battle Cry." *Los Angeles Times.* August 17.

Meyer, Philip. 2004. *The Vanishing Newspaper.* Columbia: University of Missouri Press.

Miller, Mark Crispin. 2002. "From Bozo to Churchill." *Extra!* May–June, p. 15.

Mindich, David. 2005. *Tuned Out.* New York: Oxford University Press.

Mitchell, Gregg. 2008. *So Wrong for So Long.* New York: Union Square Press.

Mooney, Chris. 2004. "The Editorial Pages." *Columbia Journalism Review.* March–April, pp. 31–32.

Morello, Tom. 2001. "The New Blacklist." *Extra!* November–December, p. 10.

Morin, Richard, and Claudia Deane. 2002. "The Poll That Didn't Add Up." *Washington Post.* March 23.

Morrow, Lance. 2001. "The Case for Rage and Retribution." *Time.* September 11.

Moyers, Bill. 2007. "Buying the War." *Bill Moyers Journal.* PBS. http://www.pbs.org/

Mozzetti, Mark, and Borzou Daragahi. 2005. "U.S. Military Covertly Pays to Run Stories in Iraqi Press." *Los Angeles Times.* November 30.

Mueller, James. 2006. *Towel Snapping the Press.* Lanham, MD: Rowman & Littlefield.

Muwakki, Salim. 2003. "When Warriors Dissent." *In These Times.* August 11.

Naureckas, Jim. 2003. "MSNBC's Racism Is OK, Peace Activism Is Not." *Extra!* April.

Negroponte, John. 2006. "Statement by the Director of National Intelligence to the Senate Select Committee on Intelligence." February 2. http://intelligence .senate.gov/

New York Times. 2004. "The *Times* and Iraq." May 26, p. A10.

Newman, Richard, Mark Mazzetti, and Kevin Whitelaw. 2001. "Fight to the Finish." *U.S. News & World Report.* October 12.

Nichols, John, and Robert McChesney. 2005. *Tragedy and Farce.* New York: The New Press.

Olewine, Sandra. 2001. "How Did Palestinians React to the Attacks on the United States? The Sorrow Unseen, the Story Unheard." *Washington Report on Middle East Affairs.* November 30, p. 16.

Orwell, George. 1992. *1984.* New York: Knopf.

Parenti, Christian. 2001. "America's Jihad: A History of Origins." *Social Justice.* Fall, pp. 31–38.

Parenti, Michael. 2008. *Democracy for the Few.* Boston: Thomson/Wadsworth.

Pein, Corey. 2004. "The Zelig of Baghdad." *Extra!* May–June, p. 32.

Pena, Richard. 2007. "Why Big Newspapers Applaud Some Declines in Circulation." *New York Times.* October 1, p. C1.

Pew Research Center. 2003. "Embedded Reporters: What Are Americans Getting?" http://www.journalism.org/print/211

Pfau, Michael, Carolyn Jackson, Elaine M. Wittenberg, Phil Mehringer, Kristina Brockman, Rob Lanier, and Michael Hatfield. 2005. "Embedding Journalists in Military Combat Units." *Journalism and Mass Communication Quarterly* 81:1, p. 179.

Pierson, Paul, and Jacob Hacker. 2005. *Off Center.* New Haven, CT: Yale University Press.

Pilger, John. 2003. "While We Are Allowed to Read Internal Emails in Whitehall . . ." *New Statesman.* September 15.

Pincus, Walter. 2003. "U.S. Lacks Specifics on Banned Arms." *Washington Post.* March 16, p. A17.

Pincus, Walter, and Dana Milbank. 2003. "Bush Clings to Dubious Allegations." *Washington Post.* March 23, p. C1.

Pintak, Lawrence. 2004. "Severed Head in the Freezer, Favorability Ratings in the Toilet." July 28. http://www.commondreams.org/

Pintak, Lawrence. 2006. *Reflections in a Bloodshot Lens.* London: Pluto Press.

Postman, Neil. 1985. *Amusing Ourselves to Death.* New York: Viking.

Prashad, Vijay. 2001. "War Against the Planet." www.counterpunch.org/ prashad.html

Prestowitz, Clyde. 2003. *Rogue Nation.* New York: Basic Books.

Price, Jay. 2005. "Hanging by a Thread." *The News & Observer.* July 10, p. A21.

Pritchard, Robert S. 2003. "The Pentagon Is Fighting—and Winning—the Public Relations War." *USA Today Magazine.* July, p. 11.

Program on International Policy Attitudes. 2004. "Americans on Detention, Torture and the War on Terrorism." University of Maryland. July 22. http://www.pipa.org/

Project for the New American Century. 2000. "Rebuilding America's Defenses." Report of the Project for the New American Century. September. www.newamericancentury.org/rebuildingamericasdefenses.pdf

"Public Support for War Resilient: Bush's Standing Improves." 2004. The Pew Research Center for the People & the Press. July 17. http://people-press.org/report/216/public-support-for-war-resilient

Putnam, Robert. 2001. *Bowling Alone.* New York: Simon & Schuster.

Rampton, Sheldon, and John Stauber. 2003a. "How to Sell a War." *In These Times.* September 1, pp. 14, 15.

Rampton, Sheldon, and John Stauber. 2003b. "The 'Sheer Genius' of Embedded Reporting." *Extra!* September–October, pp. 20–21.

Rampton, Sheldon, and John Stauber. 2003c. *Weapons of Mass Deception: The Uses of Propaganda in Bush's War on Iraq.* New York: Tarcher/Penguin.

Rashid, Ahmed. 1999. "The Taliban: Exporting Extremism." *Foreign Affairs* 78:6. November–December, pp. 25–35.

Rashid, Ahmed. 2002. "Afghanistan Imperiled." *The Nation.* October 14.

Rendall, Steve. 2001. "The Op-Ed Echo Chamber." *Extra!* November–December, pp. 14–15.

Rendall, Steve. 2003. "In Prelude to War, TV Served as Official Megaphone." *Extra!* April.

Rendall, Steve, and Tara Broughel. 2003. "Amplifying Officials, Squelching Dissent." *Extra!* May–June.

"Report on International News Coverage in America." 2003. *Washington Report on Middle East Affairs* 20, 8:16, 20.

Reporters Without Borders. 2003. "Second World Press Freedom Ranking." http://www.rsf.org/IMG/pdf/World_press_ranking.pdf

Ricks, Thomas. 2006. *Fiasco.* New York: Penguin.

Riordan, William. 1905. *Plunkitt of Tammany Hall.* New York: E. P. Dutton.

Roberts, Les, Riyadh Lafta, Richard Garfield, Jamal Khudhairi, and Gilbert Burnham. 2004. "Mortality, Before and After the 2003 Invasion of Iraq: Cluster Sample Survey." *The Lancet.* October 29.

Robison, Mike. 1985. "Narcotics Traffic Grossed $110 Billion in 1984, Panel Reports." Associated Press. March 6.

Rosenthal, Andrew. 1991. "Bush Not Pressing Kuwait on Reform." *New York Times.* March 5, p. D1.

Roy, Arundhati. 2001. "The Algebra of Infinite Justice." The *Guardian Unlimited* Archive. September 29.

Rubin, Barry. 1980. *Paved With Good Intentions.* New York: Oxford University Press.

Rubin, Richard. 1981. *Press, Party and Presidency.* New York: Norton.

Rutenberg, Jim. 2001. "Fox Portrays a War of Good and Evil and Many Applaud." *New York Times.* December 3, p. C1.

Said, Edward. 1997. *Covering Islam*. New York: Vintage Books.

Sampson, Anthony. 1975. *The Seven Sisters*. New York: Viking.

Schechter, Danny. 2003. *Embedded: Weapons of Mass Deception*. Amherst, NY: Prometheus.

Scheer, Christopher, Robert Scheer, and Lakshmi Chandry. 2004. *The Five Biggest Lies Bush Told Us About Iraq*. New York: Seven Stories.

Scheuer, Michael. 2004. "How to Lose the War on Terror: A CIA bin Laden Expert's Lament." *American Conservative*. August 2.

Schlesinger, James. 2004. "Final Report of the Independent Panel to Review DoD Detention Operations." August. http://f11.findlaw.com/news .findlaw.com/wp/docs/dod/abughraibrpt.pdf

Scholl, Russell. 2000. "The International Investment Position of the United States at Yearend 1999." Dept. of Commerce, Bureau of Economic Analysis. July, pp. 20–29.

"Self Censorship: How Often and Why." 2000. Pew Research Center. http://people-press.org/Report #39

Shadid, Anthony. 2005. *Night Draws Near*. New York: Henry Holt.

Shaheen, Jack. 1984. *The TV Arab*. Bowling Green, Ohio: Bowling Green State University Popular Press.

Shawcross, William. 1997. *Murdoch*. New York: Touchstone.

Sick, Gary. 1985. *All Fall Down*. New York: Random House.

Simon, Roger. 1982. *Gramsci's Political Thought*. London: Lawrence and Wishart.

Simon, William. 1978. *A Time for Truth*. New York: Reader's Digest Press.

Sklar, Holly. 2006. "The Really Rich Get Richer." McClatchey–Tribune News Service. September 29.

Smucker, Philip. 2002. "How bin Laden Got Away." *Christian Science Monitor*. March 4.

Solomon, Norman, and Reese Erlich. 2003. *Target Iraq*. New York: Context Books.

Somerby, Bob. 2002. "When Conservatives Smear, Pundits Duck." *Extra!* October, p. 3.

Sontag, Susan. 2001. "Tuesday, and After." *The New Yorker*. September 24, p. 32.

Spencer, Robert. 2005. *The Politically Incorrect Guide to Islam*. Washington, DC: Regnery.

Spencer, Robert. 2006. *The Truth About Mohammed: Founder of the World's Most Intolerant Religion*. Washington, DC: Regnery.

St. Petersburg Times. 2005. "Warlords Fare Well in Afghan Elections." October 5.

Stanley, Alessandra. 2001. "Opponents of War Are Scarce on Television." *New York Times*. November 9, p. B4.

"The State of the News Media 2008." 2008. Project for Excellence in Journalism. http://www.stateofthemedia.org

Steffens, Lincoln. 1957. *The Shame of the Cities*. New York: Hill and Wang.

Steinberg, Neil. 2003. "War Protestors' Worst Enemy Is Logic, Not Spies." *Chicago Sun Times*. January 17.

Stephen, Andrew. 2002. "War Comes Home." *New Statesman*. February 11.

Stepp, Carl. 2002. "Then and Now." In *Breach of Faith*, ed. Gene Roberts. Fayetteville: University of Arkansas Press.

Stewart, Potter. 1975. "Or of the Press." *Hastings Law Journal* 26:634.

Stockman, Farah. 2005a. "Afghanistan Straddles Stability and Chaos." *Boston Globe*. October 7, p. A1.

Stockman, Farah. 2005b. "Afghans Go to Polls in Historic Vote." *Boston Globe*. September 18, p. A1.

Struttaford, Andrew. 2001. "Moderately Crazy." *National Review Online*. October 23.

Truman, Harry. 1947. "Truman Doctrine." http://avalon.law.yale.edu/ 20th_century/trudoc.asp

Tuchman, Gaye. 1972. "Objectivity as Strategic Ritual." *American Journal of Sociology* 77:662, 665–670.

Uchitelle, Louis. 1991. "Gulf Victory May Raise U.S. Influence in OPEC." *New York Times*. March 5, p. D1.

Ulam, Adam. 1971. *The Rivals: America and Russia Since World War II*. New York: Viking.

Underhill, William. 2001. "Ultimate Fighters." *Newsweek*. September 28.

Veblen, Thorstein. 1904. *The Theory of Business Enterprise*. New York: Scribner.

Wade, Robert. 1996. "Globalization and Its Limits." In *National Diversity and Global Capitalism*, eds. Suzanne Berger and Ronald Dore. Ithaca, NY: Cornell University Press.

Walker, William. 2001. "Has bin Laden Slipped Into Pakistan?" *Toronto Star*. December 15, p. A25.

Welch, Matt. 2002. "The Politics of Dead Children." *Reasononline*. March.

Western, Jon. 2005. *Selling Intervention and War*. Baltimore: Johns Hopkins University Press.

Whitley, Andrew. 1991. "The Dirty War in Kuwait." *New York Times*. April 2, p. 19.

Williams, Bruce A., and Michael X. Delli Carpini. 2002. "Heeeeere's Democracy!" *Chronicle of Higher Education*. April 19, p. B14.

Wiseman, Paul. 2005. "Warlords on Ballot Worry Afghan Election Advisers." *USA Today*. September 16.

Wolff, Edward. 2001. "The Rich Get Richer . . . and Why the Poor Don't." *American Prospect*. February 12, p. 15.

Yeats, William Butler. 1974. Passages from "Easter, 1916" and "The Second Coming." In *The Collected Poems by W. B. Yeats*. New York: MacMillan, pp. 152, 158.

Zogby, John. 2002. "The Ten Nations 'Impressions of America' Poll Report." Washington, DC: Zogby International.

Zogby, John, and James J. Zogby. 2004. "Impressions of America 2004: How Arabs in 6 Countries View America." Washington, DC: Arab-American Institute/Zogby International.

Zuckerman, Mortimer. 2001. "Our Mission, Our Moment." *U.S. News & World Report*. October 1, p. 76.

Index

About the Author

Calvin F. Exoo is professor and chair of the Department of Government at St. Lawrence University. He is also the author of *Democracy Upside Down: Public Opinion and Cultural Hegemony in the United States* and of *The Politics of the Mass Media*. His numerous articles on the politics of the mass media have appeared in such publications as *Polity*, *New Political Science*, the *Journal of Ethnic Studies*, the *New York Times*, the *Times (London)*, the *Baltimore Evening Sun*, and the *Los Angeles Times*. In 2006, Exoo was selected as a Saul Sidore Lecturer at Plymouth State University, and in 2009, he was named Outstanding Faculty Member by the senior class at St. Lawrence University.

Supporting researchers for more than 40 years

Research methods have always been at the core of SAGE's publishing program. Founder Sara Miller McCune published SAGE's first methods book, *Public Policy Evaluation*, in 1970. Soon after, she launched the *Quantitative Applications in the Social Sciences* series—affectionately known as the "little green books."

Always at the forefront of developing and supporting new approaches in methods, SAGE published early groundbreaking texts and journals in the fields of qualitative methods and evaluation.

Today, more than 40 years and two million little green books later, SAGE continues to push the boundaries with a growing list of more than 1,200 research methods books, journals, and reference works across the social, behavioral, and health sciences. Its imprints—Pine Forge Press, home of innovative textbooks in sociology, and Corwin, publisher of PreK–12 resources for teachers and administrators—broaden SAGE's range of offerings in methods. SAGE further extended its impact in 2008 when it acquired CQ Press and its best-selling and highly respected political science research methods list.

From qualitative, quantitative, and mixed methods to evaluation, SAGE is the essential resource for academics and practitioners looking for the latest methods by leading scholars.

For more information, visit **www.sagepub.com**.